Design Journeys through Complex Systems

Practice Tools for Systemic Design

Peter Jones & Kristel Van Ael

Design Journeys through Complex Systems
Practice Tools for Systemic Design

By Peter Jones & Kristel Van Ael

B/S

BIS Publishers
Borneostraat 80-A
1094 CP Amsterdam
The Netherlands
T +31 (0)20 515 02 30
bis@bispublishers.com
www.bispublishers.com

ISBN 978 90 636 9634 4

Contents

The tool templates presented in this book can be downloaded from systemicdesigntoolkit.org/journeys

About the Authors

Dr. Peter Jones is Distinguished University Professor of Systemic Design at Tec de Monterrey, and an associate professor at Toronto's OCAD University. He is a co-founder of the Systemic Design Association (systemic. design) and the RSD Symposia series, and is Editor in Chief of the SDA journal *Contexts*. Peter is the founder of Redesign Network, an innovation research firm, leading systemic and platform design and research in healthcare, informatics and media, and public sector strategy. He has published three other books, including *Design for Care* (2013), as well as 50 research articles that can be found at designdialogues.com.

Kristel Van Ael is a business partner at Namahn, a humanity-centred design agency based in Brussels. She is the lead author of the Service Design (servicedesigntoolkit.org) and Systemic Design (systemicdesigntoolkit.org) toolkits. Kristel is also co-teacher in product-service-system design and lead teacher in systemic design at the University of Antwerp (Faculty of Design Sciences).

Acknowledgements

We gratefully thank our many contributors, reviewers and advisors that helped cocreate the Systemic Design Toolkit and contributed directly to the book.

Tools

— Christiaan Baelus, University of Antwerp alumnus
— Ivo Dewit, University of Antwerp
— Alexis Jacoby, University of Antwerp
— Stefanos Monastiridis, Namahn alumnus
— Koen Peters, Namahn
— Sabrina Tarquini, Namahn alumnus

Illustrations

— Alessandra Rodilosso, Namahn

Photography

— Ulla Maria Lisa Van Ael
— Jean Van Driessche
— Peter Vermaercke, Namahn alumnus

Inspiration

— Alex Ryan, Systemic Design Association
— Philippe Vandenbroeck, shiftN
— Inge Keizer, Service Design College
— Peter's graduate students at OCAD University
— Kristel's graduate students at the University of Antwerp
— The systemic design (RSD) community

Cases

Last, but not least, we thank all our clients and colleagues willing to dive into uncertainty and complexity.

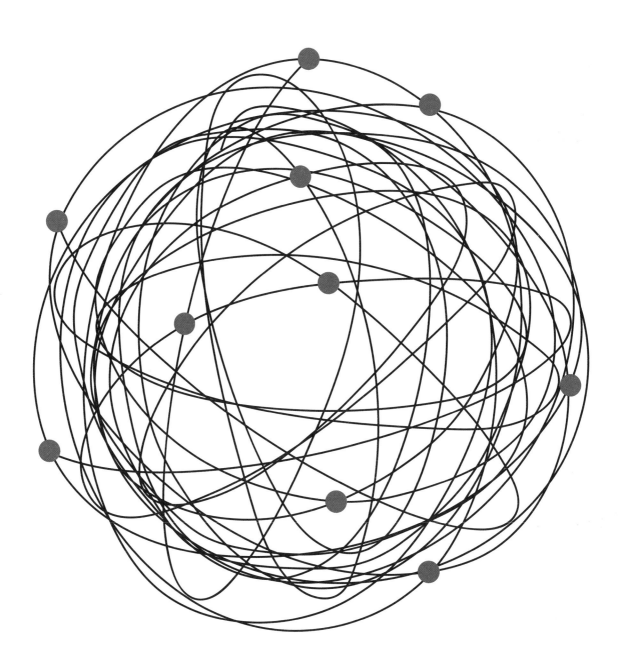

Design Journeys through Complex Systems

Systemic design for systems change designers

A Tour Guide for System Navigators

Creative professionals face unprecedented complexity, increasingly affecting our impact and influence as the 21st century unfolds. Of course, designers are supposed to thrive in such chaotic times, to navigate creative solutions within multiple intersecting complex issues, such as economic delusion, media illusion, technology evolution, information profusion, and cultural confusion. Complexity demands we collaborate. Since designers collaborate with mixed teams on real projects, we are all infused together, and this may be a story we tell to promote the agency of design.

This apparent chaos (that some call supercomplexity) imposes directly consequential demands on individual and collective cognition, as well as on the performance of decision-makers and implementers. As they are clients and fellow travellers, we might plan better preparations for the long journeys we face together into complex systems and systems change. The following is a tour guide for both expert Explorers and novice Tourists into systemic design practices, from the testbeds of practice in numerous travels of recent years.

Designers, social innovators, and business leaders are now called to address transformational challenges for which we have no relevant academic or practice training. For those employed in design agencies or creative strategy, for large-scale services or digital platforms,

these challenges are fascinating, but not quite welcome. We are not often contracted to directly design solutions for systemic problems such as regional economic rejuvenation, food webs in poverty zones, or educational systems redesign. Systemic contexts in general are problematic because they break defined boundaries that focus our work and limit project scope.

Design teams are rarely project owners; we are service providers with and for larger teams. We have to question when it's responsible to break boundaries that raise system-level problems when given a focused remit. Upselling the sponsor's brief to solve systemic problems can massively impact project scope and cost, and most clients have no organisational on-ramp into complex systems challenges. Disciplined and constructive tools are needed for stepping into systems contexts with an ever-expanding group of fellow travellers.

Design Journeys offers a repertoire of collaborative practice tools for system solutions developed and tested in dozens of projects. The book integrates theory and practices of the Systemic Design Toolkit for cocreation, in a single handbook. As a text, it informs practice and teaches relevant theories to help new system leaders coordinate much better design processes for these challenges. The Journeys methodology anchors powerful system methods from the Toolkit with cases from the two authors' years of experience in systemic design projects and method development.

Systemic Design Journeys through Complex Social Systems

Design Journeys aims to enhance practice across three broad contexts that we regularly tour with our clients or in research: public sector (government), systems change (often non-profit or development programmes), and sociotechnical services (private sector, mixed). *Journeys* travels well in education, as the Toolkit has been productive in graduate design programmes. The tools have been used extensively in virtual online courses and training, adapting the downloaded toolkit to shared whiteboards. In practice, government labs are a significant sponsor of systemic design projects, as they have the budgets and mandate to address problems at the aggregate system level and they have access to multistakeholder groups. Corporations, even when leading large consortia, do not often fund efforts beyond their organisational boundary (they have foundations for that). Our own corporate cases are typically sociotechnical systems or complex service systems, as in healthcare practice. Systems change projects have rapidly emerged from foundation-sponsored non-profit programmes, across many sectors, including the United Nations and its Sustainable Development Goals (SDG) programmes and innovation labs.

Systemic challenges often show up after a project has commenced as ambiguous issues that require expansion of a service or process design initiative. Sometimes, as in healthcare, holistic service design solutions require changes in health policy. At other scales, for example bioregional or climate planning, project outcomes might be interdependent with social movements that have no clear entry for design methods. Both complex contexts are completely different, but in distinct ways, using the same or different tools. And the same methods and tools, once learned, will be used differently in other contexts. The practitioner must learn the tools well enough to represent their value and use in each case.

Most of the Toolkit tools represent changes in practice we call *systemic management innovations* (SMIs). Management innovation[1] provides techniques new to the state of the art intended to further organisational goals. SMIs are management practices employed to enable a strategic transformation or reconfiguration of an organisation or social system, for systemic impact, and that contribute to system value. Many of the tools are admittedly structured representations of systemic methods that we have designed for collaborative engagement. The majority of methods that are so cited are also systemic management innovations in their own right, significant bodies of knowledge made coherent and useful as methods and toolkits.

Paradoxes in design for transformation

We also find a wide range of definitions and ideas around the prospect of systems change or transformation. To social innovators, systems change may be represented by a near-term positive outcome in programmes such as local food security, as localised impacts are clearly registered when situations improve. For many working with large-scale programmes (such as the UN SDGs), systems change may represent the outcome of many years of socio-economic development. At the level of economic world systems, transformative change might be represented as a definitive increase in population income levels (e.g., new middle class) or the move of a country to sustainable autarky (near self-sufficiency).

The transition from social impact to systems change[2] and transformation has progressed over a decade's evolution of social innovation, yet this emerging position is fraught with dilemmas in evaluation and conceptual definition. We are often dealing with multiple intersecting or entailed systems, as well as many changes and change influences all at once. With the implication of high complexity when working across multiple contexts, we (at least) have to ask 'which system' is being changed? Are we planning to change a service from inside its operations – as in service design, or from outside its boundaries – as in policy design? For what benefits, and for what expected or real outcomes?

---

[1] Julian Birkinshaw, Hamel & Mol (2008). Management innovation. *Academy of Management Review*.
[2] Zaid Khan & David Ing (2019). Paying attention to where attention is placed in the rise of system(s) change(s). In *Relating Systems Thinking and Design (RSD8) Symposium*. Institute of Design, Chicago. rsdsymposium.org

A clear definition of system transformation might be simply 'a deep and fundamental change of state observed in a system's structures, processes, or core functions.' Transformational change represents an acknowledged change from currently represented states, and results in some desirable and some problematic outcomes, many of which we cannot design for. Design is not control of the system but is a process that can dramatically improve and intervene in the journey of transformation. Even a change in *purpose* or values is not necessarily a system change, as an institution might change its purpose (e.g., an economic system shifts flows to the already wealthy) without changing its core functions.

As exciting as the prospect may seem to 'change the world,' the experience of leading systems change projects can be a disorienting journey without a clear destination. There are no standards or preeminent schools of thought in the evolving practices of systems change, as there are in sociotechnical systems. Reaching an agreement on end goals, means and methods, and definitions often requires seemingly endless discussions and meetings. New practitioners of systemic design will find it challenging to find the right balance of leadership and participatory process within the constant ambiguity of complexity.

Many of us may show beginner's confidence when applying known design tools for systems change and complex, multi-organisational challenges. However, complex systems (and the prospect of changing them intentionally) only get more challenging as we explore and learn together with system stakeholders. Better guidance is needed – yet a cookbook approach to methods and tools would fall far short of the power and sophistication necessary to engage systems change.

The promising potential of systemic design
Human-centred (and market-based) design creates products and services to enhance the value of an organisation's offer to customers and users. *Systemic design* advances a holistic design practice that integrates all design, research, and method skills for complex contexts. Systemic design creates no uniquely designated artefacts (such as in graphic or industrial design) but is known for systems maps – the Gigamap and synthesis map. These are tools for learning, design, knowledge creation, and action planning – maps are integral to the design journey, and are not end products in themselves.

Systemic design is a next-generation practice driven by the necessity to develop significantly better social systems, to plan and build complex services, and to convene systems transformation. It is based in pragmatism, drawing as it does from many ideas and knowledges, integrating across multiple levels and boundaries of systems practices. Systemic design is pragmatic as an active learning, not theoretical, orientation to complexity. The methods enabling systemic design are drawn from many schools of thought, from systems and design thinking, to sociology, cognitive engineering, and management theory. The objective of the systemic design project is to affirmatively integrate systems thinking and systems methods to guide human-centred design for complex, multi-system, and multi-stakeholder services and programmes.

Unlike services, systems have no single 'owner.' Nobody owns the climate or traffic, and complex healthcare breaks the boundaries of the hospital. We view systems as highly interconnected social and technological assemblages that function as a whole. Systems are networks of interconnected functions that achieve an intended outcome and can be seen as both emergent and designed. As whole systems are contained within other wholes, we often seek the next higher order, a nested or containing system, to intervene in a desired context. Today, we can view all systems as social, or as socially-entailing systems of systems. Human intervention has intervened in all aspects of the planetary ecology, rendering even natural and ecological systems socially-influenced. And even the most technical system requires services that provide direct value to people via designable processes.

Systemic design adapts the human-centred design approach to complex, multi-stakeholder service systems. It draws on well-established design competencies – form and process reasoning, social action and generative design research, design methods, and sketching and visualisation practices – to describe, map, propose, and reconfigure complex social systems.

Based on years of work in social and health sectors, we developed the Systemic Design Toolkit as a collection of systems power tools that enable service and strategic designers to bridge design research with stakeholders for complex systems. The Toolkit integrates a comprehensive set of methods in a common visual language for consistent reference across the stages of a full lifecycle systems change project. The canvases run through a complete lifecycle from start to launch over seven stages, which follow in the book. All the tools facilitate participatory engagement with iterative design for complex, multi-level contexts.

Learning by Travelling Together

The design *journey* is metaphorical, but not only so, as the book and methodology are structured to provide readers meaningful explorations of destinations in each chapter. We have designed the Journeys book to engage all travellers in a series of learning stages, as itineraries associated with the Toolkit stages and tool selection. Our objective is to narrate the learning process, anticipating the different entry points of experience and engagement, from our own experience of traversing these pathways over the years with many different fellow travellers.

We imagined the different backgrounds of our engaged readers. Throughout the book, as travel guides we speak to two primary personas, both of which are composites of the expected traveller in the learning journey.

1. **The Tourist**, who may be a first-time or interested traveller, a student, or someone learning enough to share these ideas, and

2. **The Explorer**, an experienced designer or systems consultant who may already know many tools and applications.

Many roles will find value in the design practices the Journeys methodology facilitates, including:

– Experienced designers learning systemic design tools and methods
– Learning designers developing in a field
– Managers and organisational leaders interested in the applications to large-scale problems
– Policymakers and policy labs
– Systems leaders and their organisations

Itineraries – Taking Journeys

As consulting designers and authors, we see several overarching purposes trending: complex design, stakeholder collaboration, tools for social transformation – all by systemic design. There are five major purposes of *Design Journeys*:

1. Design for systems change and systemic policy

2. Team collaboration for learning and designing for complexity

3. Design tools for complex system intervention

4. Stakeholder engagement for large-scale transition (e.g., energy, urban, climate) or transformation strategies

5. Training and education in systems methods, for systems or product/service design

Multiple purposes are often combined in complex change initiatives. Consider the worldwide UN programme for the Sustainable Development Goals, involving hundreds of UN leaders across their agencies and innovation labs; country and field-level leaders and local participants; and hundreds of civil society and NGO projects, and action networks. Dozens of specific applications for systemic design are found across the SDG pluriverse. With the overarching purpose of large-scale 'systems change' in specific cultural and national settings, we find shared systems challenges across all the SDG contexts, irrespective of the goals themselves. Why not use a common methodology across SDG programmes that might fit across many of the anticipated functions?

One of the common barriers to alignment and engagement between different stakeholders is a lack of common understanding of analysis and problem-solving methods. We find it counterproductive for such projects to require expert advisors and consultants to lead and train teams just to conduct such continuing multi-stakeholder projects. Especially since transformation programmes are commonly faced with ambiguous missions and complex social contexts, there is a real opportunity to employ convivial tools[3] that designers (Explorers) can adopt and adapt quickly. Further, we hope that all travellers might learn (as Tourists at first) and appreciate these tools as a common language and reference model, enabling alignment and coordination between the many levels and players in such systems change projects – projects that may soon become more the norm, not the exception.

📍 **Also visit**: The BIS book *Convivial Toolbox: Generative Research for the Front End of Design,* by design research professors Liz Sanders and Pieter Jan Stappers, which provides a complete methodology enabling generative research with convivial design tools for designing with, for, and by people.

---

[3] Convivial tools were named by Ivan Illich (*Tools for Conviviality, 1973*) as a mode of engaged co-production whereby simple, but useful commonly held tools could be advanced for adoption in practical settings, allowing skilled practitioners to recover agency and displace elite professionals in many walks of life.

Design Evolution into Complexity

Navigating Unprecedented Design Challenges

Design problems have grown in complexity beyond the capabilities of the creative design disciplines, and system problems have grown beyond the linear problem-solving of engineering, management, and policy. For the complex challenges of the 21st century, we require multiple disciplines, collaborating in coordinated learning teams toward a deeper understanding of contexts and social systems. Often, complex challenges will come framed by the sponsor in fuzzy, abstract terms, such as 'a better healthcare system for all,' reducing the threat of cyberattacks, or climate resilience. These are challenges that demand a deep rethinking of policy or programme planning so that meaningful interventions can be discovered through re-framing and collaboration. New frames are cocreated together, to expand the problem context to include expertise of all kinds, including the lived 'expert experience' of the victims of prior bad decisions, so we might collaborate wisely on systemic solutions and agree on action planning.

For everyone, and anyone, who may be potentially called to collaborate to address these complex social (and political) problem spaces, a significant query arises early on. What process do we agree to use? If we are dealing with complex multicausal 'messes,' or a crisis scenario, the question of process and method is not a trivial issue. If we believed that known, conventional methodologies – even systems or design methods – were sufficient, would we not see successful case studies on this or that method?

How are we then to best contribute our knowledge and perspectives in ways that accelerate learning and maximise the potential for consensus and positive progress? How do we engage an expanding variety of (potentially) leading experts who are perhaps used to leading entire programmes, as well as generalists, students, and other less experienced but passionate participants? And of course, stakeholders who might be at risk if poor decisions were made?

Activating an Integrated Interdiscipline

Systemic design developed from an integration of systems thinking theory with the practical methods of design thinking within an expanding field of research, practice experimentation, new methodologies, and engagement approaches. Academically, it is an interdisciplinary field integrating systems thinking and systems methods to effectively inform human-centred design for complex sociotechnical and multi-stakeholder social systems. As a design discipline, it draws upon theory and knowledge from systems and social sciences, cybernetics, applied research, organisational and management studies, ecology, media studies, and anthropology. With a developing body of applications in strategic planning, urban design, healthcare, public policy, and digital innovation, systemic design has become a professional practice.

We can define a system as a whole process interdependent on its constituent parts. assembly of functions and emergent interactions arising from relations of interdependent parts. **Systems thinking** analyses how the parts are recognised and interact with each other. A major goal of systems thinking is to understand the flows, relationships, and behaviour of parts within a system in order to enable the potential for changes or improvements to produce intended behaviours and outcomes effectively. The creation of any 'improvement' is necessarily a design process.

Systems thinking is not something that comes naturally to us, as most (Westerners) are trained to be linear thinkers, to analyse patterns by formula, and to observe systematic sequences as first-order chains of cause-and-effect. We also have ingrained habits of problem-solving, of perceiving situations as problems that must have solutions to be solved by linear, step-by-step processes. Therefore, we mistake complexity for complicatedness, and attempt to break down complexity into individual components in order to investigate the parts separately. When components are observed and reconnected into a system, the dynamics change precisely because they interact with each other. The weakness of the linear approach is that it occludes access to understanding the behaviour of the whole. The relationships between system levels (wholes containing other wholes) and orders of control are necessary to understand a system.

Design thinking refers to the designing process of finding meaningful solutions for human, organisational, and societal challenges. To lead in these challenges, designers listen to, learn from, conceptualise with, as well as make and iterate solutions with stakeholders. The design process always starts with a profound understanding of the needs, perspectives, and interests of the stakeholders. Design workshops are convened with mixed participants. The higher the perceived complexity of the challenge, the more stakeholders are asked to be engaged and own the cocreation of any solution, as they are experts in a lived system experience and leaders of the future model. In this process, the role of the designer is to develop a shared understanding of design context, to reframe goals and challenges, to make solutions visual and concrete, and to foster dialogue among stakeholders.

New Design, New Design Teams

Now let's seriously consider the composition and competencies of contemporary teams convening for complex systems change. Beyond the expected readers of Journeys and users of the Toolkit, depending on the system domain and expected outcome, a project team might draw on social scientists, clinicians, policy experts, engineers, investors, management consultants, or artists. Along with designers, a variety of disciplines and competencies will be necessary to collaborate across stages of work. A real and growing challenge for teams facing complex, indeterminate, wicked problems is the organisational challenge of finding, keeping, and training the right new scientists, consultants, policymakers, and designers.

Yet, if we catalogued the skill sets and profiles of the high-performance complexity team, exceptions would soon surpass the list of expert qualities. Instead, we

might imagine how the new designer will enable these disciplines to learn and collaborate. The new designer is someone who can think in systems, yet speak in stories. Someone who can sketch complex ideas in multiple formats, yet capture the ideas of the contributors with empathy. Someone who can draw on a learned range of design skills, but lends their attention to serve the team and guide its learning toward discovery and tangible outcomes. Someone who can hold images of the future[4] in focus, while working with mixed stakeholder teams on mapping the details of system interactions.

All designers are faced with increasing complications of complex projects, and the practical problem of capturing and specifying complexity to help clients understand the system impacts of product and service design. The systemic designer enters as a type of systems leader, a mixed-methods action researcher, a design facilitator for systems changes. In fact, in any challenge of significant situational complexity, the requisite skills, methods, and dispositions (mindsets) of the new designers might not be listed on any curriculum or swimlanes chart. The systemic designer will be happy to improvise in changing situations as well, to extend their knowledge beyond the expertise when needed, to locate the best-fit method when none exists, and to intuitively draw on prior experience in skilled repertoires.

Design as System Sensemaking

As systemic design grew beyond its original premise of systems thinking approaches for advanced design problems, its applications expanded from the *sociotechnical* (technology in social and work practices) to complex social systems and systems change. The field has grown quickly to advise and perform design for applications to complex societal problems, such as national healthcare services and disease management, mega-city urban planning, transition planning for energy and climate resilience, new economics, and other public policy. None of these are isolated 'domains,' as each of these are affected by unknowable dynamics

---

[4] From Fred Polak & Elise Boulding (1973). *The Image of the Future*. The future image consists of its *essence*, the dominant trajectory of events, and an *influence*, the human power of agency over destiny. Systems interventions can consider the effect and imagined outcome of any future potential.

in population and regional demographics, climate and natural ecology effects, political and regulatory influences, and technological impacts. Yet designers are not experts in these domains, neither do we necessary excel as systems analysts. The leading competency for design leadership in complexity might be a faculty we call 'system sensemaking.'

Typical systemic design challenges are socially organised, large-scale, multi-organisational, with significant emergent properties. In high complexity, design and management decisions cannot be made based on individual or in-group knowledge only. Mixed teams of the requisite mix of disciplines will often be necessary. Systemic design applies sensemaking skills such as visual storytelling and visual analysis, drawing out wisdom through dialogue, and knowledge translation through diagramming. Knowing many methods that can be selected for emerging and complex contexts proves more effective for designers than relying on the availability of deep expertise, such as system modelling.

In previous work, Jones and van Patter[5] present the four geographies, or Design Domains model of Design 1.0-4.0 (D1.0-4.0). The model expresses increasing social complexity in design applications beyond products, services, and communications – expanding the horizon and altitude of design practice (Figure 1). D1.0 (artefactual) and D2.0 (products and services) are well-known domains of skilled design practice for human use, mobilising the values of design quality, aesthetics, and usability to enhance economic value or competitiveness. Organisations and their processes (D3.0) and social, ecological, policy systems (D4.0) represent complex, non-traditional domains that require multiple, specialised skill sets for transdisciplinary projects and mixed-stakeholder teams. These design domains are practised more as a sensemaking process with system stakeholders (as designers), including but not focused on traditional creative design of artefacts or enhancing market value.

Innovation and meaning-making show up quite differently between the two market-facing domains and the two socially-complex design domains. If we posit the definition of innovation as a process that creates meaningful value for people, meaning is disclosed in artefacts and services through differentiation of qualities that reveal value, or 'differencing.' The salience of meaningful differences is represented in a market or to users through enhanced aesthetics, branded identity, and promoted features – these tactics draw on the design skill of 'making the familiar strange,' or *strangemaking*.

Sensemaking distinguishes more the organisational and social worlds, especially as uncertainty and complexity grow when stakeholder perspectives are expanded. Sensemaking can be defined as a collective attempt to form a coherent rationale to explain matters of shared concern. Does this not sound like systems thinking?

Yet, while systems thinking is notoriously difficult to learn or share, the design practices of sensemaking are much more available to elicit ideas and engage participation. While there are several schools of sensemaking, all of which may be useful or valuable in systemic design, here we will focus on how design practices created for specific purposes enable groups to make sense of systems.

The four domains require an evolution of design thinking, practice, research, and education to develop the requisite skills and knowledge necessary to address complexity that increases at each level. Completely different sets of skills and methods apply in each domain, and they are generally transferable *up* the scale (i.e., D4.0 can use skills learned in the other levels), but not *down* levels (i.e., D1.0 would not need complexity facilitation).

[5] Writing with GK Van Patter, (2013). Understanding Design 1, 2, 3, 4: The Rise of Visual Sensemaking, in *Meanings of Designed Spaces*. Authors in the systemic design corpus have proposed distinct, emerging design practices in these domains (e.g., John Thackara, Birger Sevaldson, Ezio Manzini, Don Norman).

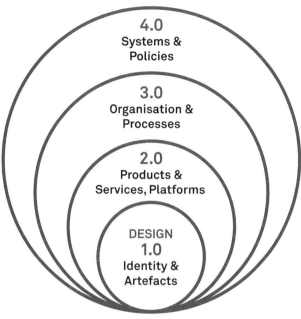

Figure 1
Boundaries of the four Design Domains

The four domains embody design processes for the following contexts:

1. **Identity and artefact design** (D1 - Limited complexity): Skilled practice for a wide range of communications, from artefact creation (graphic, ads, websites, 1-2 designers) to strategic communications as part of systems change.

2. **Products, services and platform design** (D2 – High artefact complexity): Value creation by design and mixed teams (including service design, product innovation, multichannel, and user experience); design for integration across media.

3. **Organisation and processes** (D3 – Complex, bounded by business or strategy): Change-oriented, design of work practices, strategies, and organisational structures.

4. **Systems and policies** (D4 - Complex, unbounded): Design for social transformation, complex social

systems, policymaking, ecological and community design.

Major differences in problem and system complexity are found between each level, and the skills in each domain are not interchangeable in practice. In any complex design process, the skills and tools from across all levels might be employed. Each higher domain entails and can leverage the lower ones. For example, an organisational process design (D3.0) can develop a communications design strategy with high-quality D1.0 work, and its processes can be designed following service design methods (D2.0). But a service design engagement does not typically have the skills on board, or the remit, to expand its capability to conduct organisational level sensemaking and design for culture-building.

The four domains differ in their strategy, intention, and outcomes. Each domain requires skill and coordination of distinct methods, design practices, collaboration skills, and stakeholder participation. These are not fixed requirements but merely entry criteria for skilful performance sufficient to meet the demands of that domain's complexity (or variety) in practice. The most salient of these differences is also one of the least noticeable, or recognisable as a skill – this is a skilled practice of sensemaking as facilitation. In the two product-oriented domains (D1.0 and 2.0), the requirement for leading sensemaking in complex situations is much less demanded than the design skill of distinctiveness (or *strangemaking*). Simply put, in design domains where a *product* is to be delivered, a critical performance value is the distinctive novelty the designer might realise – often considered a hallmark of creativity. Strangemaking presents the product as visibly novel, leading to desired sales, adoption, or engagement goals.

However, in D3.0 and 4.0 the desiderata are much different. These systemic contexts can be considered fuzzy situations, upstream contexts, un-briefed, non-parametric, and complex due to structure and organisation. In D4.0 systems change contexts, these problems may show up as messes or 'wicked problems.' The (Rittel) wicked problem framework[6] may be well

---

[6] Horst Rittel & Melvin Webber (1973). Dilemmas in a general theory of planning. *Policy Sciences.*

known to readers as the 10 characteristics of a dynamic problem mix that evades solutions and evaluation. The idea of the *mess* was coined by Russell Ackoff[7] 40 years ago, and technically defined as "large and complex sets of interacting problems, dynamic systems of problems." Ackoff advocated against trying to solve or resolve messes – they could only be *dissolved*, by changing the meaning (framing) and by creative planning, using design idealisation to propose different alternatives.

Such problem systems require sensemaking (in Dervin[8] and Weick's[9] sense of the interpretation of experience organisational meaning) not differencing. Everyone attempting to perform systemic work discovers that agreement on goals and actions to press the challenge require facilitated – often extensive – deliberation to elicit the 'requisite' points of view and concerns.

Design Strategies and Boundaries

How are these design strategies relevant to a systems change practice? Each design domain holds a distinct system boundary. There are well-understood differences between a simple design project (D1.0) and a market-facing product or service (D2.0). The social complexity of an organisational boundary (D3.0) entails design literacy and research insight into governance, business strategy, product line and service strategies, customer support, and management systems. The design context for a D3.0 complex system requires different mindsets, value propositions, disciplinary composition, and skills. The boundary and the social system are further expanded with D4.0 systemic design contexts. This domain includes the transformation arena (system change), ecological systems, policy design, and unbounded (messy) community and civic domains.

The primary practices taught in all design schools (D1.0 and 2.0) are premised on 'design as making,' which we do not minimise, as design craft is a foundation skill and a serious reflective practice. D1.0 and 2.0 are characterised by direct service to clients or organisations. The

standards of quality for these domains are driven by creative differentiation, for distinctive visual, experiential, or brand images that satisfy the goals of a business strategy or brief. These are defined as 'differencing' applications of design. Van Patter calls this *strangemaking*, as opposed to sensemaking – presenting the familiar as strange to enhance the unique value of design to frame ideas and capture attention.

Systemic design requires cocreating, planning, and orchestrating consensus for process or practice change at scales commensurate with the institution itself. D3.0 and 4.0 cross into transdisciplinary territory and systemic design practice. These contexts require facilitation of sensemaking with multiple stakeholders within and between organisations. Sensemaking processes are entailed in designed workshops that creatively convene these mixed stakeholders to collaborate on design proposals and reach an agreement on action in the face of high uncertainty and complexity.

The final chapter in the book (Reflections) discusses more on sensemaking as theory and process, which readers might find helpful after the development of method skills in the following chapters.

Systemic Designers are *Teams*

The strategic intent of design thinking in the organisational and social system domains is to guide teams working within these complex systems toward effective design decisions, strategies, interventions, and mixed services and systems. The Journeys methodology facilitates this process. Each tool teaches the team as much about itself – by reflecting on knowledge, goals, and tensions – as it does about the subject system of interest.

One of the first necessary design practices is to identify and shape the diversity of perspectives, experience, and knowledge in the design team to form knowledgeable, high-performance collaborations. The diversity (or

---

[7] Russell Ackoff (1981). The art and science of mess management. *Interfaces*.
[8] Dervin, B. (1998). Sense-making theory and practice. *Journal of Knowledge Management*.
[9] Karl Weick, Sutcliffe & Obstfeld (2005). Organizing and the process of sensemaking. *Organization Science*.

variety) principle comes into play as a critical method in stakeholder definition for [2] Listening to the System, as the core design team starts to realise they are designing on behalf of stakeholders of the system. The whole design team can see themselves as delegated to perform the systemic and service design on behalf of the whole system.

Because these domains of higher complexity involve significantly more social complexity parts – human stakeholders who must be consulted – system-level design becomes more of a practice of making sense of things with decision-makers and stakeholders. Design activities cannot merely happen in small groups within the studio setting, but must occur in the arenas of organisational activities and planning strategies themselves. We have traditionally faced several real barriers to increased adoption:

— Designers are not the accepted experts in any of these domains, so we may find ourselves at the edges of social programme and policy contexts.

— Social systems are not markets or customers, that we can study through research and define appropriate services. Policy labs and programmes taking this approach have often failed in projects when they do not have a service delivery level that exists within containing regulatory and governing systems.

— All social systems involve, and so require in design, the participation of a diverse range of stakeholders. The missing factor in earlier applications of design in systems thinking was the necessity of appropriate engagement with 'committed participants.' A fascination with systems methods can lead to system mapping or extremely detailed analyses based solely on external research. Until recently, we had few, if any, systems tools tested for use in stakeholder workshops.

Design Journeys integrates these domains of knowledge, using Systemic Design Toolkit methods appropriate for any stakeholder system of interest, and provides a translation of those methods to a design space for creative intervention.

Figure 2
At Namahn we have a dedicated space for cocreation with magnetic white-board walls that can be used as tabletops. Here we are cocreating for DoucheFLUX, a facility for and with homeless people.

Systemic Design Methodology

Design Journeys and the Toolkit

Design Journeys was originally developed from the Systemic Design Toolkit[1] which has been innovated and evaluated for more than five years. The Toolkit was designed from its origin as a non-proprietary collection of PDF canvases (licensed as CC BY-NC-ND[2]) with public access to a smaller set of tools in the public version. The Toolkit has been successfully adopted by organisations adopting in the public sector, social innovation, and education, as well as in small and large businesses.

We know that toolkits are a kind of translation of theory to practise by way of method, and they can have gaps and shortcomings. Any "toolkit" carries a promise to relieve the burdens of research and rigorous skill development by packaging guidelines for easier adaptation. While the Systemic Design Toolkit is used in graduate design education, most toolkits are not taught in advanced education at all. Many aggregations of resources labelled as toolkits are merely a curated set of branded training templates or guidelines provided by a popular practitioner. Also, there are so many toolkits now produced for design and innovation methods that practice leaders can be overwhelmed with choice. This is perhaps exemplified by the lead of the OECD public sector innovation lab declaring that the field has reached 'peak toolkit'.[3]

Critiques are always helpful, as there are points any new toolkit should address. The material should not be too broad, or too granular. Tools ought to be feasible to learn without extensive training, and training requirements should be explicit. The tools themselves ought to be aligned to real purposes.

The intent of the *Journeys* book is to provide the support for learning this powerful portfolio of methods, step-by-step, as well as to learn sufficient theory and application techniques to be able to apply the tools with confidence and credibility. The seven-stage Design Journeys methodology was designed to scaffold and assign a variety of tools that otherwise might be experienced as a *complicated* process, in its search to provide a framework for complexity.

Why the Toolkit

Systems thinking history shows at least four eras of systems education in management that have attempted to integrate systems thinking into management of complex organisations. In the 1960's, operations research approaches were predominant; in the 1980's, Russell Ackoff and IBM were among the systems thinking leaders; and in the 1990's, Peter Senge's *Fifth Discipline* led a management revolution. In the 2000's, we saw the rise of integrated methodologies (e.g., Michael Jackson's integrative holism), the move toward engagement (e.g., Appreciative Inquiry and Open Space), and the schools

---

[1] The Toolkit was inspired and developed in workshops at the Relating Systems Thinking and Design Symposia, with the RSD proceedings tracing its development. https://rsdsymposium.org.
[2] The Creative Commons license assigned to all tools is BY-NC-ND Attribution Non-Commercial, No Derivatives https://creativecommons.org/licenses/by-nc-nd/4.0/legalcode.
[3] Angela Hanson (2018*). Have we reached Peak Toolkit?. OECD, Observatory of Public Sector Innovation.*

of design thinking (e.g., IDEO and service design). The Systemic Design Toolkit learned from these innovations and offers an array of tools designed for stakeholder engagement that (if chosen appropriately) will support any system design context or organisation.

The methodology has been carefully constructed to address known issues and failures of these prior attempts to adapt systems thinking tools to business and public organisations. In 2009, Fred Collopy, professor at Case Western Reserve University, proposed[4] that design thinking might succeed in organisations where systems thinking had failed because its simpler, more accessible entry points allow people to try out parts, and satisfy short and long-term objectives over time. Dr. Collopy's critique noted:

> "Each of systems thinking's various manifestations demands some degree of subscription to an orthodoxy (a particular view of just what systems thinking is). And each requires that the user master a large number of related ideas and techniques, most of which are not particularly useful on their own."

Peter Jones responded[5] that the rigorous, deliberative tools of systems thinking were never designed to match the enacted and improvisational styles of modern management. Management practice is trained as if it were a quantified, scientific approach to business administration, yet in reality, managing is a mix of communications and decision support skills adapted to organisational settings. The history of systems thinking in business assumed that managers would undergo a period of training, reflection, and long-term adoption of systems methods. Instead, systems thinking – and predictably, design thinking later – became management fads. Systems thinking was popularised for a period but rarely used seriously in mainstream organisations, because of the commitment required to employ its abstract and reflective practices.

It is telling that Peter Senge,[6] author of the widely-known Fifth Discipline methodology, extended 50 years

of systems thinking to recently advocate a practice of *systems leadership* in our current era of complexity. Systems leadership develops competencies to see and engage the larger system, to collaborate toward the health of the whole system rather than symptomatic fixes, and to lead from one's own place in the system, "shifting the collective focus from reactive problem solving to co-creating the future."

The goal of a systemic design competency might be to amplify the capacities for pragmatic design and action toward change in complex systems by choosing from a powerful set of thinking models adapted for effective collaboration and design action. All of *Design Journeys*' tools are helpful when used in context, but as with any systems model, they can be challenging at first to learn and to train others. The Journeys book has been designed for use in engagements, and to ease that learning curve. In the Systemic Design Toolkit, these thinking-and-doing tools are harmonised and translated as design tools that can be used by practitioners in one to two-hour workshops with modest training. The tools are prepared as visual templates in image formats for virtual workshops, and printable at several sizes for live meetings, with a deliberate balance of design thinking and systems thinking.

Toolkit Value Proposition

The Systemic Design Toolkit is a complete set of systems methods, with over 40 modelling canvases designed for participatory workshops, following the seven-stage Design Journeys methodology. Validated through years of applications, academic training, testing, and workshops, the Toolkit bridges systems thinking, human-centred design, and service design approaches to address complex systems contexts. The Toolkit provides a full stack of powerful resources for systems change and complex design that can be learned and adapted into a personal repertoire.

---

[4] Fred Collopy (2009). Lessons learned — Why the failure of systems thinking should inform the future of design thinking. *Fast Company.*
[5] Peter Jones (2009). Learning the lessons of systems thinking: Exploring the gap between thinking and leadership. *Integral Leadership Review.*
[6] Peter Senge, Hamilton & Kania (2015). The dawn of system leadership. *Stanford Social Innovation Review.*

The Toolkit addresses challenges unique to complex systems:

— We have a clear and continuing need for powerful tools to map system contexts, human behaviours within systems, and to link services to different levels of system.

— Systemic design does not rely on 'users' only. It requires the knowledge and experience revealed through contributions by a wide inclusion of system stakeholders. Our engagement tools must reflect this difference.

— Decisions made by corporate teams for systems challenges always fail to predict future emergent problems within the next larger system boundary. Systems do not conform to a single stakeholder's interests and goals, and organisational structures prevent internal teams from truly considering the influences of other actors.

— Design thinking and product/service design have insufficient power for complex sociotechnical systems. The systemic design process allows for the sustained, iterative development of relational knowledge required to understand change points and impacts in complexity.

The most critical barrier to acceptance of design practice, and systemic design as an integrated systems practice, has been the lack of reliable and accepted methods for large-group workshops to engage real-world complexity. Creative design methodologies such as design thinking, journey mapping, and prototyping were (and are) used in many cases as a kind of compromise between well-known design practices used by firms and the desired planning and change outcomes in client and stakeholder cases. One value of the Toolkit is of course the enhanced usability of systemic thinking practices, through systems thinking methods in ready-to-use visual formats. The significant value, we believe, is that the Toolkit makes it

possible for design teams to choose the best series of systems thinking activities that match the needs and aspirations of any client problem or case. We have found that trained designers are able to use most methods with many types of stakeholders and people from all walks of life. The Systemic Design Toolkit essentially provides scaffolds and powerful frames of systems modelling and change as a new language to facilitate dialogue about problems that matter.

We discuss each of these as a tool, an open method that embodies relevant systems theory and design practices, in a fusion of concept and format. The canvas formats are created especially for small group engagement, where the PDF form can be printed and posted-up in a studio session, and image files can be posted onto virtual whiteboards for interaction with colour-coded digital notes.

Almost every tool draws on a foundational model published in systems science. The principles and steps for the use of each tool are designed to reflect the intent of the original sources, which in most cases had no interactive tool or a good visual model from which to adapt. The original papers typically present a systems theory and model, with some (e.g., Iterative Inquiry) having a basic visual reference and approach, and others (e.g., causal loops) having a visual model, but were never integrated into a holistic design process.

Each model represents a set of distinctions drawn from a relevant system theory[7] and the theories selected for the Toolkit are consistent with the prevailing models in soft systems methodology, social systems design, and newer theories such as sociotechnical transitions. As the underlying principles are consistent with each other, the maps can connect to form a series of inputs and outputs. That is, the tools can be used in an order where concepts generated in one are taken as inputs to initiate the next map in a meaningful sequence.

---

[7] We can observe that there are many systems theories, and while most of them are compatible with each other in theory (due to their use of isomorphisms that apply universally). In practice though, each system model or theory has a different best application, style, or culture. In the Toolkit, we have selected systemic methods we believe are aligned well to large-scale social system and change challenges. However, many systems theories have been left out of the Toolkit for reasons of design and their lack of fit to the design style of workshopping.

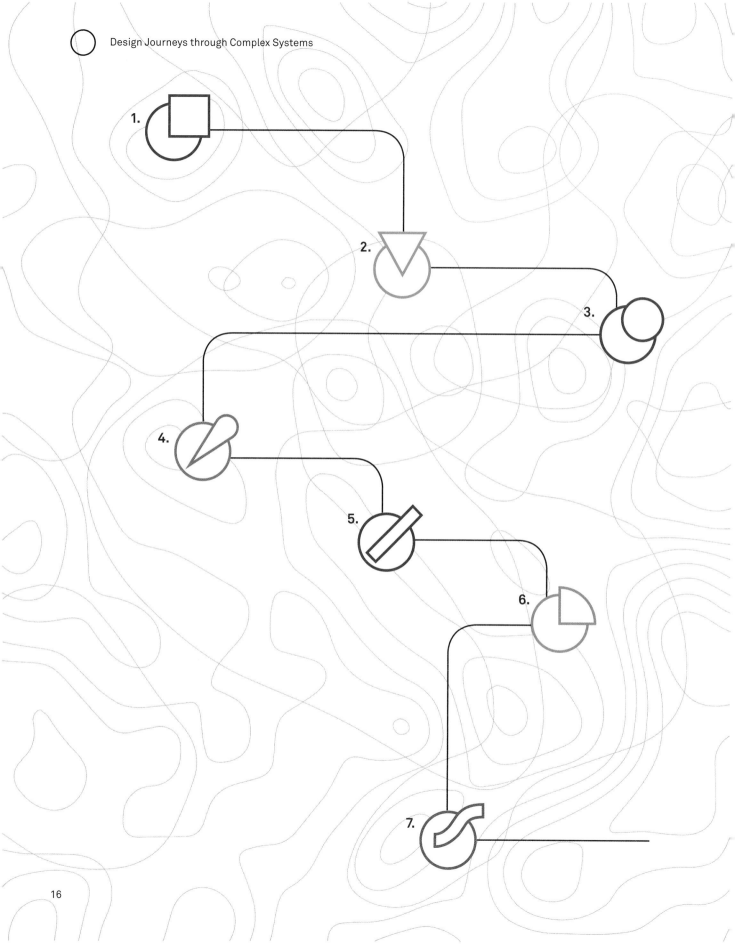

1.

2.

3.

4.

5.

6.

7.

Design Journeys: Seven Stages to Destination

The full Systemic Design Toolkit was created by assigning multiple tools, in some cases as many as seven, to a multi-stage design process that enables collaborative design for nearly every method. The Design Journeys are the unique pathways each convener takes to select and adapt specific tools as called for in any complex systems project. Design Journeys embodies a style of engagement with visual outputs that guide the quality and completeness of design and learning across stages or movements of the process. The stages are a type of *grammar*, where steps are followed (as if a syntax) for learning and to ensure a good result.

Others may find limitations to stakeholder engagement and may choose sets of stages that offer the most value in a limited timeframe. Each stage in the methodology entails distinctive differences and tools, and both Tourists and Explorers should consider the value of lesser-known tools when deciding which stages to include or shortcut.

The journeys of this book's tour follow these stages in order, like a roadmap. In actual usage, however, every project differs – some may adopt these journeys well after framing and research. Overall, the general order of the journeys shows that the first three stages explore 'how we got into this mess,' and the three latter stages plan 'how to design to change this mess.'

[1] Framing the System
The first stage frames the **scope and boundaries of the current system for the full design lifecycle process**. What are the social, physical, and temporal boundaries of the system? What is the purpose of the system? What are the forces that cause the need for change? Who is active in the system and how are the relationships influencing the dynamics? What new innovations and practices are emerging?

[2] Listening to the System
The Listening journey is a full stage of human research, **observing behaviours of the system** through engaging participants, through field studies, ethnography, participatory workshops, and social research. The tools help to prepare and carry out participatory action research and field studies. Listening provides structured tools for stakeholder discovery, and to observe, interview, analyse human interaction and activity within the system of interest.

[3] Understanding the System
Understanding **explores the forces that create system behaviours**. Well-defined systems methods are translated to design tools for finding and mapping variables and identifying feedback loops, and locating leverage points with high potential for system change. The third stage completes the 'current system' analysis, pulling together insights from Framing as well as research, integrating team learning into visual explanations.

[4] Envisioning Desired Futures
The middle stage moves the journey toward desired future systems, with several tools for collaborative foresight and defining total system value. Envisioning provides the first opportunity for reframing a systems change programme or its goals. Here, **possible futures desired by system stakeholders** are articulated and the envisioned value created by the vision is mapped.

[5] Exploring the Possibility Space
Stage [5] moves the journey toward 'the desired system' through the next three stages. The possibility space **explores the most effective design interventions** with potential for system change. Systemic design tools help define scenarios, leverage points for change, and identify the places and times for influential intervention.

[6] Planning the Change Process
The Planning stage moves the journey from abstract system models to more concrete plans for organising. This stage provides tools for planning how to **(re)organise, govern, and deliver** on system value.

[7] Fostering the Transition
The final stage in *Design Journeys* **enables the actions toward change interventions to implement the interventions and strategy for the system transition.**

A Participatory Design Practice

We developed the Journeys tools with the values of participation and collaborative learning in mind. The Design Journeys methodology supports a designerly approach to the analytical systems methods of the toolkit, with the aim of accessibility in collaborative design workshops. Workshops convened with the tools can be designed as (more or less) participatory, anticipatory, or empowering experiences.

The Journeys are staged, not to be convened as a structured design methodology, but to help the organising team separate the goals of each stage of learning, and to structure the participation for stakeholders in a clearly defined way, with a definitive logic. The Journeys design approach is all pre-development (or implementation) and can be understood as a complete metaplanning[8] and strategic design process, but applied to complex social systems and system transformation. The participatory design style is essential to system metaplanning because the planners are the stakeholders, who will be responsible for implementation. Therefore, stakeholders must also understand every step of the design planning journey.

The following principles provide a core set of process values inspiring a style for Design Journeys engagements. The values were largely suggested by vital ideas presented in various Relating Systems Thinking and Design (RSD) symposia, which, for over a decade, have grown a research community and foundation of practices supporting these methods. These are distinctly different from the (Jones, 2014) systemic design principles discussed in the Reflections chapter, that provide more functional guidance on design applications from the combined effect of unifying systems and design principles. The 10 principles are indicators for effective process design in the spirit of systems leadership, and for learning and convening Design Journeys.

Participatory

No single profession, group, or organisation can successfully address today's societal challenges alone.[9] The application of systemic design demands the participation of stakeholders across existing social systems boundaries. Unlike other design practices, systemic design has no end user or consumer. Systems have actors and stakeholders who we prefer to treat as *participants*.

Anticipatory

All systems change leads us to design for futures, but we must always ask, 'whose future?' The worldviews, goals, and values of participants in multiple future contexts are entailed and represented through futures-oriented design methods. Further, we seek to enable stakeholders with different temporal reasoning preferences to contribute to strategic foresight in systems design and change, as equally as possible.

Disclosing Knowledge

A common understanding can only truly be achieved if knowledge is openly shared within collaborations, through processes of socialisation. Experiential and tacit knowledge informing design and governance decisions are valuable when shared and understood by all. Systemic design tools reveal team and stakeholder knowledge in structured formats for effective reuse.

Experiential Presence

Systemic design becomes engaged effectively when collaborating in engaging activities that produce an intense feeling of 'here and now' presence[10] and flow in participation. During these activities, participants release cognitive commitments within the system, and can challenge and shift system boundaries and goals.

Empowering

Systemic design activities aim to help people collectively make sense of the challenge, and provide them with plans of action that they can carry out in the systems they are ordinarily entangled in. The activities transform them into agents of change in their daily field of action.

---

[8] Charles Owen (2001). Structured planning in design: Information-age tools for product development. *Design Issues*.
[9] Sharon Matthias & Jess McMullin (2017). Systemic Maturity Models and multi-organization collaborations. *RSD6 Symposium*, Oslo.
[10] Piotr Michura & Stan Ruecker (2017). Design as production of presence – systemic approach to re-designing novelty. *RSD6 Symposium*, Oslo.

Open-Ended

Unlike other design disciplines, systemic design is not bound to a specific outcome, be it a product or a service, or the creation of a single solution. Open systems demonstrate equifinality, as there may be multiple effective means to a preferred end. Systemic design aims to identify, develop, and stimulate interventions to change and adapt the system as leading processes on the way to change, supporting already ongoing stakeholder commitments.

Pluriversality

Systemic design embraces a pluriversal worldview[11] that recognises a commitment to design supporting a pluralism of cultures, societies and experiences that seek or are expressed in movements toward social transformation. A critical tension with Western or modernist universalism is implied in such plurality. Pluriversality seeks a relational appreciation among multiple ontologies that coexist, often in many territories at once, while expressing autonomy and local transformations through the power of design by co-participants.

Numinosity and Inner Reflection

While not an explicit frame of design action in most cases, systemic design recognises the mystery of human experience and the evolution of higher states of consciousness, leading to new outlooks on human possibility in nature and the universe. The emergence of the numinous, spiritual, and deep inner knowing can be integrated and honoured in approaches to creative design for higher orders of meaning, including social, cultural, and civilisational systems of meaning.

Multi-Level and Multi-Perspective

The Journeys design process continuously modulates between levels of abstraction by alternating between levels (from human-focused to very abstract) and shifting perspectives (disciplinary or expert views, or life experiences associated with the system). The tools facilitate 'zooming in and out,' moving between levels of the system and the stakeholders. Several tools help reframe boundary judgments, to accommodate different

stakeholder perspectives[12] and to transcend paradigms.

Formative

The Journeys toolkit is not merely a structured sequence of methods, but rather a grammar that connects previously isolated practices into a meaningful model. *Design Journeys* allows designers to bring the systemic design vocabulary (the methods and tools) together in a way that makes sense for a given project, commensurate with its complexity, and thus constructing a new narrative. The order of activities depends on the context of application and social dynamics of the moment.

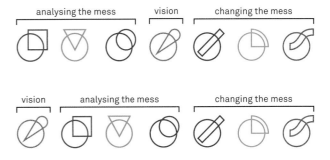

Figure 3
Blending Journeys - Visions of Stage [4] can also join Stage [1]

---

[11] Arturo Escobar (2018). *Designs for the Pluriverse*. Duke University Press.
[12] Philippe Vandenbroeck & Kristel Van Ael (2016). Codifying Systemic Design: A toolkit. *RSD5 Symposium*, Toronto.

Convening Cocreation

Facilitating the studio engagements of systemic design practices

Systemic design *requires* cocreation with stakeholders responsible for change and design decisions. The ultimate agents of system change are those who live within the system every day, who are committed to a shared future. They may not 'own' the system, but they are the system participants whose lives would be affected the most by design decisions and interventions. Real stakeholders have 'skin in the game.' They have a duty of care and to advocate for system changes that would be acceptable to others. As designers, we are usually facilitators.

In organisations and complex systems, people *are* the system. Social systems are composed of individuals acting in concert within system structures and processes. The idea of getting the 'whole system in the room' is respected throughout a systemic design process. This is recognised in the many ways we seek requisite variety in systemic design – whether it is a variety of stakeholders, representatives of disciplines and communities, or ideas and values. It may seem unrealistic to organise and aim for requisite variety at times. By following effective sampling practices and stakeholder discovery, however, participatory system convening with meaningful representation can be reached.

Convening the Journeys methodology is done with accessible Toolkit canvases in envisioning exercises, with committed stakeholders engaged in online workshops and onsite charettes. We do not recommend analytical, in-house system mapping, where one is working independently behind the scenes toward delivering a report of findings. Design is an engaged process.

The Room is Not the Territory

As the map is not the world and terrain it represents, the participants in our workshops are not actually representing the system. They are at best a good sample. Individuals represent their own interests and understandings, and no single person holds a commensurate knowledge, or the values, of a complex social group. Organisational behaviour and naturalistic decision-making, as they happen in context, are not reproduced in online or offsite encounters. A multi-stakeholder group may never have seen one another before a meeting upon invitation to the dialogue.

How do we define and qualify sufficient representation to ensure meaningful stakeholder variety? We are always working with a social simulation of the system. There may be little correspondence of features and function between brilliant, fully engaged invited groups and the social systems in which they live and work. Take this into account when making plans and decisions from the outcomes of participatory design.

Experienced facilitators of large-group interventions use the expression of 'getting the whole system in the room,' a metaphor that drives an attempt to balance representation of the direct stakeholders who live in and with the system itself. Large group processes such as Future Search[1] and Open Space[2] hold a key assumption that larger groups increase the variety of perspectives, and this variety reduces the groupthink and power dynamics within the group, and possibly for the system they represent.

[1] Marvin Weisbord & Sandra Janoff (2010). *Future Search: Getting the Whole System in the Room for Vision, Commitment, and Action*. Berrett-Koehler.
[2] Harrison Owen (2000). *The Power of Spirit: How Organizations Transform*. Berrett-Koehler.

Alexander Christakis[3] developed a foundation of systems principles that methodically result in effective group process outcomes. Following these precepts can result in similar advantages with much smaller groups, as we can form an intentional sample with just 15-20 well-selected participants that represent system variety. Over the Design Journeys stages, we can discover and integrate more participants that represent current and future system variety. These are primarily people with a stake in the system change, those who are already involved, highly impacted, or with vested interests.

In Design Journeys, a specific facilitation method is not promoted. Since many organisations will have preferred workshop approaches, we suggest an adaptive approach. It would also require far more than an introductory chapter to instruct system facilitation methods, such as Christakis' Dialogic Design or Appreciative Inquiry.[4] Yet principles from these systemic practices can serve as guidelines for design cocreation workshops.

Engagement Structure

Gaining deep understanding across widely disparate organisations and stakeholders requires more than holding large group workshops and occasional meetings. As a social system is expanded to its larger social boundary (as across an industry or community), do we plan to engage large group interventions that draw variety from the inclusion of greater numbers of participants? Or do we recruit a targeted balance of stakeholders according to their future contributions?

There are different purposes, benefits, and drawbacks to both small and large group workshops. The Journeys model benefits smaller groups for deep knowledge-sharing, collaboration, learning, and quality ideation. Smaller groups may be 10-25 participants – the sample size is relative to the entire organisation or overall system. Larger groups, generally over 40, require far more time and management of parallel production and a real focus on moderation for engagement in small groups. Breakout groups, whether virtual or collocated in person, are ideally structured to assign between 4-7 people,

regardless of the total complement in the large group. Fewer than four risks variety loss, and more than seven reduces net participation or reinforces a small number of active speakers.

Convening work with a single organisation can be done well in larger groups, as intact teams and working relationships will already be present. However, there are decreasing rates of participation and ideation in larger sized breakout groups. Larger groups often require much more time to facilitate plenary discussions, small group reviews, and transitions between sessions. Fewer maps and tools may be workshopped in these large group sessions to open the intangible, unstructured space required for dialogue.

How can we know whether we have acquired (or approximated) the requisite social variety to represent a given social system, without modelling the system and its interactions in detail? When the very identity of a social system is defined by the context cocreated by its members, we have to involve some quorum of stakeholders that other members would agree as representing knowledge and values, identities and cultures, and system boundaries. If we consider a minimum necessary set of cocreation contexts, we will find real differences in approach and can define practices aligned to these contexts.

Contexts of Cocreation

We can define four distinct forms of cocreation, based on the appropriate contexts for design, planning, or group decision outcomes. Consider the primary client or organising contexts in which cocreation workshops are conducted – how do we collaborate today? We may hold an internal working session; review and planning meetings with a core team of clients; and major engagements with organisations, stakeholders, or the public. The purpose of the collaboration defines who attends, with the immediate participants being either 1) internal only, 2) team plus external sponsors, 3) external

[3] Alexander Christakis & Kenneth Bausch (2006). *How People Harness their Collective Wisdom and Power to Construct the Future in Co-laboratories of Democracy*. Information Age Publishing.
[4] David Cooperrider, Whitney & Stavros (2008). *The Appreciative Inquiry Handbook: For Leaders of Change*. Berrett-Koehler.

stakeholders convened by the team, or 4) public meetings convened by the team. Each of these contexts demands a different convening style.

We can show these contexts in a cycle of learning and development, as shown in the diagram (Figure 4) based on author Jones' recent study[5] on dialogic design methodology. Clockwise starting from the Lab are four locations, each of which calls for different participants and facilitation:

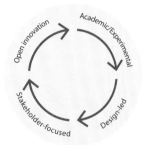

Figure 4
Systemic Design Engagement Model (Jones, 2018)

Lab – Laboratories are protected environments for controlling experiments. The Lab context is for the cocreation of planning, design, and research within a team or organisation. The Lab is a focused internal setting for the immediate team and a small number of organisational collaborators. It would not typically involve decision-makers or extended groups. A project team's 'war room' holding all the maps and plans for a project is a type of Lab.

Studio – The Studio provides a project team space (in physical space or virtually) for collaborative design activities conducted with clients and experts to develop concepts, proposals, or prototypes. A Studio facilitates socio-material constructive making, as generations of design education and practice have conducted in studio settings. While the Lab is an 'experimental' and private context, the Studio opens up a place for the 'team-plus' to productively collaborate on defined projects through all stages of work. While the typical size of a Studio with

sponsors may be 10-15 (enough for 2-3 working groups), it can expand to larger groups of 20-30, especially online.

The Studio is better defined by its activities than its physical environment. A design studio is a space where a core design team invites multidisciplinary collaboration with relevant experts, process advisors, and technical masters for hands-on constructive making, mapping, and working together. The work in Studio and Arena is the difference between private discussions and more public dialogue. Mapping workshops, prototypes, and trial sessions can be constructed, simulated, and evaluated in Studio sessions in advance of Arena engagements.

Arena – Christakis defined the Arena as the venue for engaging stakeholders representing the variety of a social system, where they are understood to represent and reflect issues of their direct concern. The Arena implies the socio-political environment of the design process or for decision-making of interest to the selected stakeholders. An Arena can represent a symbolic location of political action that influences collective decisions. It is also the closed, invitation-only corporate or organisational design session. Facilitated client workshops are often more of an Arena than Studio, and the difference is critical.

While stakeholders are selected based on their knowledge and capacity to act on it, replicating the requisite variety of an entire social system guarantees that some stakeholder positions, power, and interests will be at odds. This should be expected and planned for – working consensus on a system or future change cannot be achieved without acknowledging and negotiating real differences.

In an Arena setting we facilitate dialogue, as a methodology of structured conversation, to negotiate the social complexity and emergent issues. Proceeding 'as design' without constructive dialogue is ineffective at resolving power biases in decision contexts. People holding positional or expert power in codesign sessions may creatively engage and contribute meaningfully, but the continuity of power in a system enables capacity

[5] Peter Jones (2018). Contexts of cocreation: Designing with system stakeholders. In P. Jones & K. Kijima, *Systemic Design: Theory, Methods and Practice*. Springer Japan. Based on John Warfield (1986). The Domain of Science Model: Evolution and design. *Society for General Systems Research*.

to redirect decisions or outcomes over time. The Arena requires more discipline and constructive tension than creative contexts typically allow, through rigorous facilitation and moderating dialogue democratically.

Unlike the Studio, Arena facilitation is structured to prevent inequitable decisions or unbalanced coalitions that might offset a real consensus outcome. To signify an Arena context, sessions may be hosted in a neutral location, with the ability to design and control the environment. Since many Arena deliberations are held online in video conferencing platforms now, we might notice the lack of forms in virtual engagement for immersing stakeholders in a symbolic environment that communicates an Arena context. We may find a tendency to slip into a looser Studio mode even if a serious deliberative environment is called for, as the physical and interpersonal cues are dematerialised. We find the Toolkit structures can be selected and convened to communicate a style of articulation[6] that recreates a shared cultural experience in speech, gesture, pacing, mood, and framing of participation.

An Arena differs from the other venues in that *only* committed stakeholders are invited. As planners and facilitators, our main concern is to create a fair and productive process environment with respect to decision power and appropriate stakeholder variety.

Agora – The Agora is based on an open public dialogue as its archetypal model, such as a 'town hall' or public planning meeting. An Agora provides a gathering space in which people self-select to engage, and the variety evolves as people with an interest to participate join. While not the Athenian open plaza for public engagement, and not necessarily even a place but a context created by the invitation, the open style of participation, and the framed meaning of the event. The Agora extends open design cocreation to democratic contexts, by restoring the committed citizen as a stakeholder in a public. An Agora shows up when members of a public participate in purposeful dialogue or come together to cocreate or act on an issue or shared problem.

Agoras hold real potential for the formation of localised social influence toward promoting municipal policies and community action. The social action potential of the Agora is qualitatively different from the stakeholder-focused, problem-solving orientation of an Arena gathering.

Both Arenas and Agoras both commonly evolve coalitions for action. The Arena builds collaborative solutions or change teams across stakeholder groups. Agora coalitions take the shape of more activist-led action groups, such as Citizen Action Networks (CANs)[7].

Creating a Cocreation System

Among each of the four cocreation contexts, their most salient distinction appears to be the participants or stakeholders involved. Each context from Lab to Agora expands to a different sample and size of the group. While the Studio typically only expands to a larger working group within the collaboration, the Arena expands to actual stakeholders within the system of concern, and their contributions have an enduring impact on future change outcomes. The Arena is the primary context for deliberative design and dialogue leading to real policy or change outcomes. The Agora, being open to various publics, may draw a high variety of stakeholders, but with less immediate impact.

Stakeholder Discovery
Stakeholder selection is the first significant opportunity to shape future systems change. The insights expressed in early-stage boundary framing, actor analysis, and the vision for change set the path upon which all other stages extend. Both power and error are highly leveraged in the first design and planning engagements. As stakeholders are asked to join in cocreation, in Studio and especially Arena contexts, they become 'designers of the new system.'

---

[6] Charles Spinosa, Fernando Flores & Hubert Dreyfus (1997). *Disclosing New Worlds: Entrepreneurship, Democratic Action, and the Cultivation of Solidarity*. MIT Press.
[7] Indra Adnan (2021). *The Politics of Waking Up: Power and Possibility in the Fractal Age*. Perspectiva.

All stakeholder selection has systematic biases, as the default process involves inviting known persons closest to a project or from immediate social networks. The best way to overcome biases is to make them explicit – to use rules that accomplish a purposive outcome and are seen as fair. A recruiting process called evolutionary stakeholder sampling provides a method for selecting a range of participants commensurate with the variety of represented stakeholders in a social system's population. This process provides a justified basis for the democratic engagement of people committed to a social system, using a defined set of inclusive categories.

Moving up the complexity scale of design domains, from products to organisations, to multiple coordinating organisations, participant inclusion shifts significantly from 'users' to 'members,' then to 'system stakeholders' in an Arena. The role of a participant engaging in an app user experience entails nowhere near the social complexity or power relations involved in organisations or policy design. Yet, these Arena engagements are frequently facilitated with the same participatory and generative methods used in design thinking workshops.

The stakes are significantly different between user participation and multi-stakeholder consensus on critical issues or wicked problem systems, and the methods for professing consensus and design decisions differ not only by style but epistemology and disciplinary integration. An underinformed user's contributions to a service prototype would be unlikely to have any consequential outcomes. A stakeholder group cocreating the community's climate adaptation policy ought to require more knowledge, a personal or professional stake in decisions, and the capability to sustain action according to collective decisions.

There are many systemic and design methods considered pragmatically effective in their consultative or engagement settings. Yet, in any design process requiring participant decision-making, especially with consensus on binding actions, the participant's commitment to the outcome is a critical factor that guides method choice. Therefore, stakeholder

discovery and selection can determine the success of engagement.

Stakeholder Selection

Your participant sample defines the problem space of the system. Vision, context, and direction setting are extremely sensitive to initial conditions. Especially with an early consensus, strong visioning may create a lock-in effect, confirming beliefs among actors that their choices represent desirable preferences for future system participants.

In complex social systems, stakeholder selection can behave like a wicked problem. As in wicked problems, each stakeholder choice matters to the process outcome. Every inclusion of a participant excludes another possible choice; each category represented can occlude another category. The power balance is thrown off when too many elite participants are invited. And there is no set point at which representation would be complete.

The consequences of participation and non-participation are unknown at the time of selection, but each person's perspective counts and can be compared to potential representatives. Stakeholders as a collective share a *context* (even if solely due to their invitation to an engagement) and create a *framing* (a reference system) that can become path-dependent and irreversible.

Jones even proposed[8] that the selection of stakeholders make more difference in achieving a durable consensus than our choice of design methodology (primarily due to self-organisation). A carefully-tuned participatory design workshop with attention to process and artefacts may show no enduring influence on system change if the participants themselves have no continuing stake in the outcome. When only the design team is left to interpret for themselves the meaning of sticky notes pulled off the wall, the workshop has not intervened in system change.

In systemic design, the problem frame can change with each new selection of participants. We can see shifts between each stage of a progressive design series, and

---

[8] Peter Jones (2018). Evolutionary stakeholder discovery: Requisite system sampling for cocreation. *RSD7 Symposium, Torino.*

our goal is to sustain continuity of cocreation across engagement encounters. A typical series proceeds from visioning and problem framing, through system intervention or concept formulation, and finally toward collective action. These activities all require stakeholder-led insight and validation, and much less design guidance and content compared to D2.0 product/service contexts.

Selection Criteria

A design process becomes irrelevant if stakeholder selection does not represent the variety in the exogenous social system and fails to enrol authentic commitment from selected stakeholders. As design disciplines are predicated on a tradition of creative problem-solving and not social science research, these critical functions are often underdeveloped, especially for workshop-type engagements. When we under-conceptualise the exogenous (external, socially constructed) system, we risk failures in outcome – even when cocreation has been deemed highly satisfactory – by failing to select and enrol stakeholders sufficiently well enough to enable an effective future result in the social system.

Based on research cited previously (Jones, 2018), we indicate a model for evolutionary stakeholder "sampling" to define a fractal microcosm of the social system. Three broad categories, each with numerous variables, can be intersected to survey and identify participants to express a rich representation in smaller groups.

- Ontology – Worldview perspectives reflecting one's commitment to a domain of human experience. We have drawn on Latour's Modes of Existence typology (15 modern ontologies) for reference.

- Expertise – Selection of stakeholders by their core domain of expertise. The 'STEEP' foresight categories (Social, Technological, Economic, Ecological, Political) allow for broad ranges of inclusion.

- Social variety – Demographic and developmental characteristics representing people in the system, including age, socioeconomic, education, geographic, and ethnic factors.

The process for modelling the stakeholder sample recommends a multi-layered table, using a spreadsheet format or database. For a significant Arena event, candidate's names are assigned to category intersections, and are invited in iterations of mixed-category batches to fill positions.

Christakis defined a critical sortition of participants, assessing their 'skin in the game' using the heuristic of Five I's. Organisers should also aim to choose people who meet these criteria as relevant to the engagement issue.

1. **Informed** – Are they deeply informed about the problem and context? Are they willing to be open-minded, to learn more?

2. **Impacted** – Are they directly affected by the outcomes and decisions at stake? Are they vulnerable to risk consequences of the design?

3. **Interested** – Are they sincerely interested in the engagement?

4. **Invested** – Are they personally invested and involved in the outcome?

5. **Implementers** – Will they be involved as implementers of the plans or design?

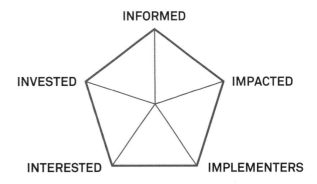

Figure 5
Five I's heuristic for stakeholder selection

Convivial Convening

Facilitating systemic design is not inherently different from other design workshops. It might appear from the (necessarily) simplified instructions that system mapping can be led as a series of guided exercises similar to generative design thinking workshops (i.e. lots of sticky notes). Mapping workshops are now often conducted online with collaborative whiteboards, and many will continue to find this an effective process for mixed stakeholder groups that might be spread across many locations. The Toolkit canvases encourage an open mapping workshop style, led by a design facilitator with an objective of active engagement from all participants.

Each tool can be used within collocated or virtual workshops. Typically, a single map is printed poster-size to facilitate a common reference point for in synchronous mapping and discussion. Colour-coded notes can be used to designate categories on the map or to reference the members of a small group working concurrently. In virtual workshops, multiple maps can be easily replicated on an online whiteboard allowing small group teams to work on their own map and narrative.

Yet, each stage, tool, and method reveals a different objective and possibility for application. It is unlikely that any two workshop series will use all the same tools in sequence. Using all 30 tools in a systemic design project would require more time and workshops than most project teams would be able to sustain. As an Explorer practitioner, learn about the value and process for all these tools and become conversant in their applications. Develop a skilled practice of selecting and connecting the best-fit appropriate collaborative thinking and design tools for stakeholder workshops.

Convening as Collaboration

Collaboration is often presented as a disposition toward participatory group work, as in 'being collaborative.' We mean collaboration as a coordinated contribution of multiple participants toward a common objective, a process than can scale from micro-teams to stakeholder groups. Collaboration can be synchronous, as in

facilitated mapping workshops, and often more effective as a serial process of parallel contributions over a period of time. Some methods (those requiring offline analysis, including causal loops and synthesis maps) will benefit from multiple contributors coordinating a serial process toward an outcome. Focused collaboration on output products can take a period of days or even weeks, depending on analysis and outputs.

We can convene systemic design at the team, project, or organisational levels. Collaboration can scale beyond the working team to coordinate multiple groups, such as stakeholder teams representing allied organisations in a large project. Such projects often involve widely-ranging levels of leadership, expertise, design skills and articulation styles. Convening large-scale projects requires an attentive presencing coordinating member roles for productive interaction in planning, group decisions, and cocreation. Therefore, mixed-member teams place a high demand on facilitation and interpersonal communications. The structure of Design Journeys tools can facilitate productive micro-collaboration in large teams, even when roles remain unclear. Skilful coordination at the project and overall programme (or system) level will help to ensure the right mix of participants and knowledge for productive mapping workshops.

Designers view collaboration as a process medium for engaging creativity, to activate participation in system engagements. Etienne Wenger's recent work on systems convening[9] describes an emerging mode of facilitating social learning in organisations and networked communities. Learning from Wenger, we can frame "occasions that promote mutual engagement" to create deeper, continuous stakeholder collaboration across system and power boundaries. Systemic designers might blend these occasions with design cocreation, extending Journeys stages with opportunities for dialogue, open forums, and visualisation. Systems convening can facilitate collaboration at the system level, with blended convening styles from focused dialogue to ideation through systemic design.

---

[9] Etienne Wenger & Beverley Wenger-Traynor (2021). *Systems Convening: A Crucial Form of Leadership for the 21st Century.* Social Learning Lab.

Style	Facilitation	Methods
Designerly	Interactive – Creative peer-to-peer idea generation	Codesign, Design charettes, Participatory design, Online whiteboard generative design
Dialogic	Inquiry – Reflective, open-paced conversation guided by questions	Dialogic Design, Structured dialogue, Talking circles, Appreciative Inquiry, Art of Hosting
Deliberative	Intentional – Structured, tightly-paced decisionmaking, agenda-driven planning	Structured dialogue, Deliberative Democracy, Planning Cell, Sociocracy, Citizens' Assembly
Dynamic	Intuitive – Loosely-structured, play-ful, embodied, or exploratory	U Lab, Open Space, World Café, Theatre games

Table 1 Facilitation Styles for Cocreation

Collegial Styles

The organisational commitment to system change is a cooperative agreement and process that entails collaboration across all phases of work and in workshops. These can be seen as scales of collaboration, or collegial styles, that engage distinct social and discursive practices.

Collegiality refers to the cooperation among colleagues to hold a shared identity and to share power and decision-making among members. Facilitation styles adapt to the necessary approaches to collegial engagement. In the mixed stakeholder settings of systemic design and change work, engagement facilitators must be sensitive to the collegial dynamics of the participants and adapt appropriately to the preferred style of engagement. Table 1 presents these four essential collegial styles, defined by their appropriate modes of facilitation and typical methods for facilitating these engagements.

All four of the styles could be employed in systemic design workshops – a designerly codesign methodology is typical but is not proscribed. The selection criteria should be based on the organisational or sponsor goals, the social culture of the participants, and the appropriate fit to the desired outcomes for the tools.

The Design Journeys methodology is flexible and agnostic to facilitation styles. Think of the collegial styles as organisational journeys into guided learning and design experiences with the tools. The use of each tool for a given productive outcome yields a well-defined complement of knowledge and learning, and these are additive across the seven stages. The engagement style for each journey will be driven by the needs of the group for their stage of work in a project.

Convening Design Dialogue Workshops

Based on a decade of development in the Design with Dialogue[10] community, a series of ritual skills has evolved as a design language for mixed-group participation. These six steps work in sequence, and transcend or adapt to many convening methods.

1. **Invitation and Greeting** – Any workshop or journey begins in the minds of the participants with the invitation and communication of the workshop from the sponsor and coordinator. When people arrive at an online or studio workshop, a welcome and invitation to participate are clearly given. Openers include a round of self-introductions, presenting the agenda, and determining any ground rules that might be preferred by participants.

2. **Circle** – In a dialogue, people sit in a large circle, with no designated head position. A talking piece can be introduced to establish a respectful speaking protocol. Even in design workshops where tables

[10] Design with Dialogue is a Toronto-based community of practice for design facilitation practice and open public dialogues on critical emerging issues, organisational and policy innovation, and sensemaking practices. designwithdialogue.org

and materials are used, an open circle situates and holds an opening question and centres the opening conversation in the circle.

3. **Vision or Goal** – Once in the circle, the aim of the session is revealed and discussed. A focus question is often used to generate deep reflective responses to frame the start. The question is asked in a way to cocreate a shared vision among the participants – the design facilitator distances from the content to ensure the sense of collective ownership is created.

4. **Small Group Dialogues** – Following an opening dialogue, multiple perspectives are developed creatively in small groups, which can be facilitated by an exercise, organising groups by themes of interest they proposed, or mixed groups for maximum group variety. A World Café style is often used in collocated group breakouts, with large sheets of paper, markers, and sticky notes to facilitate and create **documentation of the conversation and ideas.**

5. **Harvest (with Visual Reflection)** – If small group dialogues are used, have an explicit time period for meeting and finishing, with clear outcomes to encourage participation and closure. Leave sufficient time for a harvest of all the group's readouts of the discussions and concepts. If a graphic recorder is sketching the proceedings, the harvest is the key period for their visual interpretation of the discussion as well as the plenary circles.

6. **Circle to Close** – Gather everyone in a circle again to close the session with a round of final comments or reflections. This period can be as short as 2-3 minutes or as long as a final half-hour dialogue.

Double Diamond of Dialogue

Designers are familiar with the 'double diamond' model popularised by Design Council[11] that represents the procession of the design process in two broad stages of design from definition to development. Others may be familiar with its representation in systems thinking, as Bela Banathy[12] had sketched a double diamond for envisioning futures, with a diamond of vision and one of alternative solutions. Van Patter and Pastor[13] published a history of the double diamond, referring to its origination by creative problem-solving pioneers Sid Parnes and Alex Osborn in the 1970's. The common attribute shared by all these diamond models was the shape-semantics of the opening and closing angles in the two apposed diamonds, the first signifying a divergence stage, followed by the convergence.

The divergence-convergence cycle is found everywhere as a kind of design universal, but it was introduced into dialogue much earlier than design. Min Basadur[14] borrowed the idea from Sid Parnes in his research leading to Simplexity, a structured group creativity practice. Each of the eight stages of Simplexity uses the diamond as a micro-method of divergence to convergence within each stage from Problem Finding to Implementation. The diamond was adopted as an almost universal method in creativity processes for moving a group through divergent ideation, to generate high creative output, followed by a convergence by assessment and selection, with a goal of high-quality conceptualisation. In dialogue models, a liminal middle field of 'emergence' is included, showing how groups might naturally work through a large set of ideas and emergent reflection toward refinements and a narrowing of options.

Conveners can use the implicit awareness of the diamond process in dialogue as a guide for workshopping with the Toolkit canvases. These are as much a dialogue process as a design activity.

[11] Design Council (2005). *The 'Double Diamond' Design Process Model*. UK: Design Council.
[12] Bela Banathy (1996). *Designing Social Systems in a Changing World*. Springer.
[13] GK VanPatter & Elizabeth Pastor (2016). *Innovation Methods Mapping: De-mystifying 80+ years of Innovation Process Design*. Humantific. innovationmethodsmapping.com
[14] Min Basadur (2004). Leading others to think innovatively together: Creative leadership. *The Leadership Quarterly*.

Convening Online or Collocated Studios

Participants enjoy significant advantages in their engagement and learning when attending physically in-person, collocated workshops at a studio or a for-purpose workshop room. Stakeholders meeting each other in person benefit from the lived experience of place and interpersonal relationship-building that cannot be achieved in an online digital space (at least not within the space of a workshop period). We learn and create not just through cognitive activities, but through felt physical experience and social-emotional embodiment – experiences that lead to enduring memories and deep impressions from people we have worked within close participation.

The physical studio space allows for creative use of space with dedicated facilities, spacious rooms with natural light, whiteboards and walls, and breakout rooms and corners to meet. The room can be equipped with posters, markers, sticky notes, props, thinking materials, and everything else needed to set up a creative workspace.

In online workshops, the 'rooms' are set up for online breakout sessions. Dynamic interactive sessions will make use of videoconferencing software allowing breakout rooms (e.g. Zoom, Teams) and a virtual whiteboard (e.g. Miro, Mural). Remember that not all participants may be familiar with selected tools; participants can be notified in advance with a pre-workshop exercise that offers a chance to learn while doing. Ensure participants check their hardware and settings before a session, so that all may participate fully and fairly.

Just as in 'live' workshops, tools and props can be placed to steer activities and encourage creative thinking. We can redraw or adapt the tool images to tailor their labels to fit the subject. Step-by-step instructions are typically placed by the referenced tools.

Convening workshop styles

As systemic design creates from stakeholder knowledge, expect to constantly convene workshops for cocreation, co-analysis, and codesign with system participants. Five workshop styles or patterns are currently used in Design Journeys:

1. **Framing** [Stage 1] – Framing is a discovery process where the aim is to create a common understanding of an issue, the scope, and the systems involved. The approach is ideational, but the intent is to define the system and shape the future project.

2. **Sensemaking and Analysis** [Stages 2 and 3] – Once significant data is collected and immersed, a process of sensemaking and pattern finding follows. The Listening and Understanding stages are primarily data analysis, sensemaking of meaningful patterns, and critique.

3. **Reframing** [Stage 4] – The goal of reframing is to assess and reflect on the accrued formulation of issues and learning following further research and analysis. Reframing is helpful between the analysis of what-is [Stages 1-3] and the creation of 'what might be' [Stages 5-7]. Here we define the challenge, its value and opportunity, and set explicit project aims.

4. **Codesign** [Stages 5-6] – Codesign workshops are pragmatic, formative sessions that lead to tangible decisions and products. In these stages, we convene a collaborative design process to define the future strategy and organisational approaches for leading the strategy.

5. **Roadmapping** [Stage 6-7] – As indicated by the title, Roadmapping defines agreement on strategic pathways and the directions decided upon for organisational change, governance, and the phasing of a design/change programme over time.

These are guidelines for practitioners. In practice, these workshop models may not have formal boundaries, as experienced Explorers may blend workshops and tools into mixed workshop contexts.

Framing

The first stage (and chapter) involves framing, and the first workshops with any group will be framing activities. We invite clients/sponsors to join the start of a project as early as possible to initiate a collaborative approach. Typically, a core group is convened to engage a range of roles and expertise from the sponsor organisation(s), and this group may be enlarged or changed in composition as the stages proceed (from about 5, up to 10 or more). Framing involves a wide range of team members to gain early knowledge of the methods, as well as to share insights about the issues in the social system of interest. Framing workshops encourage a dialogic style of participation and can be highly divergent and wide-ranging in search of quality ideation.

We show a typical framing workshop for an agency project aiming to foster social integration. The framing workshops were held in a series. As the client understood the challenge well, and with 40 years of prior study, the workshop started with an ideal future vision. Next, we identified stakeholders across a wide range of social systems. The second workshop then invited over 80 participants from this range. This session primarily developed an understanding of the emerging niche initiatives and their characteristics within the system of social trends. This led to a definition of future interventions.

Framing the first workshops

The activities and aims of framing workshops are to create a shared understanding of:

- The scope of the system of interest

- System boundaries and relevant intersections between domains (Iterative Inquiry)

- The actors involved (Actors Map)

- A shared map of contexts (and influences) on the system to reveal points of system change (Rich Context)

- Emerging and new practices that might have potential for system change (Niche Discovery)

The outputs include the content from selected tools that enable the project team to proceed to the next stage. Some of these are directly used in Stage [2], such as the mapping of actors (and stakeholders) that we engage in Listening to the System. (A moment is often added at the end of a workshop day to prepare research questions).

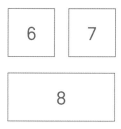

Figure 6
Sketching of the workshop flow. It's important to prepare a workshop well. We always start with the end in mind. Consider the outputs the team needs to harvest or is required as input for the next stage.

Figure 7
Use a visual agenda, sketched on a poster or as the first page structure in an online whiteboard for virtual workshop.

Figure 8
Several tools capture niche initiatives. Here a large spray of notes is posted on a larger poster (6xA1) to accommodate a larger group of participants. Here the ideal future is depicted as the metaphor of a tree, with six main leverage points defined.

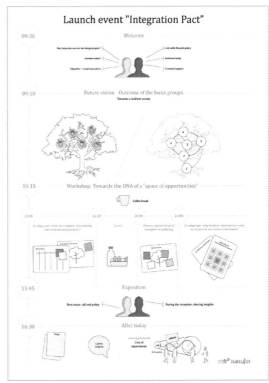

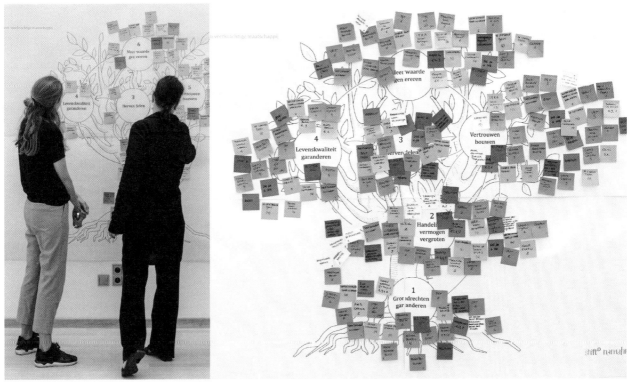

Sensemaking

Sensemaking workshops convene a collaborative approach to analysis, following a period of data collection and learning cycles. The common meaning of sensemaking is to derive meaning from information to situate oneself in a context. Here we mean it as a process of *making sense of observations and collective learning* from research and stakeholder studies. Sensemaking is often conducted in a Lab setting, with the internal design team reviewing the results of Journeys workshopping, tool canvases and materials, research notes, and other data. Studio sessions engaging sponsors can help construct shared meaning in exploring systems, what Birger Sevaldson[15] calls 'sense sharing,' a practice of extending a sense of the system with committed stakeholders.

Sensemaking creates collective knowledge from multiple observations

The activities and aims of a sensemaking workshop include:

– Understand multiple perspectives on issues within system boundaries, problems as perceived, and human issues in a system context

– Identify stakeholders and their relationships, mapping their roles and activities

– Define research questions of interest, develop and analyse findings and concepts from studies

– Discover and share meaning emerging from system and contextual analysis

Workshopping often involves:

– Analysing research materials and highlighting contributing factors (needs, drivers, barriers etc.)

– Making personas or actants to analyse activity and synthesise the results (Actants Map)

– Clustering factors into themes on (online or physical) whiteboards or software

– Analysing and linking factors (Influence Map or causal loops)

– Updating and summarising previously sketched maps

Figure 9
Clustering interview findings through the factors and themes method: first note contributing factors on post-its and next, cluster them in themes

Figure 10
Analysing what contributes or hinders to make the school system in Brussels more appropriate for the society of the future

[15] Birger Sevaldson (2022). *Designing Complexity: The Methodology and Practice of Systems Oriented Design.* Common Ground.

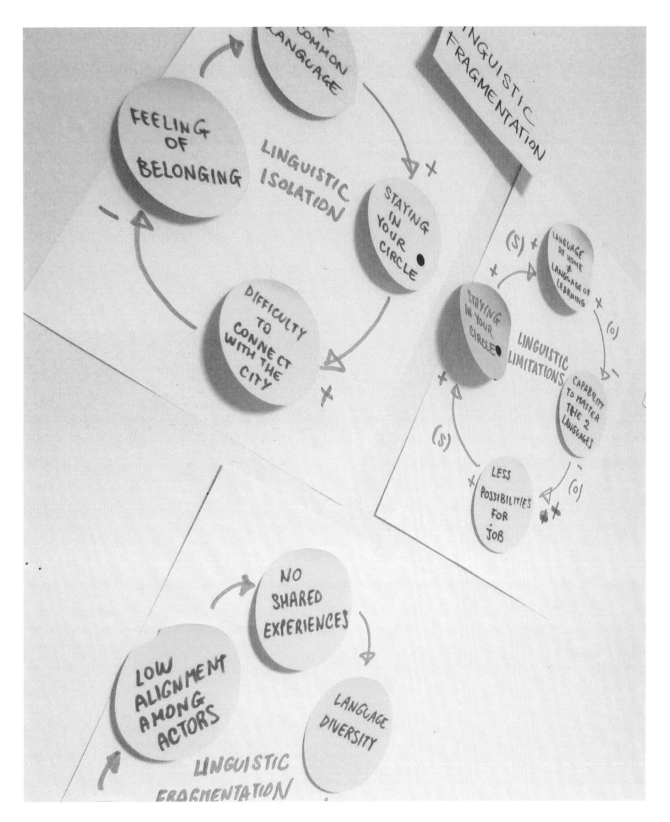

Reframing

Reframing workshops produce a cyclic feedback loop from stages that follow learning with earlier framing and boundary decisions. Reframing involves revisiting learning from earlier stages of research or design. The project team can take stock of the focus and priorities of design and the research that unfolded during the Framing and Listening stages. We can formulate design challenges in this setting with questions that revisit earlier assumptions, such as 'How might we,' 'What for,' 'For whom,' and 'Why'. The question of 'How' remains open, as the process design will *be a critical aspect of the following stages.*

Reframing workshops are convened for Stage [4] Envisioning. The sponsor core and a mixed design team provide a range of roles and expertise from across participating organisations in a Studio setting, or for a larger-scale Arena process. By this stage, the design team can be complemented with external advisors and experts.

Reframing articulates the vision, updates shared mental models

The activities and aims of a reframing workshop include:

- Communicate insights from research findings and complement with knowledge present in the room

- Identify gaps between initial and current understanding

- Define emerging design challenges within frames (Synthesis Maps)

- Model the value to be generated by the project (Value Proposition)

- Understand how emerging sociotechnical innovations can help to achieve the intended value (Three Horizons)

- Explore paradoxes in the system (Paradoxing)

To express insights from Listening research, we often cocreate personas or actant models that can be adapted and enriched by the participants. Insights can be animated by use of props, as shown in the photograph. In this case, the reframing explored new ways of living in cities – cards were created to summarise needs and desires from city participants.

Another engaging exercise is to create physical models of system research, and update and enrich the tangible concepts with workshop participants. The picture is from a workshop where Namahn designed mixed-artefact models of administrative complexity.

Figure 11
The Theory U method 3D mapping is a powerful conversation catalyst to surface the common understanding of an issue

Figure 12
Using props to communicate user research insights in a project aimed at exploring new ways of cohabitation

Codesign

The Codesign workshop might be considered the default, as a participatory design charette style used in Studio settings. In a sense, a codesign process is used throughout the Journeys, as an activity of collaborative making and ideation with design tools. Codesigning *as design* takes place in Stages 4-6, with the design of pathways, interventions, and organisational models. As a convening style, codesign assumes working with a productive intact team (not just starting out) with a clear vision and aims, and that the team can continue together in the subsequent stages. Codesign is an important style for systems change, and to expand and engage a broader sample of team members directly. Remember to continue drawing insights and show connections among the interrelated system issues, design proposals, and prototypes so that design actions are visibly reinforcing. Make sure to regularly check-in and assess these interconnections during workshops.

Organise codesign workshops soon after a reframing workshop to sustain the continuity of creative thinking and learning.

Codesign workshops are experienced as engaging and exciting by participants who can finally bring their ideas to the surface. A caution for conveners is helpful, to note that it's tempting to ignore prior research and generate new ideas that have little leverage as interventions. To avoid this, keep key reference maps and the synthesis map visually available. Make sure to refer to them often.

Be sure to validate (or ideate on) well-defined models through multiple stakeholder scenarios. Serious play or role-playing through bodystorming can be an effective way to perform and simulate scenarios in codesign.

Codesign defines the path ahead

The activities and aims of a codesign workshop include:

—   Explore possible future contexts (Future State Scenarios)

—   Define the intervention strategy to achieve envisioned change or value (Intervention Strategy)

—   Translate strategy into concrete activities and preconditions (Intervention Model)

—   Adapt the interventions to test against contexts (Contextual Variations)

—   Build shared narratives for change programmes to achieve impact (Theory of System Change)

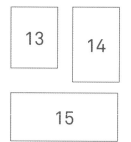

Figure 13
Mapping the stakeholders for the scale phase of the development of a network to foster SME innovation in Europe

Figure 14
Cocreating the map depicted left in a workshop with stakeholders

Figure 15
Validating concepts for a homeless service through serious play. Here we are cocreating the reception service

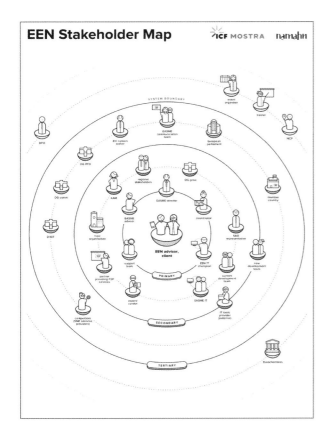

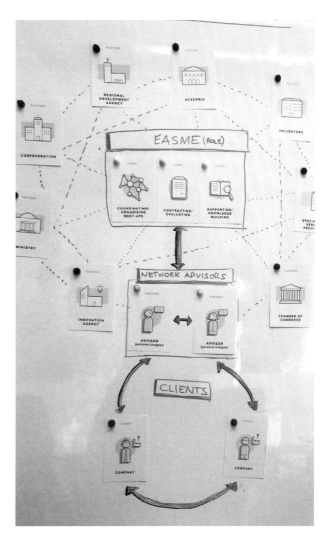

Roadmapping

Roadmapping workshops are intensive engagements, facilitated as if they were full design processes. In any context, a roadmapping session convenes stakeholders with responsibility for action to define agreement on strategic directions going forward – the roadmap pathways and the directions decided upon for organisational change, governance, and the phasing of a design/change programme over time. Strategic roadmapping has well-developed literature in strategic foresight and technology innovation, and numerous methods for convening and building roadmaps can be found. The Design Journeys methodology introduces several roadmap methods within the future system stages that are useful in extending interventions and scenarios into practical time-framed trajectories of planned or possible future outcomes.

Roadmapping helps fellow travellers carry out the mission

The activities and aims of a roadmapping workshop include:

—   Listen to the views of multiple stakeholders on future outcome priorities

—   Define time-based action scenarios using maps with structured pathways

—   Optimise potential future pathways for action

—   Explore possible future outcomes and impacts together (Outcome Maps)

—   Develop a future vision for achieving impacts through system change pathways (TOSCA Theory of Change)

—   Map out the envisioned shifts to scale from initiatives to adoption (Transition by Design)

Roadmapping is a kind of collaborative foresight process, and the convening style can be used in shorter workshops or lengthy collaborative mapping and feedback reviews. Roadmapping can engage a single tool or involve a mix of progressive system maps (Influence Maps), foresight methods (Three Horizons), change strategies (TOSCA), and transition planning (Transition by Design). Quite a few tools, even synthesis maps, could be recruited for a roadmapping session if the team is ready to shift to a planning context.

Convening a Roadmap session involves a smaller group than other engagements. A core working group of 2-3 design teams and 5-7 stakeholders is ideal. Groups over 20 can involve too much variety into decisions necessary to define points of change and impact over time. The products of roadmapping workshops include outputs of the systemic design tools, of course. However, if a single printed or PDF strategic roadmap is to be used by a stakeholder design team, a mix of tools can be uniquely utilised to present a primary pathway with overlays or change points defined by contributions from influence or outcome maps, as well as scenarios and interventions.

The photograph shows a Namahn roadmapping session where the Transition by Design map is overlaid with hand-sketched scenarios illustrating the strategic options or change points.

16

Figure 16
Mapping the transition towards a more sustainable food system using activity scenario cards developed during a previous exercise

Facilitating Cocreation

An entire book could be written on design workshop facilitation (and there are several, such as Jones' *Team Design*[16]). We have learned from our own experience that this skill is not one that can be developed well from lessons in a publication. Therefore, facilitation practice will not be covered along with the creative tools of Design Journeys. While it might be frustrating for some to learn the Design Journeys tools for collaborative cocreation with stakeholders without guidance on facilitation skills, but this would double the size of the book and might distract from the core practices published. Guidance is provided for workshop convening, structures (guidelines for each tool), and principles. But facilitation cannot be instructed by any book, it can only be learned by experience of planning and conducting workshops as a facilitator. Facilitation is truly an embodied practice learned from its engagement, and our tips and structures will only go so far.

The root word facilitate literally means "to make easy," and the task of the facilitator is to create an environment and guide proceedings so that complicated agendas (i.e., multiple tasks in order) are made easy to follow. Facilitators present tasks, direct their fulfilment within time limits, and manage agreements in accord with the culture of the participants, while expressing and reinforcing a social ecology that invites and includes full to participation. Teams and organisations depend on effective facilitation as a method for inspiring group synergy, building teams, and managing group action toward producing deliverables.

There are several modes of facilitation practice, such as the traditional process facilitator, who leads a group effectively through an agenda of topics but remains neutral to all participants and disinterested in the content. Since Design Journeys recommends facilitators know the systemic design tools, the expectation might persist that the facilitator also has content expertise. Some might indeed have expertise and might wish to shift roles between facilitator and designer. This dilemma is one of many typical cases of praxis that we cannot resolve by rules and cases in a text such as this. It's not helpful, but yet it's correct to say "it depends."

At the most basic level, every facilitator must learn at least four complex skillsets:

– Personal – Being a facilitator (embodied skills)

– Process – Structuring tasks and managing meeting processes

– Interpersonal - Facilitating to create a context, as a socio-cultural practice

– Organisational – Guiding production of deliverable materials according to agreement

Visual facilitation and graphic recording are high-value practices complementary to workshop convening. and effective facilitators learn to integrate live visual reflection and harvesting as key skills. The use of graphic recording has not been developed in Design Journeys explicitly, but every convener may find the most effective placement and provision of visual sensemaking and storytelling in their sessions.

These are necessary (but not sufficient) skillsets facilitators must learn. Participants are most concerned with experiencing and making something of value with their time contribution. Therefore, the embodied skills of listening, group sensing and feedback, time management, task pacing, appropriate empathy and distance, and physical cueing are also necessary aspects of masterful facilitation. These are best learned by apprenticeship with an experienced facilitator.

---

[16] Peter Jones (1997, 2002) *Team Design: A Practitioners Guide to Collaborative Innovation*. McGraw-Hill (1ed).

Leading Convening Models

Many facilitators start by learning a foundation method of practice that can be adapted to many meeting and workshop configurations. The following schools of practice have endured for decades as both powerful practice forms and communities of practice development.

Schools of Practice

– Appreciative Inquiry
  centerforappreciativeinquiry.net

– Art of Hosting
  artofhosting.org

– Design Shop (MG Taylor)
  matttaylor.com

– Dialogic Design (SDD)
  futureworldscenter.org

– Grove Collaborative
  thegrove.com

– *Open Space Technology*
  openspaceworld.org

– Technology of Participation
  top-training.net

– World Café
  theworldcafe.com

Communities and Resources

– Center For Wise Democracy
  wisedemocracy.org

– Design with Dialogue
  designwithdialogue.org

– Group Pattern Language
  groupworksdeck.org

– NCDD Engagement Streams
  ncdd.org

– Participedia online catalogue
  participedia.net

– Theory U (U-labs)
  u-school.org

Books and Readings

– Kelvy Bird (2018). *Generative Scribing: A social art of the 21st century*. PI Press.

– Peter Block (2018). *Community: The structure of belonging*. Berrett-Koehler Publishers.

– Alexander Christakis & Kenneth Bausch (2006). *How people harness their collective wisdom and power to construct the future in Co-laboratories of Democracy*. Information Age.

– Deloitte (2013). *Gather: The art and science of effective convening*.

– William Isaacs (1999). *Dialogue: The art of thinking together*. Currency.

– Joanna Macy & MollyYoung Brown (1998). *Coming Back To Life: Practices to reconnect our lives, our world*. New Society Publishers.

– Craig & Patricia Neal (2011). *The Art of Convening: Authentic engagement in meetings, gatherings, and conversations*. Berrett-Koehler Publishers.

– Harrison Owen (2008). *Open Space Technology: A user's guide*. Berrett-Koehler Publishers.

– Rockefeller Foundation (2022). *The Rockefeller Foundation Convening Design Guide*. rockefellerfoundation.org

– Marvin Weisbord & Sandra Janoff (2000). *Future Search: An action guide to finding common ground in organizations and communities*. Berrett-Koehler Publishers.

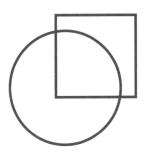

[1] Framing the System
Discovering the system and its boundaries

Framing is the first and most critical stage of *Design Journeys*. Framing is analogous to the travel plan – once the itinerary is set, plans are made, and the purpose is 'framed,' it's hard to change direction! It begins with reading the territory, mapping out a first itinerary, and planning trips. Initial conditions are set for all the design and studies that follow. Framing sets the stages, and the stage, for all concepts and models that follow.

The frame, also a boundary of the system, reveals a choice and decision – not made by the designer, but together with a team of stakeholder participants. The decision is the result of a framing process, after a series of inquiries and explorations that probe the meaning and argue for or against its inclusions. Framing constrains the range of outcomes and future possibility in every project, whether we do the framing or not. If we do not explore boundaries and assumptions, framing happens to us, by default or groupthink, and 'the system' will often be defined as provided in the client brief.

Design teams new to a problem domain will not know what unexamined positions are embedded in a problem statement. The stakeholders will not know either. In first meetings, our expectation going in will be that the client has real domain expertise, and their knowledge of the problem situation reveals the need for our project. However, that will only be *our* starting point. This difference in process makes all the difference in future outcome – the framing process leverages 'the power to change paradigms' as suggested in Donella Meadows'[1] well-known interventions framework.

While it's tempting to promote the change of system paradigms to accelerate transformation, paradigmatic contexts are highly resilient and supported by years of reinforcement. Dismantling a societal paradigm in favour a new worldview requires a very long-term focus, with continuous redirection toward the desired future frame. However, changing the paradigm that governs an immediate systems change programme (or any complex project) will be somewhat more feasible.

---

[1] Donella Meadows led a formidable career of research into deep sustainability of the world system, with an MIT research team led by Jay Forrester, resulting in The Limits to Growth (1972). She pioneered approaches to long-term engagement with complex societal problems, in the spirit of what Peter Senge (2015) calls 'systems leadership.'

Exploring the Whole System

Framing envisions the system as a whole, even before mapping its destination parts. Boundary framing establishes a common understanding of the system and constrains the space of design action. We explore and test assumptions and viewpoints to entertain a sufficient variety of alternative positions and future implications before reaching agreement on boundary, frame, and (possibly) purpose. This is a socially complex process, because our specification of a system is defined by agreement in our common language.

A whole system is a *perspective*, a shared view or mental model of the significance of the whole and the parts entailed within it – it is not a thing or a matter of fact. Systems are paradoxical – they are both metaphorical and structural, in that their definition leads to real, definable processes and services. Systems become manifested through our use of language. We speak of references to complex relationships defined within boundaries, levels, and temporalities – all these are cocreated by collaboration with stakeholder teams.

We can choose the paradigm and name the system that guides the direction of a systemic change project. The same goes for sociotechnical systems, as in healthcare and so-called digital transformation in organisations. This redirection will lead to long and often frustrating discussions. We must ask 'why to go' before 'where to go.' For systems change especially, we must continue to raise the questions of 'which system' and 'what boundary.' There are often multiple overlapping or contained systems, with independent identity for some constituents. For climate change planning, do we focus more on local impacts or contributing to national outcomes? Source causes (e.g. refrigerants, food waste) or effects (e.g. carbon measures, ecosystem repair)?

The four Framing tools all help set direction for the traveller starting out, whether on a learning journey (Tourist) or adapting the methods in advanced practice (Explorer). As Design Journey stages align to most design processes, the Framing inquiry will be compatible with the initial stage of other methodologies. Framing typically aligns with the discovery or planning workshops held with sponsors or stakeholder teams, which can be very action-oriented.

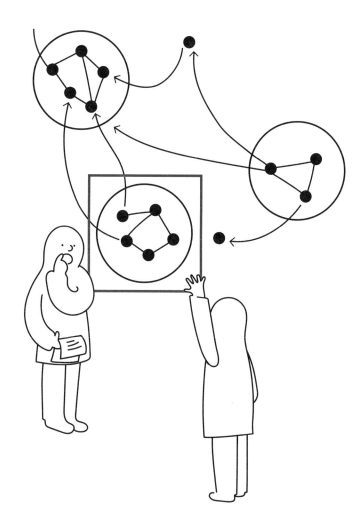

Design Journeys for Framing

Iterative Inquiry

Deconstructs a whole system into structures and processes, naming functions and identifying the purposes at each level. Discovers and defines boundaries, including system processes within these boundaries. This first tool sets the stage and defines the scope of further investigation. This tool enables a collective boundary critique, leading to the Actors Map, and processes and purposes leading to practices in the Rich Context tool.

Actors Map

Discovers and categorises system actors and actants by levels of system and relative influences. Roles and organisations (structures) are defined as actors. This leads to stakeholder analysis in Stage [2] Listening to the System.

Rich Context

Shows how a system is shaped toward change (long-term trends). Maps system context, dominant systems, and niche innovations. The niche innovations (or new practices) are inputs for the Niche Characteristics tool. Also provides inputs to the Systems Map in Stage [3] Understanding.

Niche Discovery

Explores entry points for effective system change following emerging initiatives at the niche level. As with Rich Context, this map connects to [3] Understanding.

Journeys by Stage

The flow diagram on the right proposes a typical sequence of the tools by stage and summarises the goal of the journey. The solid and dashed lines suggest the distinction between the tools for Tourists (solid), which are recommended for all, and tools for Explorers (dashed), which may require further study or time to convene well.

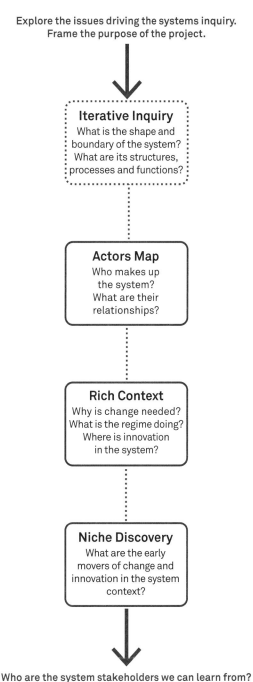

Explore the issues driving the systems inquiry. Frame the purpose of the project.

Iterative Inquiry
What is the shape and boundary of the system? What are its structures, processes and functions?

Actors Map
Who makes up the system? What are their relationships?

Rich Context
Why is change needed? What is the regime doing? Where is innovation in the system?

Niche Discovery
What are the early movers of change and innovation in the system context?

Who are the system stakeholders we can learn from? What must we learn from research? Stage [2]

Iterative Inquiry

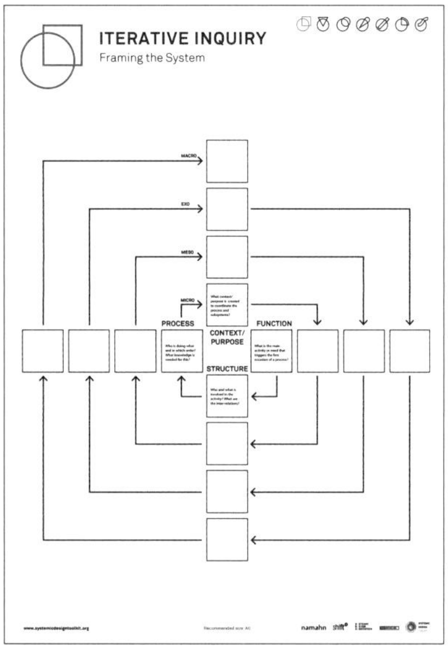

Figure 1-1
The Iterative Inquiry

- Time to Run:
  1-2+ hours
- Workshop Type:
  Framing
- Process time:
  1+ days
- Connections to:
  [1] Actors Map
  [1] Rich Context
  [3] Story Loop Diagram
  [4] Synthesis Map

The Iterative Inquiry[2] is a tool that helps to define the boundaries of a system and its subsystems or holons (other wholes contained within whole systems). The tool helps to understand system hierarchy and to investigate the purpose, functions, structures, and processes entailed in each subsystem. The Iterative Inquiry is a structured approach for boundary critique[3] or critical system reflection, a process of judgment by which the observations and values of a given choice are considered and weighed. The choice of a particular system description or its levels defines a particular system as important. It sets the limits of analysis and power relations, as well as limits the interpretation of social meaning and value implications associated with the choice.

The map defines a space for a system inquiry, which follows multiple iterations that reveal the system and its components across levels – from an initiating function out to the most inclusive purpose or the largest containing context. The starting function typically stems from a triggering situation (e.g. a common driver) that is defined as a function of the system, or as a need satisfier. Each level creates a 'ring' from function through to its containing context or purpose. At the same time, the context can become a new starting point.

We use the Iterative Inquiry to map out the structures, processes, and functions of an existing system before a project. Based on a systems inquiry method of Jamshid Gharajedaghi,[4] the process of iterative inquiry provides a visual reference to the components of a complex social system. The Toolkit provides the first visual design template that simplifies this inherently complex process diagram. The Iterative inquiry is complex due to the ambiguity of structural decisions that define each level of the hierarchy or its holons. These levels are determined by interpretation, based on the relationship of each function to the next successive function.

---

[2] Iterative Inquiry was developed by Russell Ackoff's collaborator, Jamshid Gharajedaghi, based on the (Wharton School) Interactive Management approach to social systems design.
[3] Boundary critique is a systems thinking process developed by Gerald Midgley (2000) that extends the well-known practice of boundary judgment in Werner Ulrich's critical systems heuristics (1983). These methods are forms for interpreting the social construction of naming, defining, and structuring the position of a social system.
[4] Jamshid Gharajedaghi (2004). Systems Methodology. A holistic language of interaction and design. This method was designed as a form of using iterations to understand the complexity in a system of interest, adapting a process known as Singerian experimentalism, inherent in the successive approximations of the iterations.

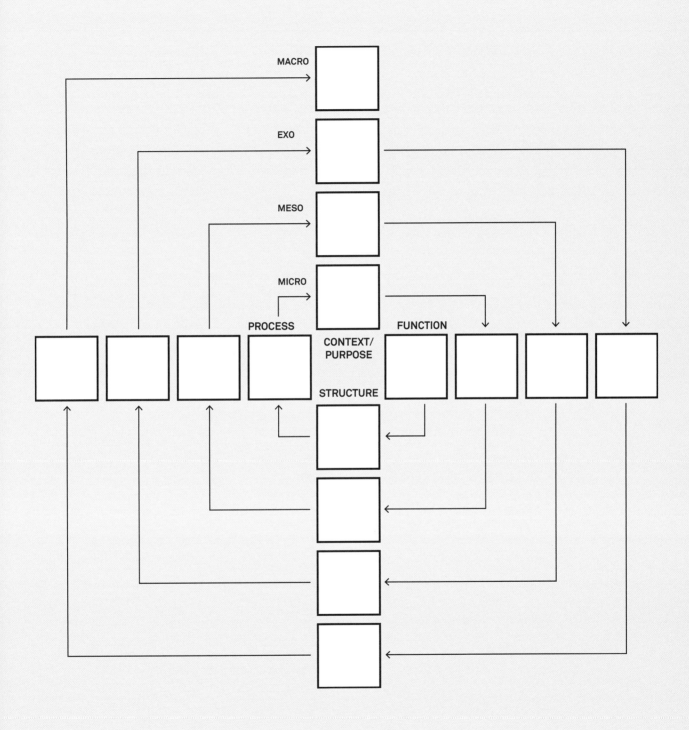

MACRO

EXO

MESO

MICRO

PROCESS

FUNCTION

CONTEXT/
PURPOSE

STRUCTURE

The Iterative Inquiry structure appears to be definitive, but a final map developed for presentation can be expressive, presented creatively as in Figure 1-3. It only requires the map to show a series of nested systems contained within an overall system.

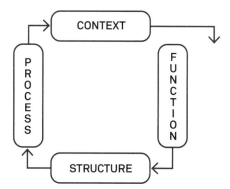

Figure 1-2 Each level of a complex system can be composed from four components within a boundary

Four stations are defined for any iterative inquiry:

1. Function – The essential or initiating action triggering system sequence.
2. Structure – Components (places, people, roles, organisations) and their relationships.
3. Process – Activities, sequence of tasks, know-hows required to produce outcome.
4. Context/Purpose – Unique environment in which system is situated, or purpose of entire cycle.

Cocreating the Iterative Inquiry

Planning and Prep

Be clear about the purpose of the exercise with this first tool. The Iterative Inquiry can be used as a powerful framing technique, or just an initial thought exercise to help define the component levels of a system. Communicate this purpose to the team before setting up a workshop and allocating time to this.

Define and label the system levels in the map, to better present the challenge or system of interest (we use micro, meso, exo, and macro to identity levels often used when designing for a social system). The tool can be edited (in the PDF file) to specify other levels. For example, in an ecosystem, we might specify niche, regime, landscape, bioregion, and ecosystem.

Mapping Method

Start at the centre of the spiral (centre-right quadrant) and name the first *function*:

1. **Function**: What is the main activity or need that triggers the first occasion of a process? Usually this is just one action. Take healthcare as an example, let's say a person has symptoms requiring medical tests or feedback. This simple initiating function of 'A person feels symptoms' is then satisfied by access to the structure and process. The choice made to define the initial function has impact on the entire mapping – which is why iteration is so important!

2. **Structures** (roles, agencies, places, settings, who and what – *nouns*): In order to fulfil the function, the system has well-known structures of parts and their connections. Depending on the system perspective, the person might use the structure of internet web search first to self-diagnose their symptoms. This might continue as the first level, or if the symptoms were felt as severe, the triggering event could lead to Emergency or Primary Care.

3. **Processes** (activities, practices, how – *verbs*): These are the activities performed within the identified structures to fulfil the function. In the web search case, the information search might involve multiple searches and pursuits to determine whether medical attention was suggested. If it was, seeking medical help would trigger the second function (and at that level, processes would include appointment, examination, tests, and result in a diagnosis and treatment).

4. **Context / Purpose** (the defining state for the entire system level): These are the contexts for the entire iteration or level and can be named as purposes. For this example, the first ring of the system might be 'Self-Examination' and the second, 'Primary Care Treatment.'

As we move up to the next level, the result of resolving the first function will define the next level of the system. If 'Self-Examination' leads to 'Primary Care' in the next cycle, a family doctor might refer the patient for further specialised care, which triggers a 'Secondary Care' context. Or if a surgical operation is needed, then a 'Specialised Care or Surgery' context may be triggered. Each of these system levels can include all of those contained in the lower levels, although not all levels are always necessary.

Delivery and Destination

Unless this tool is used as a continuing reference, it is not necessary to render a final diagram of the iterative inquiry. The final version of an iterative inquiry can be creatively rendered visually if it is to be shared beyond the project team.

The real value of the tool is in the shared learning, and development of consensus for the selected system boundary and the perspectives of the system levels that are constituted within that boundary. The image of these decisions will not always be helpful in the design process going forward, but it becomes part of the record of decision-making and analysis.

Travel Tips

Even the process of learning the Iterative Inquiry is a powerful self-starting method for learning systems theory and understanding the variables and components in a complex system. While apparently simple in structure, the mapping process can be quite challenging because it is a model from the system perspective, not a user's perspective.

The Iterative Inquiry is circular - but is not a flowchart. The arrows do not pass activity from one box to another. Iterations define each level, and iterations reflect on each update of the overall system model. The modeler or team should pause and synthesise the information into a cohesive image (concept) of the whole.

Using the Model

Not all social systems show clear dependency between system structures. Healthcare systems in most countries demonstrate clearly-bounded levels of care and medical specialisation. Modelers often show government policy and insurance regulations as a largest containing system. An iterative inquiry analysis identifies the health purposes associated with each level of function. This inquiry is produced by asking 'why' at each function to reveal the next higher function. Therefore, the first function might be 'to identify health concerns,' the second function as 'to resolve symptoms,' the third level as 'to resolve underlying causes,' and the fourth level as 'to sustain health.' By asking 'why' of this last level, we can see an ultimate level of 'to live in full wellbeing' or something similar.

The resulting model of this tool can be prepared as a visually-striking graphic reflecting colours, lists of structures and processes, cyclic lines between levels, and other clarifications. However, we often see this model as an internal product, representative of the mental model a core team might have of the system. The model can be difficult for external viewers and readers to understand, and it is not typically provided in design reports or stakeholder products. It does, however, feed directly into the other tools and models.

Case Study – Regenerative Architecture

The Iterative Inquiry is a mapping of a successive series of system descriptions from the inner-most (microsystem or deepest level) to the outer-most containing system (macrosystem, broadest boundary of expression). The number of levels or cycles within a system model is determined by the modeller – there is no guideline that limits the number of contained subsystems, as the modelling of the whole system determines the boundaries. Other than the necessity to effectively read, share, and communicate the mapping, the system levels are defined by the relations to each other, and these relationships are a determining factor.

The Iterative Inquiry map is typically named to represent the purpose of the modelling exercise, as in Figure 1-3, *Policy Framework for Green Building*.

While a common expectation of the Tourist might be that this diagram – a series of arrows connecting each station – is a flow diagram linking each function to the next steps, the purpose of the iteration cycle is actually to 'connect up,' enlarging the purpose or context at each level. This feature is indicated by the map showing four common system-level terms, from micro to macro. The levels of the system can expand well beyond four, but four is typical for this type of model. Sometimes colour-coding is used at each level to distinguish it, while each of the four areas of system definitions is matched here.

At the micro level, individual buildings can reduce operational and embodied carbon emissions. Local governments use policy and regulation to expand the number of carbon-neutral buildings and reduce urban emissions.

The global climate action system forms the next layer because all other levels of government derive their climate targets from the Intergovernmental Panel on Climate Change (IPCC) modelling and recommendations. The natural environment is the macro system, because regenerative architecture aims to enhance and restore ecosystems, not just reduce its footprint. From this exploration, we chose to focus on the two innermost system levels: buildings and municipal governments.

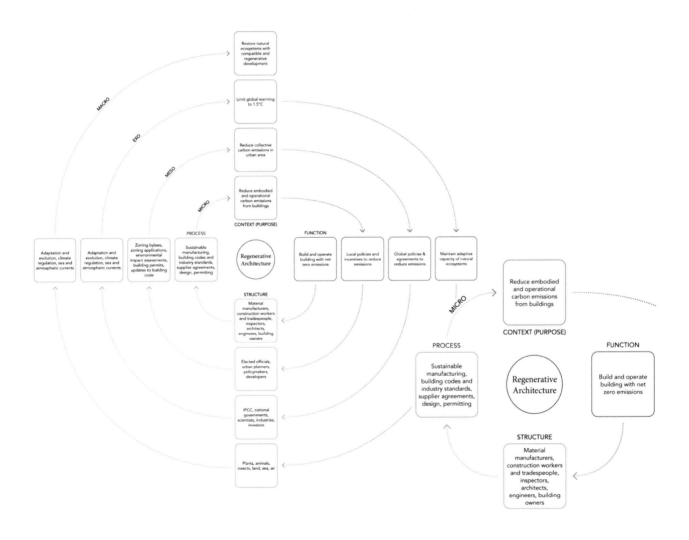

Figure 1-3
Policy Framework for Green Building. Shaun Alfonso, Carly Benson, Véronique Claude, Samah Kamalmaz, Eva Ng, Puja Prakash (2021)

Actors Map

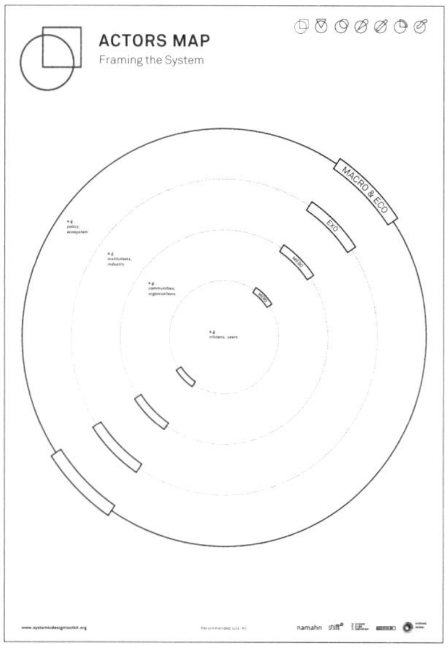

Figure 1-4
The Actors Map

- Time to Run:
  .5-1 hour
- Workshop Type:
  Framing
- Process time:
  1+ days
- Connections to:
  [1] Rich Context
  [2] Listening
  [3] Social Ecosystem
  [4] Synthesis Map
  [7] Transition by Design

The Actors Map[5] is a tool to identify and represent the key participants (organisations, individuals, human and nonhuman agents) in the system. It maps their mutual relations to the issues of concern or an outcome in the system. At the beginning of a project, an Actors Map helps identify and select the system participants to observe or interview in the case or a field study. Actor mapping in the Framing stage enables identification of human and non-human actors in the total social system. It helps to map and identify relationality within the formal structures, to uncover power relations influencing the system. Further analysis can discover opportunities for network formation and can strengthen weak connections or gaps in the social system.

The Actors Map provides a tool for iterative description of actors (and actants) in a system of interest. It can be used following the Iterative Inquiry (in which case the people, roles, and agencies in the structures can be translated into the model as actors). It is best to conduct several iterations of generating and naming actors. It is helpful to use the Actors Map early in a series of workshops or analysis, as it contributes to downstream ideation. Also teams are able to produce ready insights about system participants, leading to a quick win effect. Yet, several passes are typical before the team reaches an agreement on the map. We might refine and revise the Actors Map after a field study or use it as input to discuss intervention strategies.

Structure

There are different versions of the Actors Map in the Toolkit, but the most open-ended is shown in the model. The concentric circles show a nested system of social actors, each circle representing a level of social system. These levels are labelled by system scale, from micro to macro/eco, with open labels available for the participants to write in their own (e.g. user, organisation, society, ecosystem) to correspond to systems of interest.

Often two axes are used in the model to represent the influential relationships

[5] The actor mapping technique is based on a graphical model to visualise conflicts in Simon Fischer et al (2000), *Working with Conflict: Skills and Strategies for Action*. Geoff Mulgan & Charles Leadbeater in Systems Innovation (2013), discuss relevant power/knowledge dynamics in a well-known Nesta white paper.

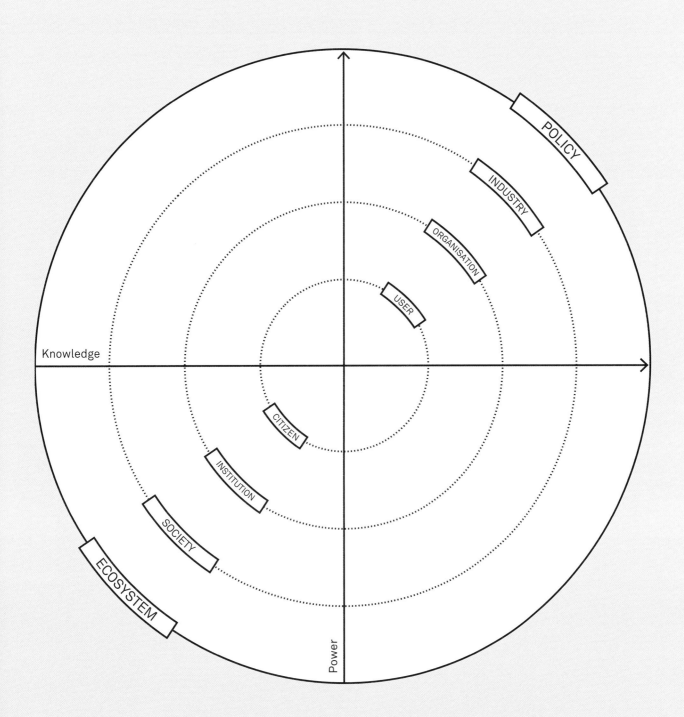

POLICY

INDUSTRY

ORGANISATION

USER

Knowledge

CITIZEN

INSTITUTION

SOCIETY

ECOSYSTEM

Power

of actors in the systems. The most typical spectra are their relative Knowledge (x-axis) and Power (y-axis) as common social forces that reveal patterns of system influence. Other dimensions can be defined as alternatives, including Connectedness, Interest, or Urgency.

Teams generate responses to the Actors Map based on their own expertise or research. Iterative review with stakeholders and field studies will update the stakeholder models developed from the map.

Cocreating the Actors Map

Planning and Prep

Define the levels that correspond to a challenge or system of interest. Each ring corresponds with the system levels from micro-macro. Place core constituents in the centre, e.g. students, patients, who represent the most micro social system. Try to find input from published reports and studies that can inform references to actors and stakeholders. If needed, create separate maps on sub-topics and/or different levels of detail to reduce complexity.

Mapping Method

1. Decide on the essential point of view (e.g. user or system). Then define the subsystems influencing the core (e.g. service providers, governance, industry sectors). Identify an initial set of key actors.

2. Start by generating notes with labels of actors and stakeholders drawn from earlier exercises. If an Iterative Inquiry was done, the roles identified as structures will also serve as actors.

3. Populate the map with notes labelled for the identified actors in a collaborative generative activity with a core team. Specify their roles. Arrange them according to their level of relative power (within the system, to change the system) and their knowledge about the issues. Note the boundaries of the system levels – power or knowledge is positioned at the edges of the boundaries.

4. Draw directional lines to indicate relationships between actors that the team can determine. Assess the quality of the relations, and use line types and colours to indicate relationship types: functional or dysfunctional; strong or weak; unbalanced, oscillating or balanced; conflicting, broken, or ad hoc; informal or emergent etc.

5. Additionally, the exchange of value between actors can be mapped, using other line types while labelling the value and return. This step creates a value network from the growing diagram.

6. Mark or group the collection of actors with similar interests and sets that may have conflicting interests.

7. Review and update the map as often as the team identifies more information about actors.

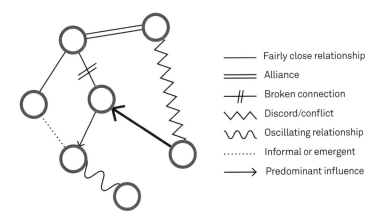

Figure 1-5
Relationships annotated on an Actors Map

Delivery and Destination

The Actors Map is a useful initial system map for all members of the design and research team. After reviewing all the notes and rendering it clearly as a final diagram, it can be shared as a defining image, as a poster, or included in a research proposal or other document.

The next step in utilising the Actors Map is to translate critical actors to stakeholders as participant segments. In Stage [2] Listening, a sampling frame is defined for planning, recruiting, and conducting interviews and observations. The Stakeholder Discovery tool defines each segment and specifies 4-6 profiles to interview for field study or virtual interviews.

Travel Tips

The Actors Map will be reviewed and updated over several iterations, with a final version reflecting the stakeholder analysis in [2] Listening. Explorers can start with a simple series of nested social systems and expand it in iterations with relevant categories, such as power/knowledge. It is only at this stage that there will be an opportunity to include a requisite variety of participants. At the framing stage, it's typical to not have access to end-user participants, as the core team will consist of organisational members, sponsors and perhaps experts.

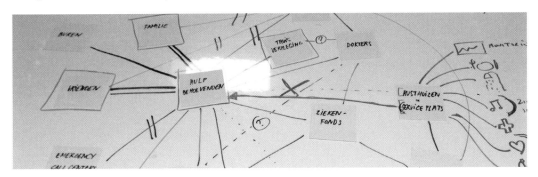

Figure 1-6
Cocreating a future Actors Map for Zyzo, a product-service system aimed at improving the daily contacts between elderly, their family and their caretakers

Rich Context

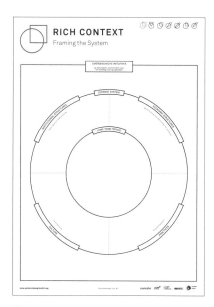

Figure 1-7
The Rich Context

- Time to Run:
  .5-1 hour
- Session context:
  Studio
- Workshop Type:
  Framing
- Process time:
  1+ days
- Connections to:
  [1] Actors Map
  [1] Niche Discovery
  [2] Research Questions
  [4] Three Horizons
  [4] Synthesis Map

The Rich Context[6] map defines connections between long-term trends in the societal environment (landscape), the current practices of the system (regime level) maintained by policies and organisations, and the emerging (niche) innovations emerging that might effectively address some of the trends.

The purpose of a rich context is to build a common understanding of the most significant system contexts in cocreation with knowledgeable key stakeholders. Typically, a sponsor team and stakeholders will have a pragmatic grasp of the existing paradigms and will know the emerging responses and innovations addressing an issue. These niche responses are often aligned with the drivers of system change. The niches, in particular, are helpful to identify actors and further direct team attention to stakeholders for interviews in [2] Listening.

Cocreating the Rich Context

Planning and Prep

Have team members conduct desk research and searches to acquire information and insight into long-term trends, current practices, and emerging niche projects or innovations that seem relevant or promising.

Mapping Method

1. Generate and post notes to define long-term trends (one topic per note) that put pressure on the system and call for change. This is the *landscape* of the context. Cluster these in the centre.

2. Now identify and post notes describing how the current regime (social and technological practices) is structured and how it deals with those challenging trends. These are placed around the centre in the surrounding band.

3. There are four quadrants – Institutional, Economic, Culture, and Practice. Post a wide range of responses to characterise the regime, such as

---

[6] The Rich Context map is based on Frank Geels (2005) Processes and patterns in transitions and system innovations: Refining the co-evolutionary multi-level perspective. *Technological Forecasting and Social Change*. This study explains the emergence of system innovations through the interaction between dynamic processes at multiple scales.

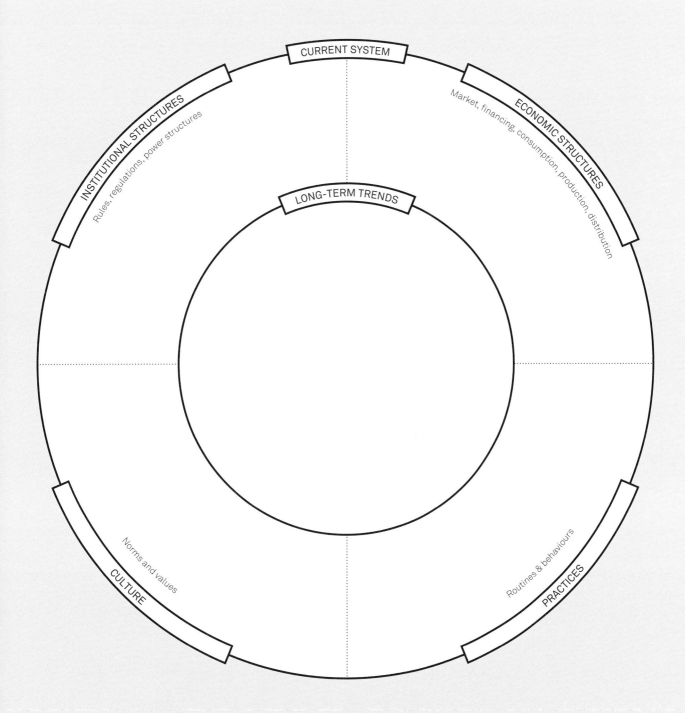

cultural preferences and shifts in social norms, expert and current practices, rules and services, technology and infrastructure, and existing networks and power relations.

4. Identify niche projects – emerging innovations that address the issue in a novel way. These notes are positioned at the outside and can be located by the same quadrant labels depending on their relevance.

5. Optional step: Draw connections between the regime-level practices and the long-term landscape trends. Also connect the niche innovations to the regime practices they might disrupt. Review the final map to Identify the most systemic regime elements (those most connected).

Delivery and Destination

The Rich Context map is most useful to the immediate design team, but can be rendered as a creative system map for documentation. The Rich Context can be used throughout the stages as a reference to the current system issues and tensions, and especially informs the systems models in [3] Understanding. It also suggests new actors, or feedback to the Actors Map, and indicates stakeholder groups to interview in [2] Listening.

Travel Tips

– It is important to be aware of the dominant regime around a defined project, as the regime can be a support or a barrier for innovation. Regime shift or the creation of a sub-regime can be part of the innovation challenge.
– The Rich Context complements the Actors Map by identifying the core and peripheral participants, some of which will be engaged in innovations changing the system over time. A second Actors Map can be constructed to present these observations or if relationships between niches and the dominant regime are non-existent.

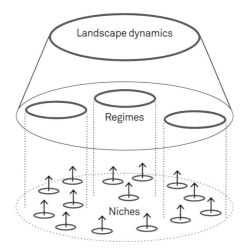

Figure 1-8
Landscape, regime and niche interactions

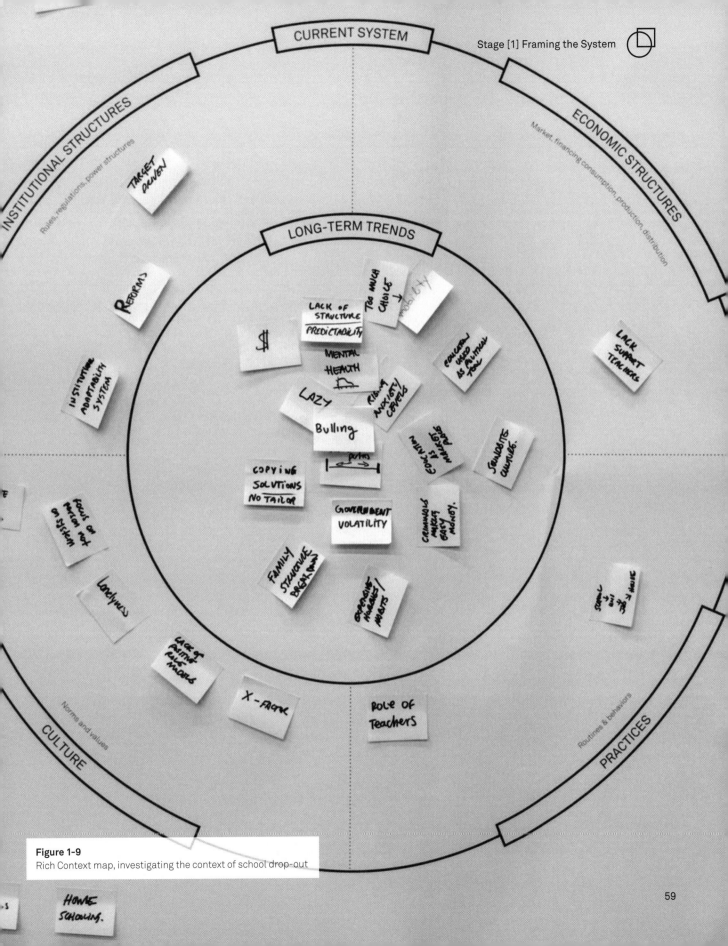

Figure 1-9
Rich Context map, investigating the context of school drop-out

Niche Discovery

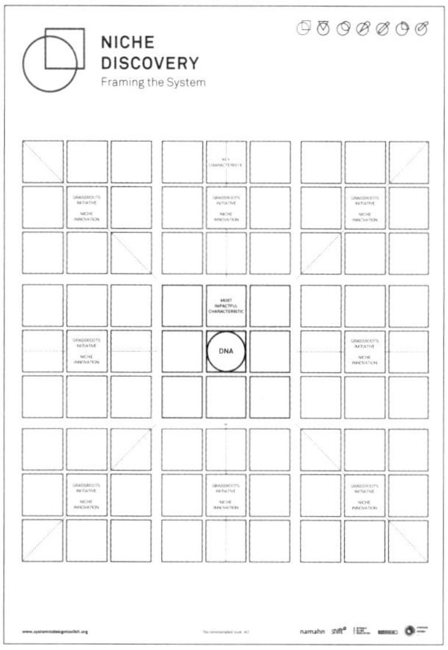

Figure 1-10
The Niche Discovery

— Time to Run:
  .5-2 hours
— Session context:
  Studio
— Workshop Type:
  Framing
— Process time:
  1+ days
— Connections to:
  [1] Rich Context
  [3] Multicapitals Map
  [3] Story Loop Diagram
  [5] Intervention Strategy
  [5] Intervention Model

With the Niche Discovery tool,[7] emerging niche innovations are explored, to identify change leaders and define their position and potential. Niches have significant influence on future systems change, and therefore have connections to many other tools in the Journeys.

The purpose of defining niche characteristics 'early' in the systemic design inquiry is to raise a wide complement of initiatives known to the team before seeking alternatives, and to understand their potential for innovation or intervention.

Sociotechnical innovations often emerge from niche initiatives that might eventually scale. Niches are 'protected spaces' such as R&D laboratories, subsidised demonstration projects, or small market niches where users have special demands and are willing to support emerging innovations. Niche actors (such as entrepreneurs, start-ups, spinoffs) work on edge innovations that deviate from established economic or service regimes. Niche actors hope that their promising novelties are eventually used in the regime or even replace it. This is not easy, however, because the existing regime is stabilised by many lock-in mechanisms and because niche innovations may have a mismatch with existing regime dimensions (e.g. lack of appropriate infrastructure, regulations, or consumer practices).

Niches are crucial for transitions because they show the emerging pathways indicating potential systemic change. Niche innovations are peripheral to the mainstream path-dependent movements, or they are too small to be considered a threat to replace the current system. The literature defines three core processes in niche formation:

1. The articulation (and adjustment) of expectations or visions that guide innovation activities, and attract attention and funding from external actors.

2. Building social networks and the enrolment of new actors, expanding the resource base of the emerging innovation network.

3. Learning and articulation processes across a growing microsystem, including technical design, market demand and user preferences, technological infrastructure, organisational structures and business models, policy instruments, and symbolic meanings.

[7] This tool is based on the Lotus Blossom ideation technique created by Yasuo Matsumura. Originally it is used from the inside to the edge, to generate ideas by association. We apply it here in reverse order, from the outside to the centre.

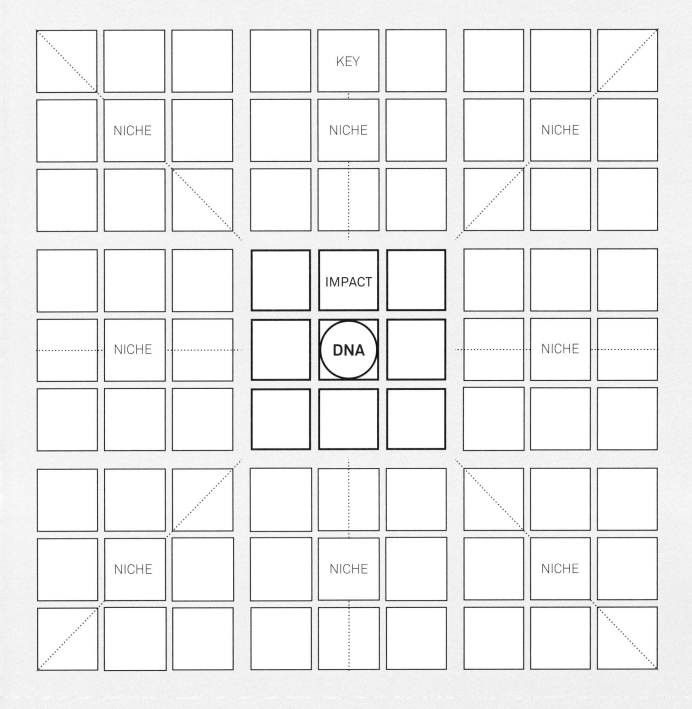

Niches gain momentum and can grow to intervene in the dominant system if the vision becomes more broadly accepted, and as learning processes in the network result in stable configurations (i.e. a formative design). As networks grow, the participation of more powerful actors and partnerships conveys legitimacy and resources to niche innovations, leading to scaling beyond the niche towards a stable level in the regime.

Convening the Niche Discovery

Planning and Prep

Well-informed participants will already be familiar with emerging innovations in the relevant fields within the system context. Workshop planners can provide homework to have people research and prepare brief exemplars of niche innovations in specific contexts of interest to share and populate the map. The map materials require no special prior setup.

Mapping Method

1. Ask participants to identify up to eight inspiring or promising initiatives that are recognised as niche-level innovations in the context of the system of interest. These are emerging innovations that contribute to the evolving purpose of system change with the potential for impact. Write names on notes (colour-coded to participants or context) to place in the boxes provided.

2. Generate for each niche initiative eight important features that uniquely distinguish the project or opportunity. Note these characteristics in the boxes around the posted title.

3. Select the eight most impactful key features that show up as recurring ideas, innovative approaches, or that could inspire future initiatives. Write these characteristics in the centre boxes. Define the central theme or model of change in the 'DNA' box if the team can identify a common theme.

Delivery and Destination

The Niche Discovery tool results in a fully-defined map of innovation concepts and possible interventions related to the system or change project. Key characteristics directly relevant to informing other models can be drawn out and synthesised in the Rich Context, the Multicapitals Model, and Story Loop diagrams in [3] Understanding, and the Intervention Strategy in [5] Interventions. Stakeholders from these initiatives can be recruited and interviewed in [2] Listening.

A system's readiness for change can be indicated by the number of emerging niche innovations. If there are no early initiatives, the system of interest (as represented) is likely not revealing signs of movement toward change through innovation. From a trends analysis perspective, it could be that they are not apparent or recognised by the team members. Weak signals may not be salient yet, or they may be obscured by competing trends.

Figure 1-11
Exploring emerging initiatives of collaboration between creatives across the Mediterranean

Light on the path

Framing the system and scoping the project are primary commitments that invest a team toward an agreed direction. If we choose a boundary that is too broad (e.g. we try to 'save the world'), the scope may be inaccessible to design intervention. Successive modelling will be filled with generalisations that fail to deliver an innovative design proposal. On the other hand, if the frame is too narrow, or short-term, the envisioned outcomes could be trivial or insufficient to the system's complexity. The organisational costs of boundary framing impacting future investment and action are not always apparent at this stage – therefore there are several tools to help.

The framing process 'discovers' purposes of system change, as this is cocreated in collaboration with stakeholders directly working with their social system. Stakeholders know their system, but as designers, we will not – we do not share their ownership. Committed system participants should ultimately agree on the boundaries defined in Framing. The designer's distance and perspective can be of great help in resolving differences and recognising the implications of different framing positions. Among the many designer's tasks are to build competency with a range of tools and methods, to design and facilitate research and workshop engagements, and to learn and evolve from stakeholder conversations.

In Framing, we can introduce critical tools of long-range foresight (e.g. *visioning*) to anticipate systems change, to cocreate and assess early design scenarios of alternative futures. Foresight methods create important temporal frames that help stakeholders assess possible outcomes from near and long-term scenarios. The Framing stage primarily focuses on the scope of system boundaries – the evolution of system change over time is developed through tools over all the stages. Yet it's often helpful to invite a foresight visioning method such as Three Horizons into early collaboration during framing.

Exploring the Territory

As with many of the Journeys methods, we can mediate an essential system process with design thinking approaches, which expands the learning and generative options by leveraging team creativity.

Framing is an essential activity for most design situations. Before a design team proceeds with creative development, a critical inquiry is performed to refine or challenge the client's brief for proposed work. Every design brief (or change programme) entails prior and often hidden assumptions, which remain influential or become problematic later if they are not consciously elicited and considered in the framing. The first stage of Framing also entails the first four (of 11) systemic design principles (pg. 228). The first four principles are relevant to rethinking the problem space, the purpose and boundaries that define the system itself, and the depth of complexity:

1. Idealisation – Locating ideals or idealised outcomes that can serve as attractors of futures

2. Appreciating complexity – A realistic appraisal of wicked problems and complexity

3. Purpose finding – Defining or evolving a focal, attractor purpose orienting design

4. Boundary framing – Defining the most effective fit of a problem as presented to a system context, testing a sufficient variety of conceptual design options before choosing boundaries

The Framing stage can set a significant path dependency that influences everything that follows. While we can return at any point in the process to 'reframe,' the design team must also recognise a necessity to revise, to create the space to reframe. Since most projects have a strong forward-moving or even urgent bias, the pause to reframe changes the itinerary and often requires a critical event or failure to even consider it.

Our framing always inherits the existing territory – the system as it exists today. Systems to-be-changed are a formative context,[8] an 'installed base' of well-known routines and path-dependent networks. While perceived problems are initial conditions that drive reform, measurable progress toward systems change nearly always occurs from policies that advance in multiple incremental steps, 'muddling through'[9] and not paradigmatic transformation. Paradigms do change, but often imperceptibly, and are recognised in retrospect. The shift in design education toward design for complexity, for example, was unheard of a decade ago. Every innovation programme, client vision, or policy solution inherits purposes that emerge from prior understanding and learning in line with the many faces of the problem. Lessons are often learned from failing to achieve a desired change in the past. Yet we cannot create a future system without dealing directly with its infrastructures, the human habitus, and social practices carried forward from its past.

The exercises in Framing help define the opportunity space and the trends within a current system. We can map out the context and create agreement about the most effective opportunities for change going forward. A new product that intervenes or facilitates a system change – such as apps that build on smartphone heart rate sensors – can frame, or envision an entire change in personal health habits, and potentially change the nature of personal health management. The formative context in this example is not the 'smartphone,' but the entire system of technology, social uses, personal behaviours, software networks, and value constellations that make such a new product possible.

The purpose of problem framing is to define a powerful relationship between a proposed action (or design concept) and the situation of concern. As designers, we often speak of problem framing, and systems thinkers are concerned with boundary judgments. In practice, these are similar methods of thought. Fit requires an iterative process of selecting boundaries and reflectively considering the associated meanings entailed by the boundary frame. For example, climate change entails an

innumerable range of possible boundaries. Productive systemic design and dialogue require participants to exchange their perspectives to understand the possible effects of action. Boundary frames might range from 'individual behaviour,' to 'effects on our region,' to 'national climate adaptation.' Each boundary has significantly different values, actions, and possible effects.

A primary function of design thinking is to obviate the necessity to analyse a problem's structure and behaviour by finding a different problem to resolve than the default situation given. Designers refer to this process as challenging the brief. Kees Dorst[10] shows how designers modify and negotiate frames of design problem briefs provided to instantiate a design project.

Dorst finds three processes we can improve in reframing: 1) Metaphor and analogy, 2) Engaging with the context, and 3) Conjecture. Metaphors are creative transformations of the problem to represent its behaviours or related elements as another model that is considered more familiar to the designers and team. In a design brief, designers might reimagine an abstract requirement (such as a website associated with a product) as another form entirely (such as a museum or analogy of a storybook). Contextual engagement refers to the approach of working with visual or verbal models (or mockups) in narratives that evaluate the functions of the brief within a context of use. Switching contexts enables the designers to reflect on the appropriate fit of the evolving idea in different uses. Conjecture asks multiple 'what if' questions of the design model and situation itself. Conjecture can be playful and non-binding, but also produces the serious effect of helping stakeholders release preconceptions of the initial frame and situation to allow something novel to emerge.

Framing and reframing are primary design practices – based on abductive reasoning and identifying new metaphors that lead us to find the right problem to solve, rather than 'solving the problem right.' Or in framing terms, we might ask, 'What is a *better* problem to resolve?'

[8] Claudio Ciborra (2009). The platform organization: Recombining strategies, structures, and surprises. *Bricolage, Care and Information*.
[9] John Flach, et al (2017). Decisionmaking in practice: The dynamics of muddling through. *Applied Ergonomics*.
[10] Kees Dorst (2015). *Frame Innovation: Create New Thinking by Design*. MIT Press.

[2] Listening to the System
Learning from the experience of system stakeholders

The Design Journeys methodology balances contributions from systems science and design-led methods in each stage. Listening to the System introduces human-centred research for planning, sampling, field interviews, and stakeholder analysis. These same methods can support a wide range of research – from rapid policy studies, design action research, or the service experience of a social system. While this 'stage' may seem presented here as one step in a linear process, in practice a single stage of research is rarely a "one-and-done" operation. Systemic design research often follows the cycles of design as an inquiry across the stages, as feedback or evaluation informing important questions. Interactive interviews, expert insights, and survey feedback can be tapped as regular listening processes throughout a project.

As with [1] Framing, research tools can be adapted for the Tourist or Explorer. Conducting research requires additional knowledge, skills, and sensitivities that take some time and training to develop beyond the scope of planning workshops. Stakeholder sampling, for example, is such an evolved but necessary skill, drawing on social research, probability distribution, and the systemic principle of requisite variety.

The Tourist might draw upon the templates for research interviews and sampling that provide some guidance to less-experienced practitioners. The Tourist approach might be best for an in-house team without formal ethnographic or user research experience. The tools can be used to spec out the desired scope of the research process, including an appropriate participant sample, a set of proposed interview questions, and a model of the activities in the system being studied.

The Explorer approach requires more experience to perform, especially for planning and conducting multi-stakeholder research. However, the Explorer mindset inspires creative and powerful approaches to system investigation, with the potential to produce extraordinary insights and results. Experienced Explorers might use the Listening tools in creative adaptations to engage sponsors and stakeholders in contributing to study design and stakeholder selection.

Researching People in Complex Systems

The purpose of Listening is to understand the goals, perspectives, needs, and drives of system actors and to identify systemic forces and issues that cause the current condition and behaviour.

In this stage, we investigate social systems and change opportunities through stakeholder studies, desk research, design action research[1], and direct fieldwork. To support in-depth study for systems change, several unique tools are available to facilitate a participatory approach to design action research. It's outside the scope of this chapter to develop or propose a research methodology, and a research strategy should be unique to each organisation. References and possible pathways are indicated throughout for the Explorer.

Research conducted in complex social systems must disambiguate multiple languages. Tourists will find (as Explorers know well) that considerable ambiguity arises in conversations about the acceptable definition of 'our' system of interest. Human research will immediately expose unresolved assumptions, as questions about the 'experience of the system' will confuse participants.

We advocate a design-led research methodology, driven by questions arising from the experiences of participants in the system of interest. Design research provides the range and flexibility of many methods suitable for the pragmatic, exploratory purpose of system research. Design-led research must sometimes be explained in context, as the adoption of findings can be a negotiated process. Ethnography and systems research are atypical fact-finding avenues in the public sector and many corporations. The findings of interdisciplinary research will be heard, and perhaps acted upon, if the presentation of new knowledge fits the culture of the sponsoring organisation. The basis for selecting research techniques can be negotiated so that findings are recognised as meaningful strategic feedback.

The Listening journey provides guidance on a systemic design approach that can be successfully integrated within a research strategy. Here, system frames are translated from [1] Framing into research questions, and system stakeholders and their perspectives are defined. In Listening, actors are sampled from the system to interview within context. Hypotheses are formulated that drive analysis and deeper understanding. Field studies, workshops, or interviews are conducted where possible to develop insights from 'inside the system.'

Evaluation is not discussed here, as the position of the Listening stage is for exploratory ethnographic and generative research to inform an understanding of current system behaviours. Evaluation is a critical research function, but largely follows early pilot studies and iteratively during implementation. Within a single chapter, the intent is to support the research role in systems change planning with design tools consistent with the Journeys – concise models of core research methods, supported by well-validated cases or references.

[1] See: Cal Swann (2002). Action research and the practice of design. *Design Issues*.
Hans Kaspar Hugentobler, Jonas & Rahe (2004). Designing a methods platform for design and design research. *Design Research Society, Melbourne*.

Design Journeys
for Listening

Stakeholder Discovery

Stakeholder analysis is conducted to understand the relevant characteristics and meaningful differences among system stakeholders, which enables effective sampling, selection, and interviewing. The tool starts an evolutionary process to engage committed participants in cocreation. Stakeholder (participant) sampling is a necessary decision and input before conducting any of the following research activities.

Research Questions

Framing research questions for any study, using a tool constructed from the Causal Layered Analysis (CLA) technique. A range of possible inquiries is generated to correspond with four levels from surface issues (Litany) to deep metaphors (Myths) as framed in this 'iceberg' model. The research questions frame and guide the direction of contextual research with system participants.

Contextual Interview

A contextual research perspective supports research tools for facilitating field observation and interviewing system stakeholders in their organisational or work contexts. A Contextual Interview tool is provided to structure an interview guide, complemented by ethnographic approaches to fieldwork and analysis.

Actants Map

The Actants Map tool facilitates modelling, summarising, and communicating findings from stakeholder research by describing activity relationships in which actors, as systemic personas, are engaged. They can be used as a first step to build Story Loop maps in [3] Understanding.

Who are the system stakeholders we can learn from?
What must we learn from research?

Stakeholder Discovery
Who are the system stakeholders, what are their varieties?

Research Questions
What are the inquiries driving the project?

Contextual Interview
How do the stakeholders experience the system?

Actants Map
What are the main relationships in the system? What is exchanged?

How can we make sense of the system?
Where do we focus attention for change? Stage [3]

69

Stakeholder Discovery

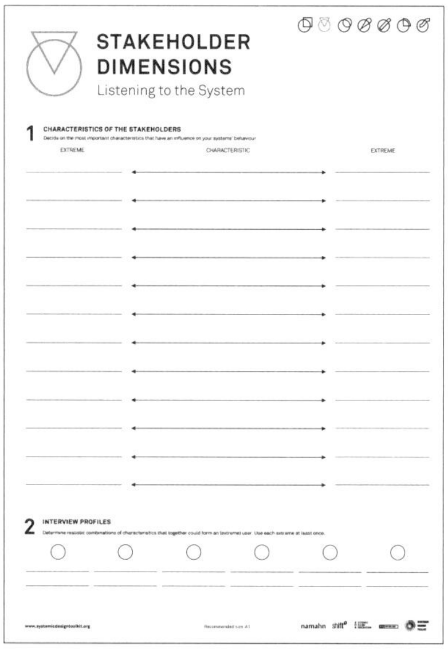

Figure 2-1
The Stakeholder Dimensions Tool

- Time to Run:
  .5-1 hour per
  stakeholder sample group
- Session context:
  Lab or Studio
- Workshop Type:
  Framing
- Process time:
  1+ days
- Connections to:
  [1] Actors Map
  [1] Rich Context
  [2] Research Questions
  [2] Contextual Interview

The Listening stage leads a human research journey, flexibly based on the type of project and accessibility of stakeholders or other participants. We start with a translation process that follows from identifying system actors in [1] Framing to defining actual stakeholders for research. Stakeholder discovery provides a set of tools for developing persona profiles and characteristics of a range of stakeholders selected from the Actors Map in Framing.

The discovery process consists of selecting, assessing, and sampling representative types from the expected social variety in the system. Recruiting participants follows the sampling definition, and is part of the discovery, as we learn as much from the recruitment as from analysis. Research tools in Stakeholder Discovery are provided in the methodology to define and differentiate the range of stakeholder segments and their initial profiles.

In the Tourist path, we explore the range of potential stakeholders to understand the variety of people (and actants) in a system context. Stakeholder Discovery lets us identify meaningful future users or system participants as segments for research and recruiting, as well as for defined personas. Therefore, this tool can be used as a basic sampling frame[2] for research and recruiting. The Explorer path expects that experienced researchers will plan interviews or field studies and can draw on several variants of the Stakeholder Discovery tools in their research roadmap. We can further develop details from the actor analysis tools in [1] Framing. The Explorer might translate from the Actors Map in [1] to determine the initial definition of key stakeholders and to sample based on power/knowledge and their requisite variety in the system.

The Stakeholder Dimensions tool (Figure 2-1) builds a set of central characteristics and ranges that are deemed important to sample from the population of system participants. These can be brainstormed by a core group in workshopping the research plan. A sampling frame (the table of desired participant characteristics) can be developed by mapping characteristics to actual segments in a recruiting strategy. They can be further articulated using a set of related stakeholder maps:

---

[2] A sampling frame is a table of the distinct different characteristics we define for each segment or category of participants in user, market, or field research for any study, whether market research, a UX analysis, or a systems study. See: Sam Ladner (2019). *Mixed Methods: A Short Guide to Applied Mixed Methods Research*.

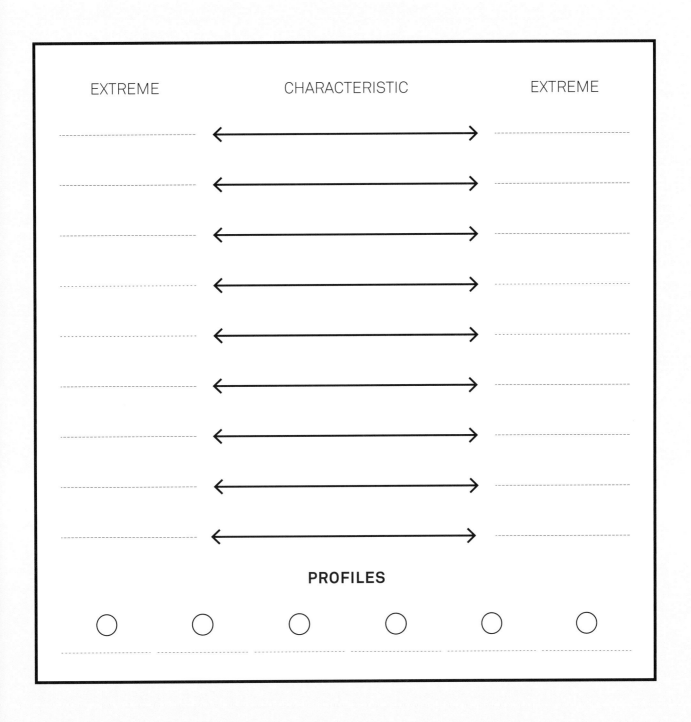

EXTREME   CHARACTERISTIC   EXTREME

PROFILES

- Stakeholder Dimensions: A spider chart of relative power/knowledge dimensions
- Stakeholder Involvement: To identify relationships to the system
- Stakeholder Profiles: To further describe named stakeholders by type (initial persona)

Cocreating Stakeholder Dimensions

A sampling frame is typically created for planning and conducting interviews and observations. The selected characteristics should be relevant to understanding the most critical ranges of invested roles in the system. Use the Stakeholder Dimensions tool to define each segment and specify a range of profiles to interview in field research or remote interviews.

Planning and Prep

Review the Actors Map and identify a meaningful selection of actors (from across the quadrants) to array a sample from different levels of the system, with roles that have a stake in the outcome. Look for a variety of demographic variables, geographies, and other variables of interest. The Stakeholder Mobilisation 'spider' map (Figure 7-1) also suggests additional variables of potential interest, including power, knowledge, or legitimacy. Actors that fulfil necessary roles can be listed as indicated from surveys or interviews of system participants.

Mapping Method

1. On the Stakeholder Dimensions tool, list the central characteristics of interest to ensure a representative sample from the population. Only list characteristics influencing the issue.

2. These dimensions can be very broad, such as age range, education, and socioeconomic context, as well as mindsets and dispositions, such as worldview, goals, or perspectives. Characteristics can also be very specific, such as job title, skills, or geographical residence.

3. List each main category in the centre column; define the extremes to the left and right as ranges. For example, a middle-age adult could be placed in the centre, with 18 years on the left and 85 years on the right.

4. Determine realistic combinations of characteristics that together could constitute a stakeholder. Mark the characteristics using dots and link these vertically using lines. Use a different colour per profile. Repeat this until you end up with ± 6 profiles per group of stakeholders. Determine combinations until each extreme is included at least one time.

Travel Tip

So-called 'extreme user' characteristics can also be defined if the study will benefit from an understanding of trends and values conflicts. For example, the category of technology orientation might allow the 'Luddite' (anti-technology) on the left and 'hacker/coder' on the right.

Delivery and Destination

The goal is to identify and recruit an appropriate range of participants for interviews and/or workshops that reflect variety in the system context. The outputs are profiles to guide selection and interviews in contextual research. If the sponsor has access to stakeholder lists that are appropriate for the research, start with their lists and have their staff send recruiting emails to enhance credibility. Create screeners for use in email recruiting or for selecting from survey responses. Recruit from appropriate lists and referrals to find participants who match the profiles for the sampling segments.

Figure 2-2
Mapping the dimensions of homeless people service providers

Research Questions

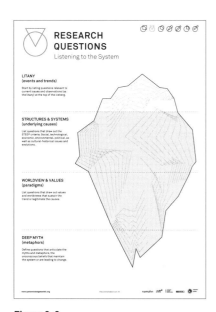

Figure 2-3
The Research Questions

- Time to Run:
  2+ hour
- Session context:
  Lab or Studio
- Workshop Type:
  Framing
- Process time:
  1+ days
- Connections to:
  [1] Rich Context
  [2] Stakeholder Discovery

There are many ways to creatively develop research questions, including generative exploration and problem finding, and good old-fashioned hypothesis formation. Causal Layered Analysis (CLA)[3] lends a method from strategic foresight useful in exploring a complex inquiry space. The CLA is expressed by four levels of increasing depth, from the Litany (events and trends) at the top, to Structures and Systems (underlying causes), Worldview and Values (paradigms), and Deep Myths (metaphors) at the bottom. The method entails conducting trends and field research that informs these levels of analysis, thus including different levels of knowledge.

The CLA is used here as an early analysis tool to create research questions associated with the four different levels. Research is driven by formulating questions that open inquiries, and we can start by simply composing a map of our evolving knowledge about the issues across these four systems strata. Of course, research questions can be defined by proposing variants of questions directly from [1] Framing. The CLA offers a versatile method consistent with the visual Journeys methodology that can be used across stages, in [1] Framing and [4] Envisioning as well.

Cocreating Research Questions

Planning and Prep

The Causal Layered Analysis can be used as a generative tool with brief preparation, or it can be filled out in advance through desk research into trends and system processes. The CLA model helps to structure questions from empirical observations (Events and Trends) to deeper issues within the system context, as well as worldviews and personal beliefs. Participants can start by identifying how their issues of interest are described in the news media, academic studies, available reports, advertisements, political discourse, or arts (fine art, film, theatre, music). A facilitator convenes the inquiry using the CLA from the top to bottom layers.

---

[3] CLA is a framework developed by Sohail Inayatullah used in foresight and futures research for questioning futures associated with multiple perspectives and participants. See Sohail Inayatullah (2009). Causal Layered Analysis: An integrative and transformative theory and method. *Futures Research Methodology*.

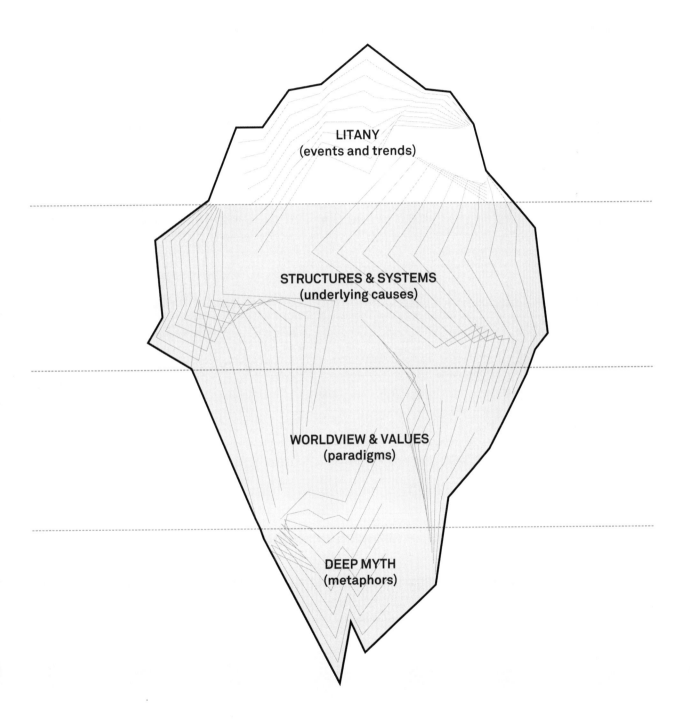

LITANY
(events and trends)

STRUCTURES & SYSTEMS
(underlying causes)

WORLDVIEW & VALUES
(paradigms)

DEEP MYTH
(metaphors)

Mapping Method

1. It helps to have an overarching research question that drives the inquiry and CLA. This can evolve during the process, but it should start as a provocative query that generates interest and has a distinct future context, such as 'what structural changes do we see occurring in liveable cities that will have impact in five years?'

2. Start by listing questions relevant to current issue, salient facts and trend observations (as the Litany) at the top of the iceberg. These are often the headline or main trend issues such as 'disincentives raise costs for driving into the city during workdays.' Events or trends derived from open news reports such as 'we are driving less and riding bicycles more every year.'

3. Underlying causes – List questions that draw out the STEEP criteria: social, technological, economic, environmental, political, as well as cultural-historical issues and trends. Draw on desk research from online agency reports, academic papers, and case studies to develop trends and ideas. Convert these to questions for research, such as 'are people walking/cycling more or less with increasing online education?'

4. List questions that draw out values and worldviews that sustain the trend or legitimate the causes. Look for clues in the language and visualisations from advertisements or political arguments, such as 'why do you choose to ride a bicycle rather than drive or transit?'

5. Define questions that articulate the myths and metaphors – the unconscious beliefs that maintain the system or are leading to change. These can be more poetic or imaginary, such as 'what experiences early in life influenced your lifelong habits?' or 'what images come to mind realising the choice of cycling to work or school?'

6. Reflect on a compilation of questions with the team and edit or add others that come to mind as filling in conceptual gaps.

Delivery and Destination

The iceberg image represents one of the classic systems models to represent the deep structure of mental models. The iceberg succinctly summarises the visible issues, deep functions, and hidden drivers of a current system, making it a useful image to build the case for change. Often the CLA iceberg is used to show the As-Is system and followed by a second, idealised iceberg to illustrate the proposed To-Be system model (building up from a changed metaphor). The CLA structure for research questions structures categories for the analysis of research findings, leading to a matching iceberg from research questions to research findings.

Keep this structure in mind when conducting interviews. Start with broad events and trends, and the underlying social causes, using the experience interview technique. Probe for worldviews, paradigms, and metaphors using the metaphor technique (see Contextual interview).

Travel Tips

The CLA tool is useful across the Journeys methodology. The CLA iceberg with research findings can be translated in [3] Understanding as an overview of the system for further analysis of dynamics within the four levels. The iceberg model is often used in synthesis maps in [4] Envisioning, as the simple visualisation lends itself to the rich picture storytelling of the system change vision. It is a very useful model in [4] Envisioning to build models of alternative futures by exploring alternative metaphors at the level of the deep system myths. The CLA can also be joined to the Three Horizons method to show a stratification of the levels of change progressing over the three curves, from lowest (deep trends) to the highest layer (perceivable narratives, the litany). These trends match the concept of 'pockets of the future in the present' in Three Horizons, as all three of the 'horizons' are distinguished by different drivers and trends that emerge over time.

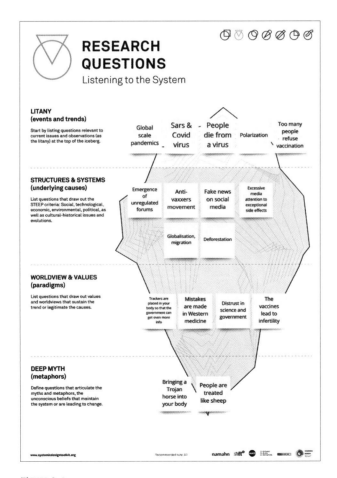

Figure 2-4
Questions tool used in online workshop to capture issues around vaccination

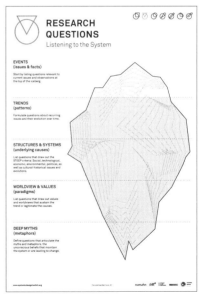

Figure 2-5
A variation of the tool with the first two levels divided up

Contextual Interview

Figure 2-6
The Contextual Interview

— Time to Run:
   1-2 hours
— Session context:
   Studio or Field
— Activity Type:
   Research
— Process time:
   1+ days
— Connections to:
   [2] Stakeholder Discovery
   [2] Research Questions
   [2] Actants
   [3] All 5 tools
   [4] Value Proposition

An ethnographic approach is taken for [2] Listening interviews to gain a contextual understanding of human behaviour in complex social systems. Ethnographic methods inform our ability to interpret culture´ and socially-constructed behaviours. Onsite field studies, more than remote interviews, are helpful to gain an empathic understanding of lived experience, with the aim of understanding perspectives, a process of *verstehen* or 'seeing through another's point of view.'

The purpose of contextual interviews is to learn about such perspectives and relevant knowledge in the systemic context. We are searching for relationships that animate the 'moving parts' of the system, significant activities involved, and positive and negative factors influencing experience. Analysis combines interview themes and findings with contextual observations of the environment, motivated activities, and interactions with artefacts.

Contextual interviews are conducted as online or in-person scheduled sessions with single participants, or in specialised focus groups using a group protocol. Understanding the social system context is helped by making visits to the place-based locations of the participants' workplace or organisation.

Convening Contextual Interviews

Planning and Prep

The Journeys handbook provides pragmatic, team-oriented tools for use in a series of connected design studios and engagements. The Contextual Interview tool draws upon the methodologies of Contextual Inquiry[4] and practical (adapted) ethnography. The tool is not a complete reference to these practices, rather it provides an entry point for the novice (Tourist) to adopt the principles of these deep foundational methodologies. Explorers may already have a methodological commitment to an ethnographic or social research

[4] Karen Holtzblatt & Hugh Beyer (1997). *Contextual Design: Defining Customer-Centered Systems*.

Stakeholder

Segment

Location & setting

Date

PHASE OR ACTIVITY

Before

During

After

EMOTIONS AND DYNAMICS

WHY QUESTIONS & CONTEXTUAL QUESTIONS (POEMS)

practice, but we expect many will find value in the use of these new tools in workshopping research materials with project teams. This simple, extensible tool combines key categories advised for inquiries to understand stakeholders within social systems, a set of broad questions based on systems principles, and an observation tool for conducting disciplined observations of behaviour in service and system settings.

The purpose of the Contextual Interview tool is to provide a first-stage tool for identifying the stakeholders, settings, and categories of interest with the team's stakeholders in the studio setting. We do not expect Tourists or Explorers to use the tool as a printed guideline for conducting interviews, but as a reference to gather team inputs and agreement before conducting in-depth individual or group interviews and observations. The Contextual Interview tool can be used for studio testing and pilot testing the interview process. A specific interview guide (and a handout or poster for mapping narrative timelines) is typically customised and pilot-tested for use in the field research.

Mapping Method

The Contextual Interview provides an outline to guide the team planning and collaborative construction of field research, ethnographic observation, or rounds of interviews. The tool itself is structured like a synthesis map (used in [4] Envisioning) that compiles segments. A team research lead should typically follow the design exercise with individual development of research materials, including interview guides with specific questions, and observation frames based on the POEMS[5] reference in the tool. (The POEMS frame refers to annotated observations of People, Objects, Environments, Messages, and Services.)

1. The stakeholder type and their location or setting are key factors to define for any study. List the segment categories associated with the system framing (e.g. clinicians, health-seekers, health policymakers). Note the types and roles for each segment from stakeholder analysis and discovery (e.g. family doctors, nurse practitioners). Identify their work location or activity settings.

2. Define the categories of information that will help identify and analyse behaviours shaped by activities and services in the system. A basic outline of seven broad types is given below.

3. Determine the kind of data that would be helpful for future design decisions. Will it be more helpful to learn about everyday activities occurring within a typical day, as in a medical practice or a field aid worker? Or are the system activities spread out over longer periods of time, such as the months of experimentation and analysis conducted by life scientists or policy planners?

4. Consider the other categories that might be useful to inform the field study. These may not all be necessary for each or any given study, but choose from among the types, and later develop interview guides that inform these questions.

5. Review the POEMS observation guide, which can be used and adapted as a guideline for field study observations. Used with the team in studio, the focus is on identifying appropriate settings that can be arranged for observation and reviewing with the team the focus of observation.

[5] Vijay Kumar & Patrick Whitney (2007). Daily life, not markets: Customer-centered design. *Journal of Business Strategy.*

Delivery and Destination

The Contextual Interview tool is first used to collect inputs from the Studio team to construct interview and observation guides. There are two versions of the tool available, the research planning tool (A) and a template for interview data collection (B). The planning tool A is useful to map out the categories of interest, the desired focus of study and interviews, and the system levels to observe. The design research team can produce print or structured guidelines from the tool to use in fieldwork or interviews. Version B can be used as an interview protocol in the research. Even though the tool is a structured outline, the interviews could follow as open, semi-structured, or structured techniques. The final guideline should reflect the realistic amount of time available in the interviews requested, which are typically no more than an hour, and for higher-positioned individuals, even half an hour. Interviews must retain a high degree of flexibility to obtain meaningful data while covering the majority of questions within each of several interviews.

Field Methods in Use

Determine whether the focus of the context in the interview is a *system activity*, such as the participant's everyday work practice, if studying a sociotechnical system such a healthcare. The other context is the *experience* of a system, for example if studying the system of consumerism. The same tool can be used, but the interview and interpretation are quite different.

System Activity

1. Start by building rapport and understanding of the activity or problem context. Ask participants to describe relevant experiences in the situation over a meaningful period of time (day, week, year). Depending on the activity or problem, focus on a particular period triggered by an event (e.g. getting ill) or even a typical day (e.g. at school). Inquire about the context in which experiences occur – a simple drawing of the timeline or a curve of the activity or felt experience can be useful.

2. Identify significant events or touchpoints and ask for a description of the actors involved. The POEMS observation frame can also be used here (People, Objects, Environment, Message, Services).

3. Continue to follow the experience timeline and ask to identify key events leading to cycles or outcomes. Be sure to ask about the current state of the person in this timeline.

4. Consider other actors involved, human and non-human. Sketch the relations between actors in the system and ask for elaboration on each relation: What is the quality of a relationship? What typical activities are involved? How have relations changed over time? What are the goals of other actors?

5. Elaborate on the needs, values, motivations, and barriers that influence participation in the system. Draw out their perception of social influences and how dominant narratives have formed.

6. Ask to describe their involvement in the current system using metaphors. Ask to explain the metaphor. Ask to propose a metaphor for an ideal system.

"I teach in a pretty **challenging** school. As it is supposed to introduce students to practical jobs, we have a **variety of situations**. In one classroom, you might have students with **low self-esteem**, **autism** or **low concentration**.

I started two years ago and first I was really **stressed**. I am **young** and difficult students would **not recognize my authority**. They would rebel to test you, to see if you can handle them.

Now it is getting better and better. You need to **be strict first**, but also **patient** and **creative** with your teaching. **Showing gratitude**, keeping a few **simple rules** and **giving rewards** is very important for them. After a while the students will **respect** you more and you can **build a connection**. I love that. I even helped a student find a holiday job once: he was so grateful that he brought back Turkish sweets from the bakery. I know there are difficult situations, but these episodes make my day and feed my **passion for the job**.

Great colleagues play a role as well, especially when dealing with difficult cases: together, we try to do our best to **monitor the pupils** and give them **personal guidance**, which I think it's the best thing. The school puts a lot of effort, but unfortunately it does not always succeed."

Figure 2-7
Highlighting the influencing factors, relations, and loops in an interview transcript

System Experience

1. Ask participants to describe experiences over a meaningful period of time (contact moment, week, year) from the beginning (the trigger) to an end point (e.g. the follow-up). Inquire about the context in which the experiences occur.

2. Using a curve, ask to explain how that experience felt in the experience (positive and negative). Elaborate on the moments when the curve changes according to experience (rising or falling back) and ask about the events or circumstances that caused these outcomes.

Steps 3-6 above can be used to continue this interview.

— The contextual interview can be understood as a sensemaking process for both interviewers and participant. Use open-ended questions to learn about experience, and ask about the perceived gaps in the experience or the system.

— Ask people to suggest metaphors for the current system, and for an ideal system. Continue to ask why questions (e.g., the education system is like a swamp because you have to wade through it. Ideally, it would be a rainforest because…). If a metaphor does not immediately come to mind, ask the person to sketch an image or give a hint, such as suggesting a common object or reference.

Documenting

Remote interviews are invariably video recorded, yet be sure to also take notes (with a partner) to capture insights, emphasise key points, and record POEMS observations. It's always best to record notes during or immediately following interviews. Collect materials collected from interview notes and interview (audio) transcription, and any artefacts photographed or identified into dedicated research folders or a tool such as OneNote. In [3] Understanding – translation from human experience to system patterns and models. Therefore, in interviews, look for or prompt to learn:

— Factors that are influencing the behaviour of people in sustaining or negative ways
— Causality relationships; how power, message, or system functions influence behaviours
— Factors contributing to continuous growth or decline
— What maintains inertia and obsolete patterns, preventing system change

For example, the research associated with Figure 2-6 includes an interview with a secondary school teacher talking about the challenges in a school with huge dropout rates. This would clearly be a loop – the reinforcing growth of an underside pattern.

The most relevant methodology in social systems inquiry is ethnography, a practice cultivated from cultural anthropology to study people 'in situ' in their everyday life and work, to understand cultural practices and the meaning of artefacts, symbols, rituals, and behaviours in context. The naturalistic orientation to ethnographic research draws on non-intervening observation and progressive interviewing as the researcher becomes socialised and experienced in a culture or community. Ethnography is not a method or tool, but a skilled research practice drawing on various techniques to inform a deep understanding of human behaviour in social system, including:

— Observation (using structured observation frames)
— Field interviews and notes
— Formal informant interviews, including contextual interviews
— Artefact collection and analysis
— Participant-generated data (diaries, photo journals, image collections, collages)
— Participatory narratives
— Field case descriptions (notes, sketches, diagrams)

Figure 2-8
Examples of props used to prompt in interviews

Use of contextual cues (props): The photo shown is related to interviews conducted with pregnant women in poverty. In this case, we used props during the interviews which helped to steer the discussion. Props can be 3D objects, but also simply a visual note or index card depicting situations, events, or surfacing metaphors.

Observation as Foundation

In ethnography, the basic orientation to the field is as a curious, alienated (non-belonging) observer.

– Train yourself to observe details in all settings
– Observation frames (POEMS or other) – Use even if an experienced researcher
– Photography – Take more than necessary, but do not rely on photos, use structured notes
– Video – Consider video as a different method, not a substitute for observation

Data Collected from Observations

– Context – How architecture and social settings influence behaviour and interactions
– Cultural data – How people exhibit culture and symbolic identity in these settings
– Activities – What tasks, routines, habits, and services are performed?
– Messages – What displays, language, signs, and meanings are observable?
– Temporal patterns – How do behaviours vary by time of day or season?
– Social cues – How are social contexts and rules guided and constrained?

Interview Structures

Be prepared to conduct the appropriate interview type for the context. Also be prepared to change interview structure should the situation call for a more participatory approach to data collection.

— Open-ended or informal interviews
— Structured (scripted)
— Semi-structured (interview guide)

Information Collected from Interviews

Collect as much data as possible, but do not exhaust your welcome with participants and sponsors – research is consensual and participatory. In one hour or less, there will be minimal time for contextual observation as well as interview. If invited to a participant's work location, use the time, if possible, for a brief tour of the location. Take photographs, not video, if these are allowed for team research use.

— Background – Collect sufficient contextual background to enable understanding of the findings when analysed later
— Etic data – Responses to questions prompted by a priori categories of interest to the project
— Emic data – Naturalistic, self-disclosed responses from participants reflecting their interests and concerns, especially of interest when data is not directly related to the study questions, but revealing previously unavailable knowledge
— Behavioural data – Description from observations of work or activities in context
— Opinions – Note the expression of opinions and views relevant to research variables
— Feelings – Note the expression of emotional responses to issues and their relevance to understanding the person in context
— Knowledge – Identify and collect references to knowledge informing the research and system context

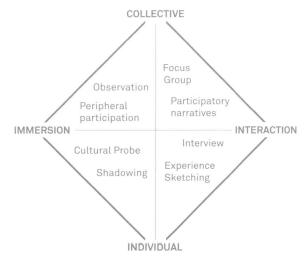

Figure 2-9
Ethnographic methods for immersive and interactive data collection, by individual or collective responses

Actants Map

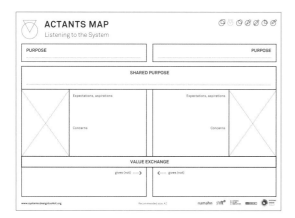

Figure 2-10
The Actants Map

— Time to Run:
  30' per actant
— Session context:
  Lab
— Workshop Type:
  Sensemaking
— Process time:
  1+ days
— Connections to:
  [1] Actors Map
  [2] Contextual Interview
  [3] Multicapitals Model
  [3] Story Loop Diagram
  [4] Synthesis Map

The Actants Map provides a tool to understand and map out the distributed and dominant relationships in any social system. The tool also identifies the factors (variables in the next step) that are influencing this relationship in a positive or negative way. Actants are identified from each (important) relation discovered with the Actors Map and as surfaced in research interviews. They will serve as input in the next steps.

The Actants Map was inspired by Bruno Latour's Actor Network Theory[6] as a method to enable mapping exchanges between actors and activities that represent enactments of or in a social system. An actant is something or someone acting in the system or being affected by it. An actant can be a human (actor) or non-human. Non-human actants are usually technical, such as smartphones or interactive devices, cars, landscapes, or buildings. Biological actants (such as a water body, trees, animals) can also be mapped. Latour suggests we can locate actants by following their role in a network and analysing how their enactment makes a difference in the course of another agent's action.

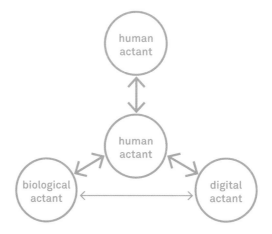

Figure 2-11
A human actant can interact with other human or non-human actants

[6] Bruno Latour (2007). *Reassembling the Social: An Introduction to Actor-Network Theory.*

PURPOSE	PURPOSE
....	....

SHARED PURPOSE

....

	Expectations, aspirations	Expectations, aspirations	
	Concerns	Concerns	

VALUE EXCHANGE

gives (not) ·····>	<····· gives (not)

The concept of a *shared purpose* in the relationship draws on the motivational aspect or 'object' from Activity Theory.[7] While the Actants Map models just the relational interchange between *two* actants at a time, and their orientation toward the objective of a social system relation, multiple maps can be sketched up and arrayed to illustrate relations within a network.

Cocreating an Actants Analysis

Planning and Prep

Review the outputs from the Actors Map and other research interview findings. Identify the relationships most relevant to the emerging issues defined in the system of interest. Salient 'paired' relationships are those representing direct work or social activity, such as doctor-patient or other service provider relationships where value is cocreated together in the shared purpose. Who are the leading system participants or stakeholders, what types of users, what are the most surprising insights?

When setting up the tool for a workshop, have pairs or small groups cocreate different actants maps to develop a range of relationships in the Actor-Network of the system. Use the Actors Map to locate preferred actant pairs and have teams develop and share their tool findings after 20 or 30-minute sessions.

Method Mapping

1. Review interview notes/transcripts from the field studies. Find a relationship between the two roles expressed in their exchange (e.g. student, teacher). For each of them, find a picture or photograph that can be used to express the actant role.

2. Note the purpose (goal for the activity) or the function (if non-human) at the top of each actant column of the Actants Map tool. Identify and name the shared purpose between the actants, if this can be determined.

3. List the aspirations (hopes), expectations, and concerns of each actant for the purpose in this relationship between actants. What socially formed roles do they play, what personal expectations do they have for each other, and what might concern each?

4. Identify and name the value exchange – the value cocreation accomplished between the actants. Propose the value given, or taken, and messages found as exchanged between the actants. What do they give to and receive from each other?

[7] An activity system tool is also provided in the extended Systemic Design Toolkit, not included in the book. See: Yrjo Engeström & Annalisa Sannino (2020). From mediated actions to heterogenous coalitions: Four generations of activity-theoretical studies of work and learning. *Mind, Culture, and Activity*.

Delivery and Destination

Especially where multiple actants are modelled, the resulting maps can be rendered for sharing with team members to reveal and discuss patterns of experience within the system and for finding critical feedback loops. The interests and concerns, and value exchanges can serve as inputs for the Multicapitals Model in Stage [3] Understanding the System. Multiple actants maps can be aggregated to build activity networks to scale the analysis across the system or be used in synthesis mapping.

Travel Tips

— The actants model can be used to prompt interview insights. Ask participants to share their understanding of relationships, shared value, and influencing factors.

— If the focus of the map is to narrate and analyse a shared experience (e.g. teacher and student experience in school) the tool template shown below suggests a good technique. In this variation, the curves of each actant's experience are drawn over each other and the differences between both actant's experiences are analysed.

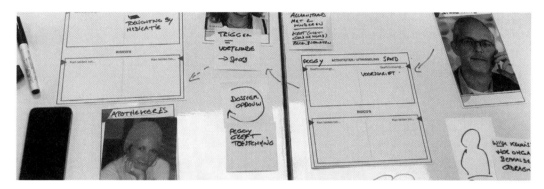

Figure 2-12
Mapping multiple actants in the care system using cards

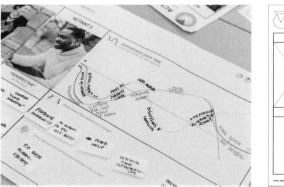

Figure 2-13
Mapping the school experience of two actants, a student and her teacher, within a common period of time

Light on the Path

For both Tourists and Explorers, an incomplete treatise on social and ethnographic research might be found frustrating. These are relatively new applications for mixed-methods field research into complex social systems. For Tourists, we could say much more about practical design research, especially to help those making their first forays into studying complex systems. Experts or Explorers might want more depth of specificity in the unique applications of human-centred design research and ethnomethodology to complex systems and change.

Research Pathways

In complex systems research the design team is faced with myriad possible complications and tensions. Any single research methodology will likely be insufficient (or misleading), at some point in the process. Design Journeys proposes human-centred design research for early exploratory studies, primarily through ethnographic field research. However, limited user studies cannot possibly explore the deep understanding of a complex social system, industry, or policy area. The Listening stage should be considered more of a research planning and initial research into these questions. Some organisations, with recognised need, budget and staffing, will proceed with continuous field and systems research in parallel to the other Journeys stages.

Among the complexities to be resolved in research practice are the competing perspectives to be expected between a creative design team, a planning group, stakeholders, or sponsor/clients. While not experts in research, each role will inherit a preferred style of findings and an implicit epistemology. Systems theories underpinning the Journeys tools and models express a *constructivist* perspective[8] through the participatory construction of stakeholder-defined representations. A human-centred research epistemology is consistent with constructivism, as is the cocreative approach to research through stakeholder engagement. Ethnographic methodology

is interpretivist, anti-positivist and consistent with constructivism. Interpretivism forms knowledge claims based on the validity of human experience, from inductive observations of social behaviour.

The interpretive perspective informs human-centred research, participatory engagement, but not generally strategic planning or systems analysis. These methodologies have been deeply informed by the cybernetics and social systems perspective that systems are socially constructed by members of a system through language. This is central to the persistent argument against systems as 'things' that exist in the world. A serious contribution from natural science and engineering approaches is also necessary in systems research, even if not part of the engagement approach of Design Journeys.

The use of the Toolkit informs decisions for complex sociotechnical systems, policy proposals, and high-stakes systems change interventions. Real projects with concrete outcomes and significant investment require an objective view of a shared external reality in which system interventions are constructed as real-world events. In design as well as systems research, we must recognise the philosophical implications behind methodology. A recognised paradox is found in the relationship between constructivism and critical realism[9] that orients design to material artefacts and change outcomes in the real-world contexts of organisations and technical systems.

Observing the System Experience

Consider how a complex social system becomes an increasingly intertwined, interactive combination of people, processes, and cultural practices. A 'system experience' can be studied from internal and external, objective and subjective, human and system-centred perspectives. The system *experience* as such lives inside the experience of everyday people engaged in

---

[8] See Bruno Latour (2003). The Promises of Constructivism. *Chasing Technoscience: Matrix for Materiality*.
[9] John Mingers (2014). *Systems Thinking, Critical Realism and Philosophy: A Confluence of Ideas*. Routledge.

the practices that construct the system. But it is also constructed by objectively observable, interacting external events and social forces. Are not these structures and forces also independent of the selected participants we happen to recruit for interviews? If our participants failed to show up for work, these forces would continue without them. How do we best study both and reconcile their findings?

Otto Scharmer[10] speaks of sensing the interiority of social fields, from different points of view: an internalised, first-person perspective, a relational view, and external third-person view. To understand these perspectives, we can observe behaviours of individuals in system activities, within relationships, performing work; the structures of their organisations; personal interactions in their community lives; social and instructional structures such as organisations and agencies; social practices and norms; and shared cultural practices, such as in arts, education, and entertainment.

When we translate from the abstraction of 'actors' listed on a model to real people, the experience of people within a system can be quite ambiguous and difficult to qualify. Our targeted system of interest, let's say the system of preventive healthcare, might not be of central significance in the experience of the participants, or well-understood by them. We also have to ensure that the most deeply invested participants (perhaps primary care clinicians in this case) are not overly influential in the research. This type of influence will unduly bias the research and our interpretation of system experience if we rely on their contributions without balance from peripheral, or future, emergent beneficiaries. If we are working with health system leaders, a small number of patient and physician interviews will not inform us of the whole system context. System participants might understand parts of the system with which they interact, but will have no insights into the whole or the parts with which they have no experience.

Any one of these levels of context might be central in the experience of selected stakeholders. Field research

will be greatly improved if we can gain agreement on a shared model of the social system and the variety of stakeholders in the system. This understanding also reinforces the necessity to balance the strongly interpretive with critical realist or system-centred perspectives.

The diamond model in Figure 2-13 presents a range of methodologies applicable across systemic design. The four points represent intents of the research, with Understanding and Prediction anchoring a scale between interpretive and positivist schools. Change and Design, while not epistemologically divergent, represent differing aims of research application. Design Journeys is primarily oriented to understanding systems for design and change, and the tools are constructivist in approach. Journeys draws on methods keyed in the legend as Generative, Interpretive, and Participatory. Ethnography (which includes hermeneutics) and sensemaking are clearly interpretive modes, oriented to Understanding. Evaluative and Analytical methods are common in classical systems studies, and are more oriented to prediction (explanation). Both perspectives are necessary, albeit at different stages in a design or change process.

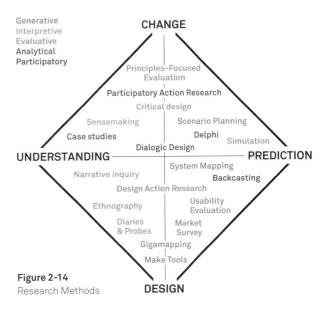

Figure 2-14
Research Methods

[10] Otto Scharmer in interview from Melanie Goodchild (2021). Relational Systems Thinking: That's how change is going to come, from our Earth Mother. *Journal of Awareness-Based Systems Change.*

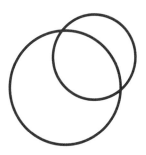

[3] Understanding the System
Seeing systems, learning from systems

In Stage [3] Understanding, our purpose is to learn and define the structures, influences, and flows in a system to form a shared mental model of its complexity, to inform design and strategy decisions. Understanding helps us 'see the system' through collaborative study of systemic behaviours, a holistic view that is created by balancing human-centred design research (Stage 2) with the dynamic causal relationships of complex systems. A durable understanding develops that leads us to a common and coherent narrative about the core system issues and the problematic feedbacks that sustain undesired system behaviours in wicked problem contexts.

The Systemic Design Toolkit crosses several complementary schools of systems thinking in a journey that develops this understanding: Social systems, system dynamics, and critical systems, as well as complementary schools of thought, including ecology, cybernetics, and complexity science. System understanding requires both systems *analysis* (within the tools) and *synthesis* (building team knowledge by active learning and sharing the models). By visualising systemic behaviours, we can map relations and ordering structures in social systems and define the powerful effects of feedback loops.

At this stage we are making sense of the current system, to explain it to ourselves, without yet making informed arguments for system change. These four tools are valuable for presenting a discovered core issue, for justifying the most effective places to intervene, or to locate the conditions for transformation to occur.

System understanding maps out the structure of a complex challenge - how we locate the sources of pain, the root causes of undesirable outcomes, and barriers to change discovered in complex systems that interact and persist. System models are synthesised through workshopping generative exercises to visualise the flows and feedback processes contributing to common mental models of a shared complex system. A model of the *whole* system emerges from a learning process accelerated by the sensemaking tools in the journey that powerfully reveal complex system relationships and interactions. The construction of a whole system view creates a shared coherence, and understanding of insights developed together, as rationale for an effective system story.

Modelling Complex System Behaviours

Understanding methods are helpful for understanding the factors contributing to our observations of complexity. The four tools are not meant for classical systems analysis – that is, a dispassionate analysis of systems and relationships as they currently exist. They can be used as mapping templates for desktop exercises, but we find they work best to engage a small team in an active collaboration of sensemaking through modelling.

Each tool enables a different view of system complexity and the insights for intervention. Designing system value or intervention proposals can draw from any, or all, of the maps in this journey. The tools are flexible and can be trialled (in a Lab context) to define initial models for validation and dialogue. Partial maps, as prototypes, can be taken into Studio settings with stakeholders as proposed starting points, to accelerate the shared learning process and generate iterations of new ideas.

The tools range from large-scale system maps, unique adaptations (Multicapitals stock and flow), and classical system models (Story Loops). Each tool contributes a distinct value to developing understanding, yet they are not all necessary in every project. The systems mapping tools are based on qualitative, soft systems approaches, as are typical in social systems. The system archetypes are standard models in system dynamics (hard systems) and represent recurrent processes that can be modelled and simulated. The Social Ecosystem is a multi-layered social system model, and the Influence Map embodies a method for leverage finding in system change. The Multicapitals Model bridges the Rich Context tool from [1] Framing to the range of tools in [3] Understanding. They can all be used by Tourist practitioners, except the Influence Map and full causal loop diagrams are more Explorer methods, as they will require more practice and learning to lead in collaboration.

The team participation of cocreating and making sense of the system analysis generates the shared language and common mental model about the boundaries, problems, and consequential effects of the system. This understanding leads to visualisations informed by the research narratives, creating patterns for 'system stories' from the mapping and learning journey.

Design Journeys
for Understanding

Social Ecosystem
The Social Ecosystem defines social systems in which personas, organisations, and communities participate to help the design team identify values and criteria across all levels of a complex system. This tool complements the Influence Map by finding influential social structures and relationships between groups at different scale levels.

Multicapitals Model
A unique systems map for stakeholder mapping of multiple capital stock and flows, the Multicapitals Model tool provides a choice of two capitals models or a trends map (categorised by the STEEP trends). The multicapitals model describes the material and informational stocks observed in the system, and leads to mapping flow relationships within the system, providing guiding input for the next two stages.

Influence Map
A powerful canvas tool for describing system influences and leverage pathways, with guidance for influence structures such as outcome mapping (used in Stage [5] Interventions). The Influence Map helps identify high leverage activities, contributing factors to a theory of change, and can be used to find loops for Story Loops (causal loop diagrams).

Story Loop Diagram
A variation of the canonical causal loop diagram, constructed from system narratives discovered in research during [2] Listening. This tool is a next step from the Multicapitals Model, defining causality in system flows. In this mapping, the stocks and flows are represented in continuous causal relationships (the loops from flows) and possible points for intervention can be found.

System Archetypes
System archetypes represent recurring patterns of system behaviour. These are both common and typically dysfunctional, so the patterns can be used as a diagnostic tool when analysing causality for Story Loops.

**How can we make sense of the system?
Where do we focus attention for change?**

Social Ecosystem Map
How have social systems and structures evolved?

Multicapitals Model
What are the capital stocks of interest and how do they build and flow?

Influence Map
How do social and causal functions influence each other across the system?

System Archetypes
What common systemic issues are found?

Story Loops
What are the continuous sources of problematic effects in the system?

How might we redesign system conditions that might lead to preferred futures? Stage [4]

Social Ecosystem Map

The Social Ecosystem Map adapts the socioecological system model[1] from systems psychology to provide a canvas for mapping the progressive series of nested social systems within a societal or cultural context. The Social Ecosystem Map provides a research-based tool for mapping social systems and their relations within and across multiple system boundaries.

While the Actors Map provides high structural consistency, the social ecosystem's purpose, system theory, and levels are different from the actor-network style of map. The concentric rings define boundaries of social systems that are traversed and learned through human development. As a child grows socially from the centre unit out, navigating each level of social system as they develop, we generalise from this universal social ecology. For most types of activity, we participate in one sphere of the map geography at a time. As adults we navigate all levels of social structure together, and have continuous relationships within each sphere of activity, but we often separate experience differently, at home, at work, and in public life, as common examples. For general purpose social systems, these same levels reflect the proximity of these social systems to the personas or populations of interest placed in the centre. These are in effect all the social worlds within a national or cultural boundary (the macrosystem), and within that, the natural ecosystem. These sociospatial relations occur within the procession of time, the Chronosystem, implied by arrows indicating continuity of participation over time.

Cocreating the Social Ecosystem Map

Planning and Prep

The socioecological model is used in this tool to map how the social, cultural, and ecological environment influences the behaviour and development of people, and to show how social relations change over time (i.e., Chronosystem). Initial inputs to inscribe the Social Ecosystem Map include the actors, organisations, and social systems found from the Actors Map in [1] Framing, as well as the actants, new groups, and relationships emerging from the experiences observed in [2] Listening. While roles or titles are often used to reference the actors, these are translated

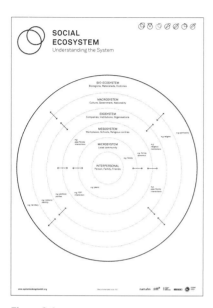

Figure 3-1
The Social Ecosystem

- Time to Run:
  2-4 hours
- Session context:
  Lab or Studio
- Workshop Type:
  Sensemaking
- Process time:
  1+ days
- Connections to:
  [1] Contextual Interview
  [3] Multicapitals Model
  [3] Influence Map
  [3] Story Loop Diagram
  [4] Synthesis Map

[1] The model is based on Uri Bronfenbrenner's bio-socioecological model of human development. The adaptation to social systems is developed by the author, Jones (2017). Social ecologies of flourishing: Designing conditions that sustain culture in Astrid Skjerven & Janne Reitan (eds) *Design for a Sustainable Culture: Perspectives, Practices and Education*.

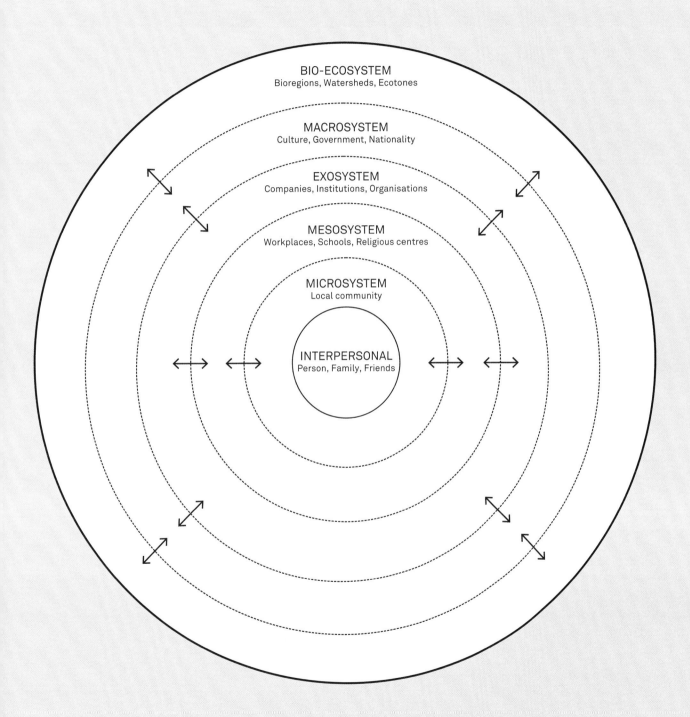

BIO-ECOSYSTEM
Bioregions, Watersheds, Ecotones

MACROSYSTEM
Culture, Government, Nationality

EXOSYSTEM
Companies, Institutions, Organisations

MESOSYSTEM
Workplaces, Schools, Religious centres

MICROSYSTEM
Local community

INTERPERSONAL
Person, Family, Friends

into named social systems for mapping a social ecology. Individuals are not referenced unless they are referenced in the centre (as they are often specified as personas in the microsystem).

Mapping Method

At the centre of the circles, list one or more of the actors (or segments), referencing personas where applicable. Because this map is already quite densely represented with labels, a persona image can be used as a signifier. An image or sketch can represent characteristics of the chosen actors. Factors like age, geographical relationship, socioeconomic status, and health status may be meaningful to the social relations.

The steps in the Social Ecosystem Model are flexible, as the intent is to create a multileveled model of the relations between social systems across levels. There are 'force lines' to indicate relational dynamics within and across levels for use as observed in the models. Six levels (adapted from Bronfenbrenner) are defined in successive levels of scale and complexity:

1. **Centre**: Individual actors are represented in the abstract as this is a system model. A persona represents one instance of a class. One actor is usually (not always) indicated, as the immediate family (a kinship relational social system) is also implied.

2. **Microsystem**: The most proximate social systems relevant to the actors – the everyday social contexts in the geography and society. Add notes to show the closest relationships that directly interact with an actor – e.g. workplaces, school groups, the neighbourhood. Post notes between the actors in the microsystem sphere that have influence on the central actor but are not authoritative – e.g. members of a team, volunteers, a conflict between peers.

3. **Mesosystem**: The meso level shows structured community and organisational settings in which people participate on an ongoing basis, e.g. the company structure, a school, church, or religious community, the local community in a city.

4. **Exosystem**: Bronfenbrenner's term refers to the external structure of social systems, here we refer to as the corporate identity of a company, an industry, healthcare institutions, municipal or regional governments.

5. **Macrosystem**: The macrosystem is the largest social sphere, the predominant or national culture, the political context and economy. Map the factors related to the political, cultural, economic, and social contexts influencing quality of life and the social worlds of the actor – e.g. cultural belonging, spiritual identity, information and media sources, national heritage, population demographics.

6. **Bio-ecosystem**: Map the influencing factors of the natural environment – e.g. watersheds, woodland and riparian ecologies, health of flora and fauna, biodiversity, pollution effects. Use two colours if mapping change over time to indicate improvement or deterioration.

7. **Chronosystem**: Temporal relationships are drawn by adding arrows between actor references within or across levels, and by defining changes over longer periods of time by use of a long directional arrow.

Delivery and Destination

The social ecosystem is a dynamic model enabling us to locate relationships (the parts) within a complex whole place-based or societal system. The mapping can show a critical analysis of social determinants of health or a problems in an actor's environment. It is well-suited to map the developmental journeys of actors, and to explore transitional events that occur in an actor's lifeworld. The social ecosystem can also show scenarios of preferred normative future outcomes. Jones' model of the socioecological system (2017) shows value criteria and indicators developed from research that can measure progress toward flourishing at each level, from micro to ecosystem, for social, organisational, and ecological contexts.

As with any other final version map, an image can be shared for continuing analyses or use in reports.

Case Example

As depicted in the research of Paczka Giorgi (2023), Figure 3-2 shows a social ecosystem for Canadian immigrant women within ethnocultural communities. Showing developmental relationships to people, institutions, and forms of nature in the city using line types from the Actors Map, this model highlights the availability of nature in urban environments as the shared context in her study.

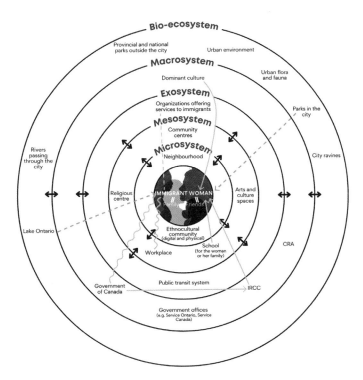

Figure 3-2
Luz Paczka Giorgi, *Imagining an Equitable Mental Health Ecosystem*. Design for Health, OCAD University.

Multicapitals Model

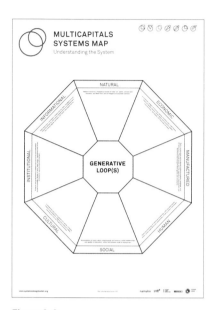

Figure 3-3
The Multicapitals Model

- Time to Run:
  1+ days
- Session context:
  Lab + Studio to revise
- Workshop Type:
  Sensemaking
- Process time:
  1+ days
- Connections to:
  Desk Research
  [2] Contextual Interview
  [4] Synthesis Map
  [5] Future State Scenarios
  [5] Intervention Strategy

The Multicapitals Model provides a fundamental system map that can be used across the Journeys. Multicapitals are multiple stocks of capital (sources of value that can produce additional resources). The tool is an updated stock and flow diagram – an alternative to the more linear 'bathtub' models often used to describe system flows. The diagram uses a simple design canvas to enable a gradual discovery of the deep underlying system structure and its observable, symptomatic outcomes as they appear in major trends or indicators.

There are two forms of multicapitals models in the Toolkit – the STEEP trends and the multicapitals. The analysis process can also map system influences or system flows. This flexibility provides for a modelling tool that can be used with stakeholders to identify the elements of a system and the problematic issues, as they understand the situation. Conducting several passes if necessary to map elements and their causality or influence relationships. This flexibility allows for both Tourists and Explorers to use it effectively.

The Multicapitals Model allows for:

- Defining and agreeing on problematic issues requiring resolution within a system context
- Describing and diagnosing the current state and functions of a given system
- Creating a shared understanding of system complexity and map the essential elements and relationships
- Facilitating consensus regarding the most critical problems in the system of interest
- Locating opportunities for feedback, intervention, or change
- Interrogating the system across multiple categories to ensure completeness across the manifestations

A good reference to an eight-capital model and its use in modelling community resources was published by Andre Nogueira[2] and colleagues.

---

[2] Andre Nogueira, Weslynne Ashton & Carlos Teixeira (2019). Expanding perceptions of the circular economy through design: Eight capitals as innovation lenses. *Resources, Conservation and Recycling*.

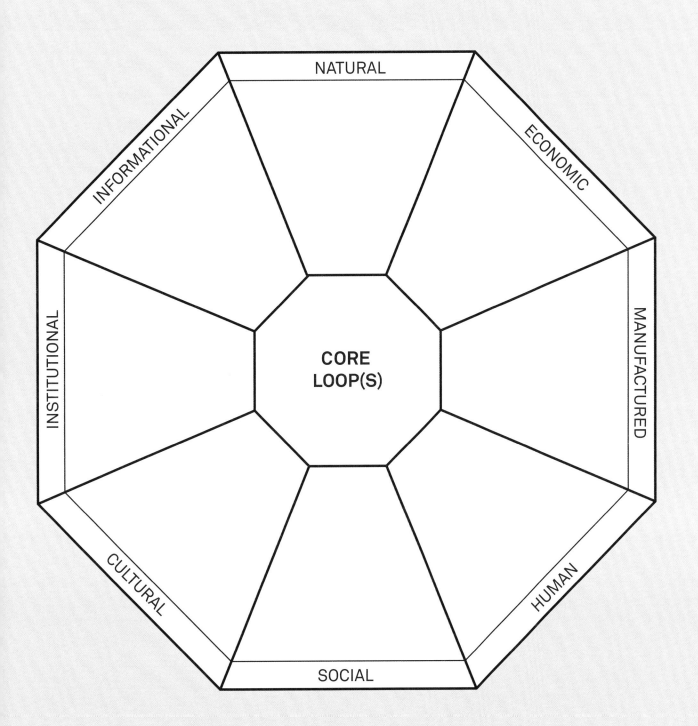

Cocreating the Multicapitals Model

Planning and Prep

The Multicapitals Model allows finding and mapping resources as system flows in a dynamic process. Decide whether to map the current system flows or an ideal future system context and represent this to participants. Be sure to trial the map with the team in a Lab situation first before taking it into the Studio with clients.

Mapping Method

As with many of the tools, the Multicapitals Model provides summary instructions on the canvas, but these should be seen as minimal reminders. The Multicapitals Model can be cocreated with stakeholders leading them through a staged process, starting with stocks and flows, and translating to Story Loops for further analysis. The following steps are suggested, for both initial and extended maps:

1. First, **identify the system of interest** by agreeing to boundaries and a descriptive name.

2. **Define an issue or problem state**: Start by defining a central challenge or issue of the system (in the centre). The challenge can be diagnostic (assessing potential harms of the issue) or aspirational (depicting the desired forces). What are the undesired behaviours and effects of the current state system? What are the painful and persistent issues stakeholders and policymakers want to solve? **For an aspirational vision, define the purpose**: What is the ideal outcome desired, or as intended by the new system?

3. **Identify stocks (noun objects) and their flows in the system**: The design team may draw on desk research, or if participants are domain experts, they might be asked to define and discuss the material and information stocks, as well as their uses and supplies to other entities or stocks. For example, an economic system would show forces of production, supply chains, pricing, consumer demand and demand creation, and incentive policies that might involve all the capitals.

4. **Connect these elements** using arrowed lines to indicate relationships. Label some lines to describe the influence or flow as a system relation. If modelling types of relations – such as decisions, money, or information – the flow lines can also be indicated by colour, weight, or line style as a graphic technique.

5. **To go further: Identify influence variables and loops** in the system model. *Variables* are those elements that will change over time and influence the system. Loops are 'reinforcing' (+) positive feedback or 'balancing' (-) negative feedback.

6. **Optional**: Draw the relations between all elements on the map. Mark relations that are substantially reinforcing (positive growth loops) or balancing ('negative' or limiting feedback that maintains a state). Show where leverage or interventions might be best indicated based on the current model (but do not yet commit to these placements, it is an early analysis!).

Definitions

The multicapitals are so-named after the theory of multicapital flows managed for sustainable development. In the first r3.0 whitepaper[3] Bill Baue describes multicapitalism as a process of respecting all necessary capital flows in the ecosystem, with the purpose of maintaining the carrying capacities vital capitals (natural, human, social, intellectual, constructed, and financial) and respecting normative thresholds. Mark McElroy further states in the paper that "vital capital is a stock of anything that yields a flow of valuable goods or services important to human well-being." He notes, as do most in the field, that the choice of capitals is relevant to the design context, there is not a consensus set or number. Baue and Mark McElroy define 8 capitals in sustainability terms relating to the thresholds and allocations of the measured uses (four of which are economic). We use eight capitals that balance the human contribution, and the following definitions of the capitals are defined for use in collaborative mapping.

7. **Natural**: Natural resources, biophysical stocks of water, air, plants, animals and microbes, and their flows and exchanges as ecosystem services.

8. **Economic**: A combined category of financial capital (monetary and credit flows), financial assets (stocks, bonds, gold), and economic capital (real economy, real assets, and business services).

9. **Manufactured**: Build, constructed and produced material products, buildings, and infrastructure. Physical assets and the capacity to manufacture and distribute and transport these goods and structures.

10. **Human**: Stock and exchange of individual knowledge, craft and specialised skills, human experience and capabilities, primarily within individuals.

11. **Social**: Accumulation of social value, societal goods and services, social relationships, and quality of interaction, within and between small to large groups.

12. **Cultural**: Civilisational and cultural goods and values, artifacts, artwork and artefacts, religions and cultural creeds, national and cultural rituals and practices.

13. **Institutional**: Political and governmental institutional structures and embedded formal knowledge. Bodies of laws, legal codes, regulations and review procedures, security and enforcement.

14. **Informational**: Data resources, information infrastructures, data management and networks (flows) for information dissemination and development. Can include digital, symbolic, and biotic information forms.

---

[3] Bill Baue (2020). From Monocapitalism to Multicapitalism: 21st Century system value creation. *R3.0, White Paper No. 1.*

Delivery and Destination

The Multicapitals Map is useful as a rich system model that shows the team's current thinking about important capital stocks, and their flows and connections within a complex system. The poster or whiteboard image can be maintained as a reference for ongoing analysis and updated as new information is learned.

For typical use as a deliverable, a simplified illustrated version of the map can be made as a reference for design documentation or client sharing. Often, category labels and lines will be simplified, with the core loop and main leverage points highlighted. The map can be used in a Story Loop workshop that could follow this exercise.

Travel Tips

The map helps participants understand a wider variety of system functions than they might otherwise discover by focusing on actors, causal loops, or other functions. Some might find it difficult at first to identify good examples of all eight capital types, if they are not familiar with the extension of the system concept of capital stocks and flows. Refer to the article to clarify distinctions, e.g. between human, social and cultural capitals.

Several workshop tips include:

– Encourage iteration of proposals by collaborative workshopping and analysis.
– Name the map with a definitive noun phrase that any reader would understand, such as 'Healthcare access in underserved communities.' Never name a model by reference to 'the system.'
– Describe the activities, or the conflicting or problematic relationships, and place these in the centre. This can be a system loop (archetype) or just a text note for the system purpose or desired outcomes.
– It helps to generate metaphors to define core loops. Try to identify one or more system archetypes in the core. Identify the core variables in the loops and build the engine on the map.

Figure 3-4
Cocreation of a Multicapitals Model in a workshop

Influence Map

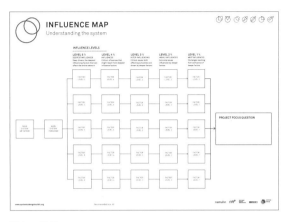

Figure 3-5
The Influence Map

— Time to Run:
2-4 hours
— Session context:
Studio or Arena
— Workshop Type:
Sensemaking
— Process time:
1+ days
— Connections to:
[2] Contextual Interview
[3] Story Loop Diagram
[4] Synthesis Map
[5] Outcome Map
[6] Theory of Systems Change

Influence mapping is a general technique for locating the patterns of influence in a complex system. There are a number of types of influence maps, each with a specific strength for identifying leverage or root causes in a problem mapping, or *problematique.*[4] The problematique is a type of influence map of issues and their relationships, used to determine the best pathways for systems change. Influence maps are nodal networks, plots of named issues as nodes connected by influence logic, defined by the functions of the connecting relations.

Rather than specifying a particular mapping method, we encourage Tourists to adopt the influence map tool as an adaptable roadmapping technique. The goal of the resulting roadmap can be used by a stakeholder team for iterative learning and dialogue as a formative strategy is developed. Over the stages of the Journeys, the Influence Map can evolve with updates and engagement, updating the team's mental model of the problem area and approach to change. There are several systems change planning methods in *Design Journeys* that capture learning, leverage points, and theory of change ideas that can be used as planning roadmaps, including the following types (and their journey stage):

— Influence map networks [3]
— Three Horizons model [4]
— Outcome (impact) maps [5]
— Theory of System Change [6]
— Transition by Design [7]

Cocreating the Influence Map

Planning and Prep

There are several purposes for which we might use the Influence Map tool. The information necessary to build the map and locate influences will not yet be available until at least Stage [3] Understanding. The most important

---

[4] The global problematique was developed by Hasan Özbekhan, and later interpreted by Christakis and Warfield, to map influence relationships and overlapping impacts across continuous large-scale societal problems. The problematique is a mapping of complex situations in which pathways for resolution might be found through leverage analysis or stakeholder assessment.

INFLUENCE LEVELS

**LEVEL 5 **
DEEPEST INFLUENCES
Deep drivers, the deepest influencing factors that can affect the entire network

**LEVEL 4 **
INFLUENCES
Critical influences that might result from deepest influence factors

**LEVEL 3 **
INTER-INFLUENCING
Critical issues both affecting outcomes and driven by deeper factors

**LEVEL 2 **
HIGHLY INFLUENCED
Outcome issues influenced by deeper factors

**LEVEL 1 **
MOST INFLUENCED
Challenges resulting from confluence of deeper factors

FACTOR LEVEL 5	FACTOR LEVEL 4	FACTOR LEVEL 3	FACTOR LEVEL 2	FACTOR LEVEL 1	
FACTOR LEVEL 5	FACTOR LEVEL 4	FACTOR LEVEL 3	FACTOR LEVEL 2	FACTOR LEVEL 1	
FACTOR LEVEL 5	FACTOR LEVEL 4	FACTOR LEVEL 3	FACTOR LEVEL 2	FACTOR LEVEL 1	**FOCUS QUESTION**
FACTOR LEVEL 5	FACTOR LEVEL 4	FACTOR LEVEL 3	FACTOR LEVEL 2	FACTOR LEVEL 1	
FACTOR LEVEL 5	FACTOR LEVEL 4	FACTOR LEVEL 3	FACTOR LEVEL 2	FACTOR LEVEL 1	

contribution is the generation of actions or propositions. The nodes are defined by activities and functions – the Iterative Inquiry and Rich Context are useful references for functions. The Influence Map and Story Loops inform each other, capturing different dynamics of the system.

Workshop setup: Working with map logic requires collaboration with smaller groups. Determine whether to work in a small group (3-6 participants) or if a large group is invited, to break out into teams of 4-5 per group, that can be organised by domain expertise (multiple thematic maps) or by carefully organising to maximise variety within each group (microcosms). Each method has its strengths, and both avoid the outcome of randomness or by affiliation.

Multiple teams can be based on thematic categories (e.g., STEEP) or be assigned to create team maps according to their own focus or areas of knowledge. A common final map can be aggregated from the constituent maps produced in each team.

In advance of workshopping the Influence Map, a focus question is developed that will elicit responses from all team members that can be arranged by leverage and influence. The focus question is cocreated by the organisers and core group as the key issue most relevant to the envisioned future context. A typical focus question has the structure of '(what) are the most significant (challenges, factors or barriers) facing (we, our stakeholders) in the next (10, 20) years?' Each term in brackets is a variable for the focus question, as these will specify a consistent set of responses to an agreed-upon context of shared importance.

Mapping Method

The procedure for cocreating influence maps differs by method. There are two starting points for all map types – forward-chaining *abductive* logic, and backward-chaining *retroductive* logic (backcasting). There are also two mapping types based on the original algorithm used in Interpretive Structural Modelling.[5] John Warfield's method builds a network from left to right, while the Christakis method[6] (used in software such as Logosophia) is bottom-up, as the Journeys tool depicts. In the influence map the user notes are typically either challenges (problem statements) or actions ("solutions"); both can be called factors, but a map would use only one type.

The abductive forward-logic requires discipline in facilitation. A relational network is constructed from a bottom-up ordering, based on the leverage of each factor (the written notes) on its subsequent outcomes. To define leverage, the bottom factor or challenge is located as the 'deepest driver' of the entire network (in the tool it's shown as Level 5: Deepest Influences, but this could be as many levels as necessary). Successive iterations are used to discover and compare between the highest-leverage candidates for deep drivers. As the tool visually indicates, there can be just one deep factor, but more than one are always possible. With multiple root level drivers or challenges, each often links to its own influence path. We can also test the deep root factor for its reach upward to all the challenges or actions connecting to the top. The top-most factor is considered the 'most influenced,' as it is driven by everything linked below it.

[5] John Warfield (1974). *Structuring Complex Systems*. Battelle Memorial Institute.
[6] Alexander Christakis & Maria Kakoulaki (2021). Objectifying intersubjectivity through inclusion for a scientific [R] Evolution: Avoiding polarization by engaging stakeholders for saliency, priority and trust. *From Polarisation to Multispecies Relationships*.

The series of factors are connected in single-arrow line graphs extending from bottom-up until a terminal function is determined. This is often a major emergent issue such as 'social inequality' or 'climate change', which is an effect of being influenced by all the contributing factors driving upward to it. Abductive mapping steps can be followed as such:

1. Instruct team members to write **short challenge statements** that answer the focus question. Take 5-10 minutes to do this in silence. Have members share their statements and clarify them to ensure that each statement is understood by other members. (Nominal group technique)

2. **Locate influential propositions**. Using abductive (forward) logic, start with a hypothesis that one or more factors will be highly influential to many others. Select a small number of statements and position them in an initial ordering toward the deepest level of the map (Level 5). if one clearly influences the other, place the most-influential factor in the deepest-level box and the other one following it, connected by a directed arrow line.

3. **Structuring**: Select a larger number of statements (10-15) and arrange them around the template. Review these to compare with the ones already set in the diagram. Determine influence relationship between pairs using the query 'will action on challenge (A) make *significant* progress on the other challenge (B) as well?' Not all the notes have to be used – if there are duplicate ideas, these can be joined.

4. **Analyse** the significance of the relationship between each pair of factors. Compare the ideas and define the direction and strength of the relationship. If challenge or action A has a *significant* effect on B, draw an arrowed line from A to B and define this relation. The structuring question is usually worded to describe progress relationships of the effect of the resolution of challenges on other challenges. If actions or barriers are defined, rather than challenges, these can also be compared by relative progress.

5. **Continue to compare** actions C, D, and so on with the others. Draw lines between their influence relationships. As the network grows, multiple paths from bottom-up will be defined. The tool is designed to allow either one factor at a level, or multiple – each having its own connections to the other challenge factors from the bottom-up. Their influences should become intuitively apparent as the team builds the network up, but it will become complex quickly.

6. **Iterate on the process** with members until the selected factors or challenges have been integrated into the influence relationships (or found 'not significant'). The top-most actions are outcomes with no leverage on the others – these are the 'most influenced.'

7. **Walk through the logic of the map** with members, from both bottom-up and top-down. Try to rearrange factors in the order of their influence connections. Meanwhile, construct a verbal narrative to explain their relations from the perspective of discovering the deepest influential root functions.

Delivery and Destination

As with other tools, the Influence Map can be edited and composed as a deliverable and presented in the bottom-up style, or left-to-right by translating the boxes and arrows. This tool can be used for several purposes. In the Stage [3] Understanding, the purpose is to create a first mapping of the influence or leverage relations within a social system or change programme. At this stage, it is not necessary to define a strategy for action or planning.

An influence map that shows a clear logic from connecting multiple challenges can directly inform a transformation strategy, such as the Outcome Map in Stage [5] Exploring and the TOSCA theory of change in [6] Planning. A transformation roadmap can be used as a team artefact and also serve as a planning system.

This map shows the subset of factors voted as most significant in relation to the urbanisation focus question. Factors are displayed by relative order of impact from the highest leverage on the left (or bottom, as shown in the software) to the most influenced to the right.

Case Study – Imagining Canada's Future: Southern Ontario Panel on Urbanisation

OCAD University faculty and graduate students organised a Dialogic Design co-laboratory for a Social Sciences and Humanities Research Council (SSHRC) project with five universities as a panel to advise SSHRC on future research agendas. A selected group of experts and affected stakeholders were invited, chosen based on requisite variety to the issue. Southern Ontario stakeholders were selected and convened to provide SSHRC with strategic foresight for a Canadian research agenda based on future societal concerns for urbanisation. While the panel workshop was completed in one day, preparation for the session required two months of planning, framing, and recruiting. Panellists were selected for depth in a category, cross-panel diversity, and geographic representation (following the evolutionary stakeholder discovery process described in Convening Cocreation). The results of a day-long workshop of structured dialogue are reflected in the Influence Map, which was used as input into the Imagining Canada's Future research agenda.

The 13 challenges arrayed in the diagram were selected following reflective clarification, categorisation, importance voting, and the unique structure voting enabled by software using the Interpretive Structural Modelling (ISM) algorithm to translate group voting to influence relations.

The research question was to examine the factors of increasing urbanisation and rank the significance of key regional and global drivers of change. Of the 'top ten' issues derived from the influence map of 13, it was significant to note that the 'top three' deep drivers were all mutually reinforcing loops, between three factors later refined as:

1. Advancing a diverse and inclusive society
2. Enabling equitable access to ICT
3. Governing ourselves responsibly

The major issue of our time, climate change, was pushed to the right as a highly influenced outcome and not a deep driver of the other ten. Instead, because of the logic of the ISM influence engine, factors such as 'Stewarding regional ecosystems' and 'Indigenous land rights' were found to influence the progress of climate change.

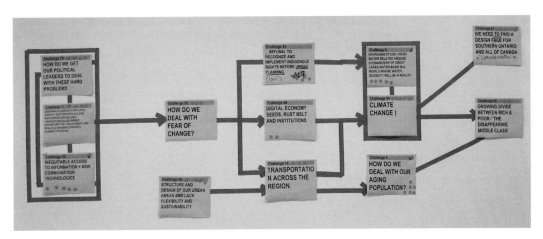

Figure 3-6
Influence map generated by ISM software and posted on whiteboard for stakeholder dialogue

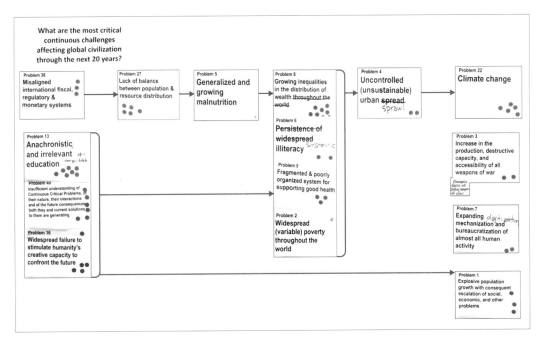

Figure 3-7
Influence Map displayed on whiteboard in Dialogic Design workshop

Story Loop Diagram

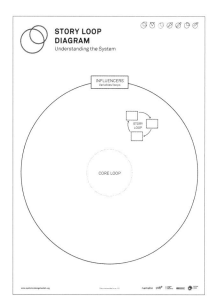

Figure 3-8
The Story Loop Diagram

— Time to Run:
.5-1 day
— Session context:
Lab + Studio to revise
— Workshop Type:
Sensemaking
— Process time:
3+ days
— Connections to:
Desk Research
[2] Contextual Interview
[3] Social Ecosystem Map
[3] Influence Map
[3] Archetypes
[4] System Value Proposition
[5] Future State Scenarios
[5] Intervention Strategy

A Story Loop is a causal loop diagram constructed and presented as a system narrative of problematic dynamics in a current system. It addresses a drawback of classical causal loops on which they are based, which is that stakeholders must be trained in CLDs to make sense of them. As with a causal loop, the purpose is to discover potential leverage points in the system dynamics, identifying the areas where intervention is likely to have the most impact.

Story Loops are defined from research findings and some analysis, and can be developed from desk research and expert understanding. They are more powerful when presenting systemic research findings from a meaningful set of participant narratives. The Story Loop provides a useful tool for sensemaking of social complexity, and for developing a shared understanding among stakeholders about the most salient issues, interdependencies, and causal relationships between system variables.

The contextual focus of the story loop differs from the causal loop known from system dynamics. The emphasis of the story loop is the human story, to describe experience in the system and not the flows of system variables . The story loop can help visualise the systemic relationships of social events, incentives and responses, emotional states, and conflicts.

Cocreating a Story Loop Diagram

Planning and Prep

Review and provide research findings from [2] Listening in both summary and detailed (e.g. spreadsheet) forms. For workshopping, have an updated Iterative Inquiry or Rich Context available from [1] Framing.

Loops are built up from variables representing a stock or a level, and their connections as flows. A variable is a noun representing a state that can increase or decrease – as a measurable quantity, such as 'price.' Make sure not to mix them up with static elements (such as 'a unit of land') as this will not lead adequately to show flows or leverage.

Mapping Method

1. From available research, distinguish between the narratives of current system behaviours and 'aspirational' narratives (a description of a desired state). Give priority to current system data.

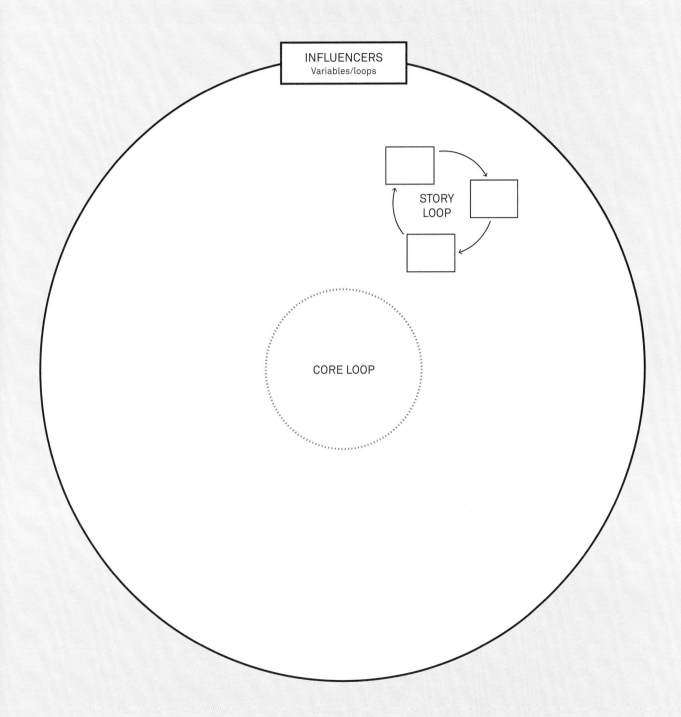

INFLUENCERS
Variables/loops

STORY
LOOP

CORE LOOP

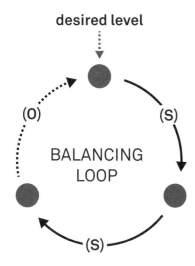

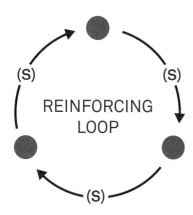

Figure 3-9
There are two basic loop types: Balancing loops and reinforcing loops

2. Elicit variables from the data by attending to potential system factors. Identify initial variables – nouns that designate things or processes with the ability to change by influence or over time.

3. Write the (O) selected noun-variables on notes. Be precise; each variable should express a measurable quantity. These are 'neutral,' in that the language should describe a variable from a neutral position, e.g. 'health status,' not 'better health.'

4. Create links between the variables indicating their influence on each other – the arrowed lines describe an increase or decrease in the same (S) or opposite (O) direction. Draw loops (between at least two factors) and identify reinforcing (+) or balancing (-) flows.

5. Use the labels of each loop as a point of reference to create new, potential core variables. Use another colour for this. Try to identify a dominant 'engine' of the system being mapped.

6. Arrange the story clusters around the core loop. Now see how all variables in the different stories influence each other and the core loop. Draw additional arrows where necessary.

7. Identify potential leverage points - these are variables with high connectivity. Determine whether they are drivers or blockers (recognisable by the number of arrows going out or in).

8. Discuss and define the loops as the team develops an understanding of system behaviour over time.

Delivery and Destination

Causal loops are notoriously difficult for inexperienced readers to understand. The Story Loop approach can present the loop dynamics as a formal complex system model for audiences that have worked with these models. It can also be simplified in ways to express the core loops as a salient finding, locate leverage points, and point to system issues. A simplified version can be presented as a core loop and the main leverage points/loops to use in workshops or reports.

Travel Tips

— Use simple noun phrases to describe the variable. One way to test a variable is to place the words 'level of …' at the beginning of it. State the variables as neutrally as possible and do not include qualifiers such as 'increasing' or 'decreasing' or value terms, such as 'better.' These are the changes represented by the notations on the link line, or the flow.

- As in math, two negatives (or opposing flows) yield a positive or reinforcing direction. If there are two (O) arrows in a loop they should be regarded as one loop in the same (S) direction, yet opposing the desired direction. If applicable, indicate delays in the system by a double line across a loop line.
- When the variables and links are well-defined in a causal loop diagram, identifying leverage points becomes relatively simple. We can determine whether variables are drivers or blockers, based on the relative number of arcs or arrows connecting to the variable or leading from it to other factors.

- Appropriate interventions are defined depending on whether a driver, or a barrier or bottleneck is found. A driver is recognised by a high 'out-degree,' with a larger number of arrow arcs leading from the variable; whereas a barrier or bottleneck variable is recognised by high in-degree, with more arrows leading into the factor. The system dynamics can be evaluated qualitatively, with the strength of the relationship determined not by computer simulation, but by the number of times an issue was raised during interviews or as observed in analysis.

Looping, Step by Step

1. Write your variables around a circle. Consider if and how the variables are connected to each other and draw an arrow wherever you see a cause-and-effect relationship. Indicate the way they effect each other (S)ame or (O)pposite.

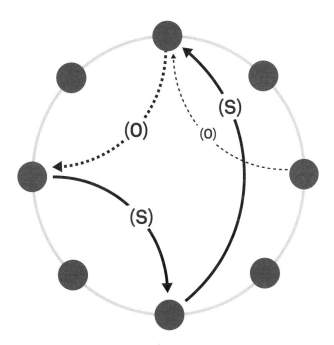

Figure 3-10 Connection circle

2. Identify the balancing and reinforcing loops and draw these loops again using circles. Indicate if they are balancing (B) or reinforcing (R) in the middle.

3. Label the loop with a brief description, summarising the dynamic of the loop. Note that balancing loops bring the system back into the initial state – preventing the loop from escalating or changing too much. Reinforcing loops lead to escalation. Both can be helpful or counterproductive, depending on the context.

4. Draw casual relationships between the variables of the individual loops. Add other variables (the ones that are not in loops) if these variables are important to understand the behaviour of the system.

5. Identify the leverage points and loops in the model. The leverage points are based on the most connected nodes. Those with high 'out degree,' or more arrows extending from the node, are the most influential. Those with high 'in degree,' or arrows-in are potential barriers and bottlenecks.

Travel Tips

The Story Loop model can be seen as a series of continuous touchpoints in the Front Stage of a system, similar t to the concept in service design. The contextual focus of the Story Loop is human experience, or the system as experienced. The Multicapital (stock and flow) model can be described as the Back Stage, as it focuses on capital material flows, stock accumulation and material exchanges (e.g. money, goods, knowledge).

The correctness of a loop can be assessed by mentally running the flow in the opposite direction from a model as defined, e.g. if A decreases and B also decreases, the opposite flow must also work: increasing A should lead to an increase of B.

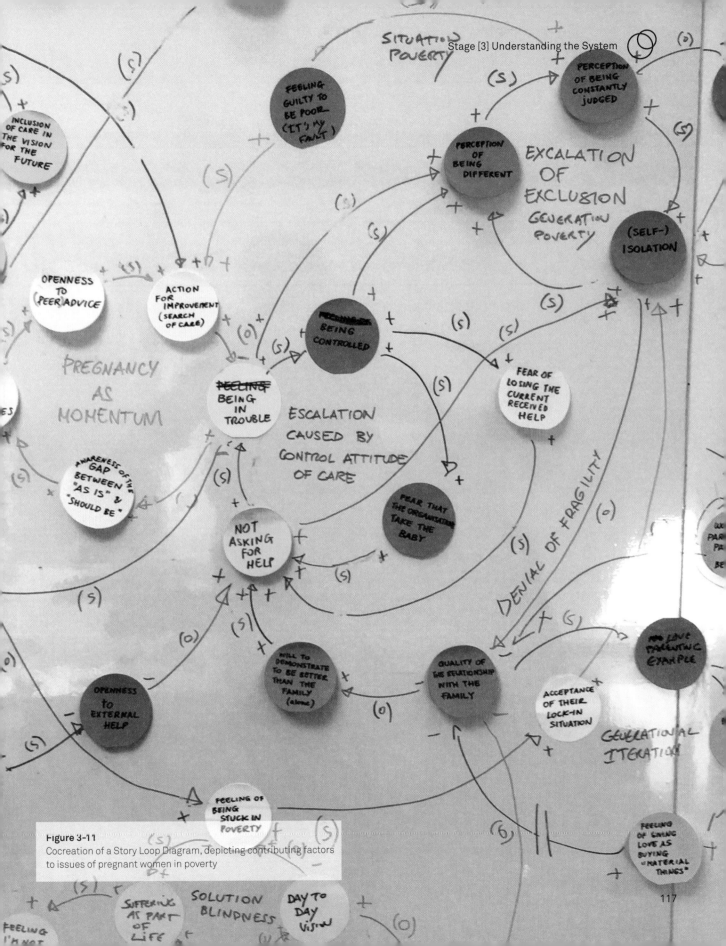

Figure 3-11
Cocreation of a Story Loop Diagram, depicting contributing factors to issues of pregnant women in poverty

117

System Archetypes

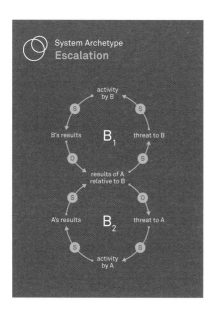

Figure 3-12
Archetype Cards can be downloaded
from the Journeys website

System archetypes are recurring, highly-regular patterns of behaviour. The leading systems thinker Peter Senge dubbed these 'system archetypes,' defined by a series of common, mostly dysfunctional, frequently recurring patterns within organisational systems. Quite often one or two archetypes can be found to indicate a central problem in the system of interest. In these cases, an archetype can be used as a core loop in Story Loops or systems maps.

All systems maps are techniques for visualising a system and reaching agreement on its composition, salient aspects, opportunities for efficient action, and ultimately, a shared meaning. Even though there are many ways to map a system, the causal loop systems map is practically a standard technique for 'systems mapping.' Causal loops are powerful tools as their models surface the forces in the system by visualising dynamic structure, system flow, and the interrelations between the continuous functions in any system.

Causal loops are a fundamental model used in system dynamics. They can also represent stocks and flows, and viewed as continuous patterns of feedback. Positive (or reinforcing) system flows increase a stock by feedback that increases its gain. Negative (or balancing) loops are feedback that decrease or limit a stock. Error correction, or limit switches such as thermostats, are examples of negative feedback loops. System models can be developed by linking multiple loops to describe complex system behaviours using a simple notation of circles (for stocks or system states) and curved unidirectional arrows (for flows or feedback).

System dynamics modelling was developed by the first generation of systems scientists, starting with Jay Forrester at MIT, who developed the original World3 Model simulations used by the Donella and Dennis Meadows team for the Limits to Growth[7] book.

Understanding the System Archetypes

According to William Braun,[8] there are four generic archetypes:

1. **Underachievement**, where intended achievement fails to be realised (e.g. *Eroding goals*)

[7] See Donella Meadows, Randers, & Meadows (1972). *The Limits to Growth*. Club of Rome.
[8] William Braun (2002). *The System Archetypes*.

2. **Out of control**, where intended outcomes fail to be realised (e.g. *Fixes that fail*)

3. **Relative achievement**, where achievement is only gained at the expense of another (e.g. *Success to the successful*)

4. **Relative control**, where control is only gained at the expense of others (e.g. *Escalation*), where one party seeks domination of a situation that triggers a reaction from a party that is threatened by the action).

Cocreating from Archetypes

Planning and Prep

Learn the archetypes by familiarising the team with the Archetype Cards (from the Toolkit online). These can be pasted as images in online whiteboards. Further study is recommended from Braun's *The System Archetypes* (available on the Journeys website). Have other Toolkit models available – the Multicapitals Map, or the Rich Context from [1] Framing are useful tools to identify the patterns of problematic situations for archetypes and other causal loops.

Mapping Method

Review the findings and stories from the research in [2] Listening and locate a situation (or vignette) that may demonstrate a continuous, systemic problem. This could be a simple situation that might be expected to unfold as one of the archetypes. For example, an aid organisation that continues to deplete resources in a social development programme without seeing continuing benefits might be losing effectiveness due to one of the archetypes, such as Eroding Goals or Tragedy of the Commons. The following steps may be helpful:

1. Identify a situation from mapping or research findings with repeating characteristics that might be 'archetypal.'

2. Choose an archetype that fits the problem context as closely as possible. Unlike drawing a causal loop from 'scratch,' this is more of an abductive process, of successive approximation. The idea is to propose an archetype that might explain the observed behaviour, and map the increasing or balancing forces to see if it fits.

   For example, the case study archetype that follows is 'Fixes that Fail.' In this situation, a consumer makes a purchase to fulfil a need or want, it has the unintended consequence of fulfilling an emotional response. While this feeling may seem desirable, it fails to fulfil the underlying need.

3. Label the variables – the changing stocks or factors of the problem – as neutrally as possible to describe the continuous situation. New modelers (Tourists) often label the factors or 'bubbles' in terms that express their preferred value, such as 'better health'. Variables should be labelled instead as 'health status' in this case, where the sign on the arrow defines the value (e.g., reinforcing health in the Same direction or decreasing its value by Opposing).

4. Label the links based on the actual behaviours, try not to fit the links to the situation.

5. Find other situations that might be similar archetypal patterns. 'Shifting the Burden' is similar to 'Fixes that Fail,' and it was also found in the consumerism case. Figure 3-16 shows how consumer buying behaviour creates a side effect of guilt for not addressing the underlying concern.

Delivery and Destination

The archetypes are useful on their own as they can be used in 'system storytelling' to highlight primary problematic issues in the Understanding journey. They are often used to express hypotheses about the most central symptomatic issues that indicate systemic problems in a situation. Archetypes can be placed centrally in systems maps and used as the basis to extend and develop more complex and interconnected causal loop diagrams.

Building on Archetypes

Four common archetypes we might observe in any complex situation are those termed as:

1. **Success to the Successful** – The common situation when good performance is rewarded with more resources, creating a continuous loop of increasing resources to a party and enabling disproportionate outcomes.

2. **Fixes that Fail** – When a 'quick fix' to a problem results in unintended consequences that reinforce the underlying root problem.

3. **Tragedy of the Commons** – A situation that occurs when resources (or responsibilities) are provided to multiple parties, and they are exploited by one or some at the expense of the others.

4. **Shifting the Burden** – When unproductive actions are taken to resolve the tensions of a symptom, while leaving the underlying systemic situation unresolved, typically ignoring a situation that regresses.

Often, multiple archetypes are discovered when diagnosing a problem system. The complex situations that inspire the motivation for reform often result in several symptomatic problems readily recognisable once the vocabulary is learned. This vocabulary is revealed in the system archetypes, of which a well-defined set of commonly occurring patterns are defined.

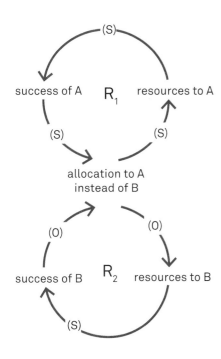

Figure 3-13
Success to the Successful archetype

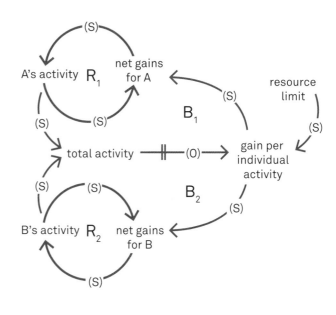

Figure 3-15
Tragedy of the Commons archetype

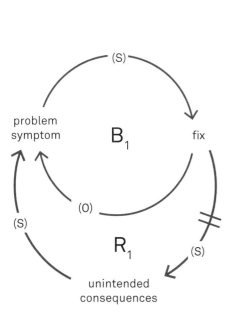

Figure 3-14
Fixes that Fail archetype

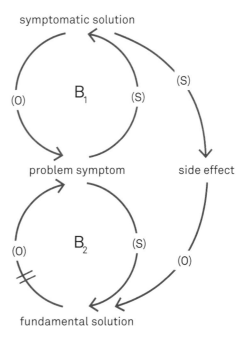

Figure 3-16
Shifting the Burden archetype

Case Study – Why We Buy: Consumerism and Mental Health

The archetype example is drawn from an in-depth synthesis map and analysis conducted by a university team, on the underlying causes and maintenance of consumerism. The 'Shifting the Burden' archetype is well-known from management theory. In everyday business affairs, companies seek to find the most efficient and low-cost solutions to issues, and to balance priorities. However the complexity of problem resolution leads to resolving the symptoms of problematic situations while avoiding responsibility for solving the fundamental problem. Here there is a tension between the relatively simple and low cost 'symptomatic solution' to a visible problem, and the desired, long-term outcome as a fundamental solution to underlying systemic issues that cause the undesirable pattern of behaviour.

In the case of 'retail therapy' as described in the study, 'Why We Buy,' OCAD University graduate students[9] investigated the complex patterns of consumerism.

When we understand the act of purchasing as an emotional response, this archetype helps outline how that act is a symptomatic solution. When we feel unfulfilled and turn to buying to feel better, it does not address the core emotional issue of an individual's unhappiness. The process of 'retail therapy' or consumerist buying shows up as a coping mechanism. While this action can be momentarily soothing and sufficiently distracting, it ends up producing unintended consequences – a side effect of guilt and shame for spending money and making an unnecessary purchase. That guilt might propel the individual to seek out help and support by way of counselling or emotional therapy and address the underlying issue of unhappiness. However, people are human and therapy does not end such emotional cycles. Eventually, we become unhappy again, and the consumerist cycle repeats.

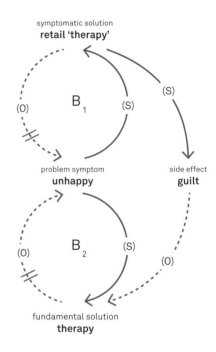

Figure 3-17
Shifting the Burden archetype applied to the case

---

[9] Nicole Brkic, Martha Chomyn, Alejandra Farias Fornes, Razane Hanna, & Amy Morrell (2021). *Why We Buy*. OCAD University, Toronto. The full synthesis map is available for download on the Journeys website, and an interactive Kumu model of this diagram is linked from the site.

The fully-developed causal loop diagram in Figure 3-17 provides a more complete model of the consumerism trap and individual behaviour cycles. In the centre, the core loop of Pursuit of a Better Life, Purchase, and Earn Income show the primary reinforcing loop that drives many of the downstream loops. The Shifting the Burden archetype was used as an initial analysis, that expanded into the complex sophisticated model that portrays the dynamics of identity, self-worth, purpose, work, and consumer behaviour.

Colour-coding reveals analysis insights from the design team. A legend on the original diagram shows: Dark circles are causes, and white circle are consequences. Same directionality is indicated by a solid line, and opposite by dashed lines. The colours refer to the association with STEEP indicators (see original on the website).

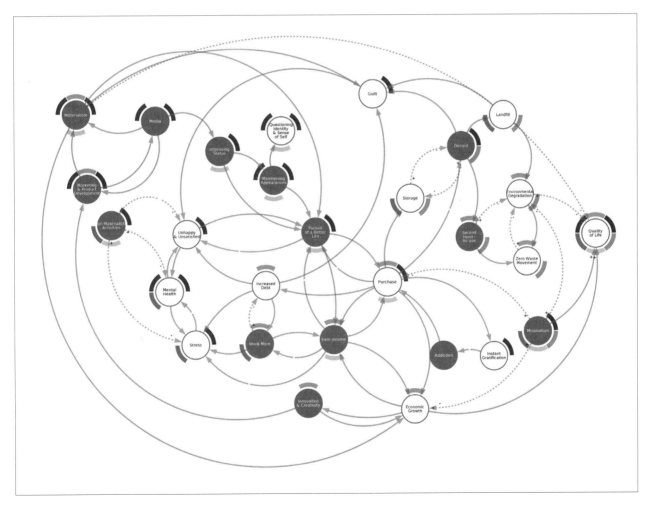

Figure 3-18
Causal Loop Diagram, Why We Buy, Brkic, Chomyn, Farias Fornes, Hanna, Morrell (2021), OCAD University, Toronto.

[4] Envisioning Desired Futures
Imagining and cocreating possible future systems

How do we begin to design comprehensive interventions for systems change? Tools in [4] Envisioning help us shift from the sensemaking of legacy systems to envision future systems and services. We suggest Tony Fry's disposition of *futuring,* not as a mode of future visioning but an orientation toward future sustainment of flourishing. We promote cocreative design practices here that shape the evolution of preferred systems with stakeholders. Systemic design instils a futuring mindset, a long-term view that guides the emergence of preferred future outcomes through a continuous cocreation of system value. Envisioning proceeds through early prototypes and design concepts for system transformation, societal innovation, and sociotechnical services within these systems.

The goal of a single, perfect future, exciting yet speculative, is always unproductive to pursue. Multiple futures are possible because people live within multiple social systems simultaneously, that evolve at different rates. Future value is realised through foresight that confers optionality, the availability of more alternatives and opportunities that accord to a strategy as the future unfolds. Value options are increased through multiplicity, a worldview of pluriversality, cultivating multiple pathways for expression and realisation.

The idea of 'pluralising the future' means not only to define multiple future scenarios so that we can better sense and adapt as events unfold. It also means that we co-produce the emergence of multiple futures by design interventions, as new shared practices that become part of our cultures. These practices evolve new social systems, with potential to change organisational, technological, and economic systems.

Four power tools are presented here in the spirit of Buckminster Fuller's precept of 'building new models that obsolete an existing system.' By envisioning a desired future, we construct new models that might have potential or attractor value to displace the existing system (i.e., those systems analysed using tools from the first half of Design Journeys). Envisioning tools offer collaborative methods for designing conceptual system prototypes. These include design templates for system-level value propositions, futuring proposals, and scenario tools for composing multiple prospectives. Many use the Systemic Design Toolkit to employ futuring methods for strategic planning and visionary business planning. As *reframing* practices these methods provide guidance for convening visioning engagement, and for meta-planning for system or organisational transformation.

Cocreating future system value

Among the many clever cautions of systems sceptic John Gall,[1] a physician and early critical realist, was the 'Electric Turtle Effect.' This is stated as: "In setting up a new system, tread softly. You may be disturbing another system that is actually working." Gall also said, "if you can't change the system, change the frame – it comes to the same thing." These wise insights suggest a principle that 'the best intervention is the least that makes the most difference.' The stages that follow provide for many opportunities to design interventions. Balance the drive to 'design a better system" with the knowledge that many intervention attempts, like startup experiments, could fail at first. Large social systems have inertia, and they push back against change.

While idealisation is a critical aptitude for system leadership, the stark reality and maddening persistence of established systems requires human skills necessary for the long view – forbearance, compassion, and faith. The purpose of Envisioning is primarily to cocreate mental models of sociotechnical or system change outcomes as system blueprints for preferred futures. Design Journeys provides collaborative practices to facilitate vision-led requirements for desired new systems, structures, processes, and functions. Using synthesis and antithesis (paradox), we move from systems *analyses* of the current system, toward the strategic potential of what design change *ought to be*. In this stage, four tools (plus a set of informative cards) are recommended to design and prefigure future system(s) as both designed and emergent evolutionary outcomes through systemic design.

---

[1] John Gall (1975). *General Systemantics*. Quadrangle.

Design Journeys
for Envisioning

System Value Proposition

Enables the definition of **total system value** constructed
by contributions from all perspectives and proposals for
value creation, across levels of a classical nested system
perspective. The resulting shared image of 'system value'
serves as a guideline to realise the ultimate benefits
through the project.

Three Horizons

The Three Horizons framework is represented here at
this stage as a systemic futures method that translates
future trends and desired outcomes to evolutionary
cycles of innovation and impact over long-time cycles.
The Three Horizons is a well-known method that enables
the collective formulation of future system evolution and
focuses the team's present-day innovation and systems
change goals.

Paradoxing

Paradoxing is a dynamic technique of introducing
paradoxical concepts as imaginative provocations in
value creation, as a tool for inspiring open and lateral
responses in design planning. Since paradoxes become
apparent when defining and explaining 'value,' using
a set of cards with binary options enables workshop
participants to playfully embrace and creatively exploit
the paradoxes in the system.

Synthesis Map

A synthesis map visualises system analysis and
proposed design interventions by integrating multiple
models into a single visualisation, often enhanced
with metaphor and visual rhetoric. Synthesis maps
are complex, yet accessible system stories – visual
narratives meant to be readable and usable by
stakeholders. Unlike other design tools in the Journeys,
the synthesis map can be shared in public presentations
as well as with the team.

How might we redesign system conditions
that might lead to preferred futures?

**System Value
Proposition**
What value can be
cocreated for all
stakeholders?

Three Horizons
How is the envisioned
future emerging and
what transitions will
help achieve it?

Paradoxing
How can we use
apparent tensions in
the system to our
advantage?

**Synthesis
Map**
How can we visualise
the whole system as
learned thus far?

What are the best strategies for systems change?
What intervention are good design options? Stage [5]

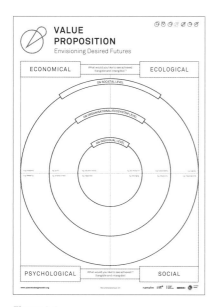

System Value Proposition

The System Value Proposition[2] tool adapts a business-modeling method for creating a value proposition to guide strategy, positioning, and prototyping. The Design Journeys methodology provides a specific tool that enables teams to define approaches to system-level value.

System value is a relatively new concept used to represent the mix of value realisation in large-scale systems such as energy, city building, or healthcare where multiple beneficiaries receive value from services provided by a system. The tool provides a flexible model of system value that can be used in any context from organisational strategy to social programmes to planning. Like the well-known Strategyzer[3] Value Proposition tool, the format can be used to define value proposals that can be presented as full value propositions for a new service or system proposal.

The system value model assigns a value schema in three nested levels , associated with *micro*, *meso*, and *macro* perspectives: These are labelled for individual (all people), organisational, and societal/planetary. Four dimensions capturing perspectives of *economic*, *ecological*, *psychological*, and *social* value form the concentric circles into quadrants.

Cocreating the Value Proposition

Planning and Prep

It will be helpful to inform participants before a value proposition session to prepare some initial ideas to frame the unique value offered in the proposed system change or service system. People can investigate relevant trends and competing ideas to suggest as concerns in the mapping process.

Start with the standard circular template as shown. It can be adapted to make it more relevant for any given project, by relabelling the levels (e.g., 'community' instead of 'ecosystem'), refining the perspectives (e.g., spiritual instead of psychological), or adding other levels (e.g. 'planetary').

Figure 4-1
The System Value Proposition

- Time to Run:
  1-2 hours
- Session context:
  Studio or Arena
- Workshop Type:
  Reframing
- Process time:
  1+ days
- Connections to:
  [3] Story Loop Diagram
  [4] Three Horizons
  [5] Intervention Strategy
  [6] Theory of Systems Change

[2] This tool is based on the value framework presented in Elke den Ouden (2012). *Innovation Design: Creating Value for People, Organizations and Society*.
[3] Alex Osterwalder, Pigneur, Bernarda & Smith (2014). *Value Proposition Design: How to Create Products and Services Customers Want*. John Wiley & Sons.

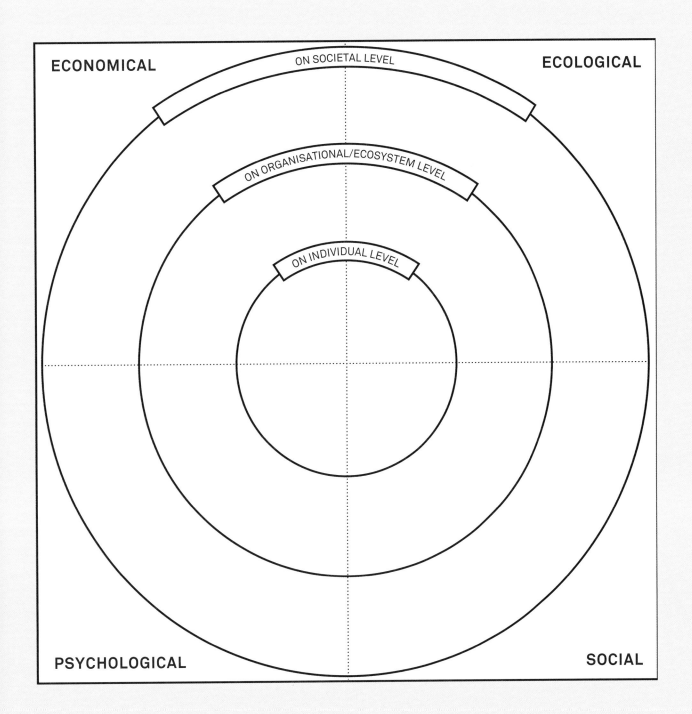

ECONOMICAL

ECOLOGICAL

ON SOCIETAL LEVEL

ON ORGANISATIONAL/ECOSYSTEM LEVEL

ON INDIVIDUAL LEVEL

PSYCHOLOGICAL

SOCIAL

Method Mapping

1. Post up the Actors Map or stakeholder analysis from previous stages. Select meaningful actors that serve as beneficiaries and assign them to the different levels on the canvas (if individuals, place in the centre).

2. Review the themes and leverage proposals from the Multicapitals Map or Story loop Diagram. Identify value cocreated with and for the actors from these ideas, associated with the four dimensions in the quadrant (economic, ecological, psychological, social). Write value proposals and benefits for these on notes in the circles and zones. Generate themes and ideas that apply to all in the centre of the canvas.

3. Consider each of the other levels in turn and identify the potential benefits envisioned for single organisations, the ecosystem or network of organisations, societies and regions, and the planet (if so choose to).

4. Synthesise these proposals into broad themes or phrases that summarise each level and quadrant. These become the main themes of the system value proposition.

5. Consider potential value destruction or any negative value cocreated in this context, in the levels and quadrants. What possible loss of current value, even if indirect, might result from the value proposals?

6. After iterations and review, a final system value statement can be developed following this format: 'The (envisioned programme) provides new benefits for stakeholders, for people by (summary benefit), organisations involved (summary benefit), and for the planet/system/ society (summary benefit), and supersedes/surpasses other programmes because (unique position of the intervention).'

Delivery and Destination

The system-level value proposition can be synthesised into main themes and defined with an overarching value statement using icons or graphics to illustrate a final deliverable version. The contribution this tool makes to a developing project is that it helps develop a positive mental model of the shared value and values that will be cocreated by the change organisation and stakeholders. The System Value Proposition tool defines some of the first indications of interventions that can be defined across the system levels – the focus of the next stage.

Travel Tips

Some examples of system value cocreation and value goals for people (individuals) (P), organisation (O), or society (S) might include:

- Economic value: Value for money (P), profitability (O), prosperity (S)
- Ecological value: Energy efficiency (P), sustainability (O), liveability (S)
- Social value: Belonging (P), reciprocity (O), community participation (S)
- Psychological value: Happiness (P), shared values (O), sense of safety (S)

In preparation to workshop this tool, inspire and engage participant imaginations by making a mood board (with pictures) or a drawing of the ideal future.

The system value tool can be introduced in different moments in the systemic design journeys. It can be used at the beginning of the project or between systems mapping in [3] Understanding and intervention strategy in [5] Exploring to ensure that the stakeholders embrace collective benefits when planning areas of interventions or ideating.

The tools can always be adapted to the project context and interests. The tool image in Figure 4-2 shows how a political dimension was added to better define the map dimensions for a project investigating European innovation systems.

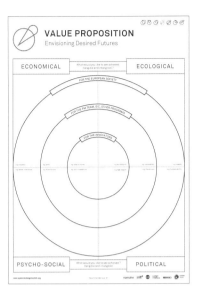

Figure 4-2
The tools adapted to a political context

Figure 4-3
Mapping the value of music sharing to foster intercultural connection

Three Horizons Map

Figure 4-4
The Three Horizons

— Time to Run:
   .5 – 1 day
— Session context:
   Arena or Agora
— Workshop Type:
   Framing, Cocreation
— Process time:
   2 + days
— Connections to:
   [1] Rich Context
   [2] Contextual Interview
   [3] Story Loop Diagram
   [4] System Value Proposition
   [5] Intervention Strategy
   [5] Outcome Map
   [6} Theory of Systems Change

Three Horizons[4] is a core methodology in strategic foresight, valued in practice for its ability to integrate complex systems in the temporal dimension. Like other tools from Envisioning and later stages, Three Horizons maps out strategic pathways, following a unique model of three overlapping time horizons. Trends, values, and interventions proposed in analysis are shown in temporal relationships to reveal preferred future outcomes. There are similar logics between Three Horizons, outcome mapping, and Transition by Design. Three Horizons (3H) can be applied much earlier in engagement, to set a long-term vision in [1] Framing, and can also be used as a transition roadmap in [7] Transition, and in the Envisioning stage for defining future value.

The purpose of Three Horizons mapping is to discover the relationships of change and innovation over the shift of temporal transitions toward preferred future outcomes. The 3H model creates a profound vision for change planning and can be used as the primary method in creative futuring workshops with stakeholders.

The 3H introduces the powerful idea that multiple futures coexist in any present moment. The three overlapping horizon curves provide a heuristic for determining the strategic fit of actions chosen to promote a desired future vision, versus a continuation of default 'business as usual' or non-desired outcomes. The heuristic draws on three of many possible future trajectories:

Horizon One (H1) is shown as sloping down from a present peak, suggesting the inevitable decline of unsustainable or obsolete practices in the receding landscape. Horizon Two (H2) represents the 'turbulent transition' to the desired future, but entails the innovation potentials necessary for bridging from the declining H1 into the desired future. Horizon Three (H3) portrays future outcomes desired by stakeholders in the exercise, as essentially the shared vision. H3 is conceived of as a longer-term future (at least 10 years,

---

[4] Bill Sharpe, Tony Hodgson et al (2016). Three Horizons: A pathways practice for transformation. *Ecology and Society*.

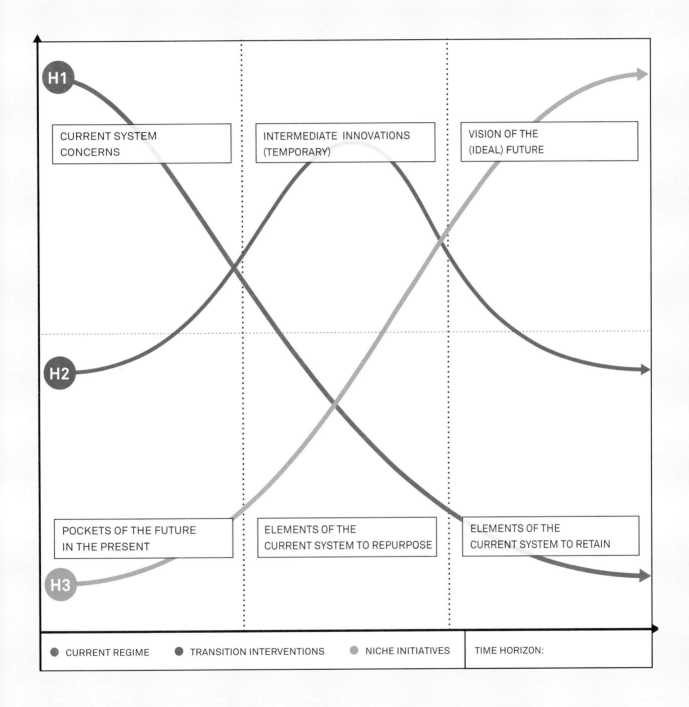

H1

CURRENT SYSTEM
CONCERNS

INTERMEDIATE INNOVATIONS
(TEMPORARY)

VISION OF THE
(IDEAL) FUTURE

H2

POCKETS OF THE FUTURE
IN THE PRESENT

ELEMENTS OF THE
CURRENT SYSTEM TO REPURPOSE

ELEMENTS OF THE
CURRENT SYSTEM TO RETAIN

H3

● CURRENT REGIME   ● TRANSITION INTERVENTIONS   ● NICHE INITIATIVES   TIME HORIZON:

and often 20 or more) with outcomes potentiated by transitioning actions that promote positive interventions in the near term.

A key concept in 3H is the imaginary of the desired future observed in the present, as in 'pockets of the future in the present.' The innovation and change projects of H2 are championed to lead the unfolding future along the desired pathway, through adoption and socialisation of bridging innovations that lead the third horizon and its values to emergence. 'Innovation' is broadly conceived, as any practices of technological, social, political, or cultural development might disclose opportunities for transition into the third horizon.

Cocreating the Three Horizons

Planning and Prep

The Three Horizons map integrates ideas from medium and long-term trends (Rich Context), emerging niche innovations, emerging systems (Story Loops), and desired future outcomes (System Value Proposition). If the team has completed these models, they can be revisited in the review of materials in planning. The STEEPV (Social, Technological, Economic, Environmental, Political, and Values) framework can also be used to structure identified weak signals and trends.

There are several variations of the 3H process, that are more or less appropriate for future visioning, change transition, or long-term foresight planning. The flexibility of the 3H as a visioning method allows framing and reframing, cocreation, and roadmapping styles. We suggest a basic model for Tourist practitioners in the steps that follow. (Explorers can find references to advanced methods online).

The mapping method can be adapted to convening workshops with groups of any size – from groups of 5-10 in concurrent sessions, groups larger than 50 in small groups, as well as in rotations between mixed teams and experts.

Method Mapping

1. With a whole group involved in the exercise, start with **Horizon 3**, not the H1 first horizon. H3 sets the idealisation for long-term future vision (desired future outcomes that will evolve). Focusing questions to inspire ideation can include: What is our vision of the emerging future? What are the desirable future outcomes we envision today? What long-term trends are driving towards these outcomes? Do not edit or constrain the ideas proposed, as they can be sorted out later.

2. Next, generate and brainstorm the salient trends of the present era in **Horizon 1**. These are primarily current practices now declining in their fit to the emerging needs of the societal system. Identify the main trends of the current period that seem to be ascendent and even critical. Many features of H1 will remain and transform through Horizon 2.
Ideation questions include: What are the main trends today that appear to be ascendant and continuing? What are the prominent trends that appear to be declining in significance? What is valued today, but taken for granted? What current evidence suggests the established system is

under strain, shows a decreasing fit to the emerging conditions, or is even failing? What are the elements of the current system we should retain?

3. **Horizon 2** is ideated last. Here, we propose the innovations, emerging trends, and new practices that are becoming apparent on the horizon, and that might connect the aspirations from H1 to the desired future of H3. The constructive ideation in H2 develops what will become the near-term strategy for motivating changes and adopting appropriate innovations leading to the desired future. Focus questions to use in H2 include: What innovations do we know about (anywhere in the world) that are responding to the pressures for change and might be growth points of the future system? How can we use them to transition? What examples (from anywhere in the world) do we know about where elements of the future systems we have described already exist? Can we repurpose elements of the current system to support our new goal?'

4. Spend additional time identifying the key transition trends and proposed activities or outcomes that bridge the horizons. Take note to locate near-term transition drivers and innovations in the H1-H2 overlap (the iceberg form can be used to show these trends) and also in the long-term trends in the H2-H3 bridge. While visible in H1, these emerging innovations are the trends in H2 that will become innovations drawing the present toward the Third Horizon.

Delivery and Destination

Three Horizons lends itself to visualising future trends maps, documenting high-level plans, and capturing transition strategies as a collaborative roadmap. In strategic and community planning workshops, we have created large posters of a 3H rich picture as a composite, working with a graphic facilitator live sketching the 'harvest' or read-outs of small group work to draw and integrate a visualised composite. After internal (sponsor) reviews and updates to resolve duplicate concepts and temporal inconsistencies, these graphic recording murals can be rendered as large posters, images in reports, or as part of synthesis maps in a complete system story.

As the 3H diagram is constructed, note that the regular-shaped curves of the canvas tool are not necessarily the shape of the future trends growing into each horizon for most trends. Using the whiteboard or changing the final diagram, shape the curves of each horizon to show the growth curve, continuity (e.g. flattening top), or steep declining curves in each period. Look at multiple examples of 3H sketches to inspire the team's thinking.

Travel Tips

In Three Horizons, the H2 phase is considered the 'turbulent transition,' a messy period of change. This is a critical period of innovation adoption, or failure to adapt to some trends. This is the temporal cycle where trends emerging today will be challenged, modified, or re-appropriated – often to emerge in a completely different form as societal forces move through the influence of these trends together. In map design, imagery can be introduced to portray transition dynamics. As Three Horizons is often used in programme planning, some practitioners draw 'bridges' or straight lines extending from H1 to H2 at the point where the lines cross, and a similar bridge from H2 to H3, to suggest paths of direct adoption through planning. Key transition strategies can be defined here to indicate how the organisation might draw on emerging innovations to facilitate early transition to the new regimes of practice.

Participants in Three Horizons workshops may find that they have mindsets in common with those who share similar interests toward future timeframes for vision and action. Author Tony Hodgson recommends strategic dialogue between proponents of the three positions, who may be recognised by mindset, and not necessarily by allegiance to a timeframe. Those who are committed to the effectiveness of current systems in H1 might see H2 as innovative but risky, and may filter out the ideas of the H3 future. Those already mentally living in an H3 world may treat H1 as if it's already obsolete. The innovation champions of H2 can adaptively mediate between H1 and H3. They will be seen as entrepreneurial by H1 and an ally to the H3 futurists, and can translate the H3 ideas effectively into the contemporary mindset.

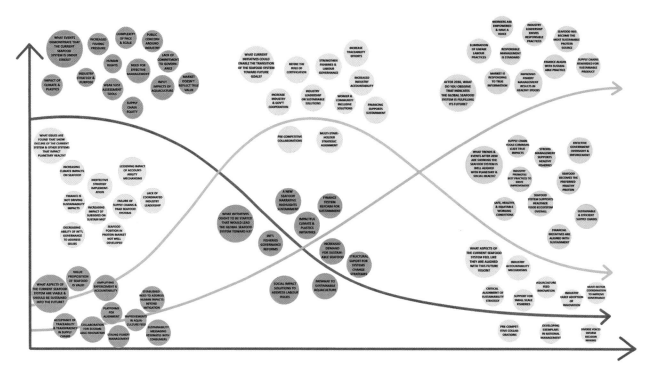

Figure 4-5

Three Horizons Map for Sustainable Seafood (Modified by permission, courtesy of Ian Kendrick, Bounce Beyond)

To illustrate the visual presentation of a Three Horizons final product, Figure 4-5 shows a working image from a series of Three Horizons maps created by Bounce Beyond for a sustainability strategy for the Seafood 2030 industry association, one of the Next Economy initiatives of Bounce Beyond. The full mapping was composed by acquiring responses to a series of questions (similar to those in the steps) from a large online survey. The design team analysed the responses, and assigned labels to clustered groups, creating themes from the inputs as shown in the coloured circles. While Three Horizons can be done as a one-day interactive mapping process, as a typical workshop approach, this rigorous methodology required a series of outreaches, analysis, and reviews. This final presentation summarised significant themes in each of the horizons:

- H1: Coordination failure of the global seafood system caused by overwhelming complexity.
- H2: Industry leadership of the system supports and drives adoption and development of innovation in the system to run and change the system.
- H3: Industry strategy driving an aligned seafood system that respects and evolves with ecological, social and economic needs.

The full Three Horizons analysis was a primary method of Bounce Beyond's engagement, for developing the Seafood2030 industry strategic plan (A New Paradigm for Sustainable Seafood Strategies), a 2023 report that includes other systemic approaches methods, including the CLA for issue mapping.

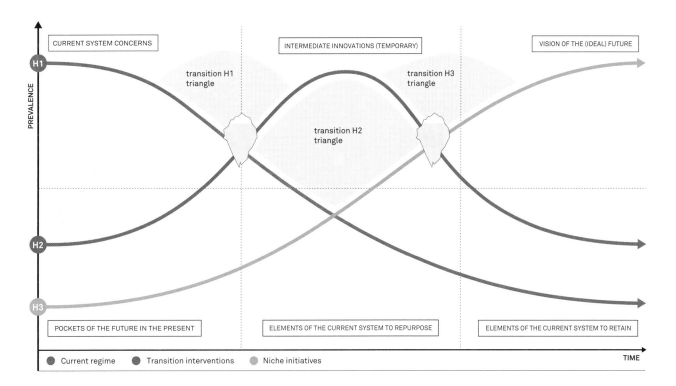

Figure 4-6 Three major transition points in the Three Horizons model

Tony Hodgson describes the positionality and interactions of the quintessential characters of each of the three horizons as attitudes towards futuring. The H1 persona can be thought of a someone invested in the current paradigm, perhaps not entirely business-as-usual but who is more wedded to incremental reform than visionary system change. The negative position of the H1 persona is that of someone hanging on the past and impeding change. They are in direct opposition to the H3 position of high-risk, long-term vision.

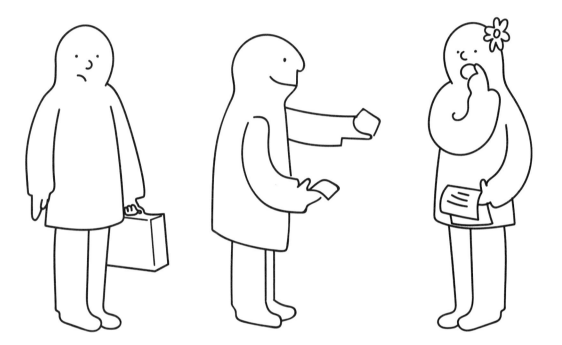

Figure 4-7
Interacting Personas of the Three Horizons

The H2 persona can be seen as an entrepreneurial character, seeing the opportunities for near-term innovation beyond the current system, but also sympathetic to the visionary – even if many of the H3 ideas are seen as impractical. The H2 innovator can form good partnerships with both H1 and H3 positions, so their pro-futuring and prosocial attitude is essential to successful change.

The H3 persona may hold to a long-term vision and may have strong views of how to accomplish the change. Theis inspiration and energy are essential in the mix, but their view of those beholden to H1 might be dismissive. The H2 innovator will be helpful to translate in dialogue from the visionary to toady's practical leader who may take some time to learn and be convinced. All three personas are always at play within the drama of creating a Three Horizons strategy that can be enacted.

Case Study – A Serious Game for Policy Makers

Namahn collaborated with the Transitions Lab of the Flemish government to create a 'serious game' for policy design, inspired by Three Horizons and the Meadows interventions strategies. Policy researchers Peter De Smedt and Kristian Borch[5] describe this serious game as a transition mapping for transformative change, a fundamental system-wide change in system structure and function. Using a prototype approach, the team evolved the serious game as a participatory policy tool over a three-month period. The team drew upon experience in system thinking and systemic design, serious game development, innovation systems, foresight, and behavioural insights. Since its development in 2018, the current version of the gaming tool has been further used and tested in training and policy workshops.

Figure 4-8
A serious game combining the Three Horizons and the Intervention Strategy levels. In the photograph the game is tested during the Joint Research Centre (JRC) FTA2018 conference - Future in the Making (courtesy of Peter De Smedt, DKB)

[5] Peter De Smedt & Kristian Borch (2021). Participatory policy design in system innovation. *Policy Design and Practice.*

Paradoxing

As we closely observe insights and design proposals for high complexity situations, we encounter paradoxes[6] that are seeming contradictions. These might be dismissed as irreconcilable, thereby choosing one of the positions or extremes. By doing so, we will make a conceptual error. Cognition seeks to reduce uncertainty in complexity, so often people quickly choose a position, not necessarily as an ideological choice, but for the sake of making progress. There will always be tensions and discontent in dealing with complexity, but we stand to lose a unique chance to learn and adapt if disregarding the function of paradox. In a paradoxical situation, the seemingly contradictory factors are both true at the same time and can be embraced together in design conversations.

Cocreating with Paradoxes

Paradoxing is a technique, not a tool. Namahn's Paradox Cards can be used to draw out and creatively exploit the perspectives in paradoxes within all types of design and complexity contexts. Images of the card set can be used for online whiteboard exercises or printed out for reframing workshops. The following guidelines will help in getting started.

Level One: Spotting Tensions in a Complex System

- The first level of use is to raise awareness of tensions in a complex system, which could be on different levels: On a societal level, between organisations, within a group, when designing products and services, or even to resolve conflicts within one's family. Moreover, if the same tension is present on multiple levels, a theme is discovered that can be resolved in the different tiers.

- Managers and team members can explore dominant tensions at play in their organisations and the dynamics of their influence. A typical example

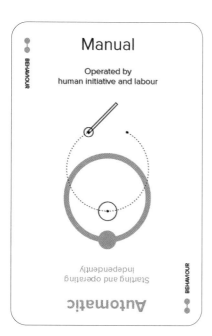

Figure 4-9
Paradox Cards can be printed or posted online

- Time to Run:
  1-2+ hours
- Session context:
  Studio or Agora
- Workshop Type:
  Reframing and Codesign
- Process time:
  1+ days
- Connections to:
  [2] Contextual Interview
  [5] Intervention Model

[6] Inspired by Kees Dorst (2006). Design Problems and Design Paradoxes. *Design Issues*.

A non-exhaustive list of paradoxes:

Emergence

- Tradition vs. Change
- Instability vs. Balance
- Revolution vs. Evolution

Appearance

- Durable vs. Momentary
- Close vs. Distant
- Visible vs. Hidden

Power distance

- Flat vs. Hierarchal
- Bottom-up vs. Top-down
- Centralised vs. Distributed

Collaboration

- Autonomous vs. Dependent
- Consensus vs. Imposed
- Teamwork vs. Competition

Business model

- Private vs. Public
- Paid vs. Free
- Non-profit vs. Profit

Connectivity

- Isolated vs. Networked
- Delayed vs. Real-time
- Once vs. Always

Understanding

- Complex vs. Simple
- Intuitive vs. Taught
- Machine vs. Human

Behaviour

- Passive vs. Active
- Automatic vs. Manual
- Serving vs. Leading

Governance

- Trust vs. Control
- Self-organised vs. Arranged
- Reactive vs. Proactive

State

- Static vs. Dynamic
- Closed vs. Open
- External vs. Internal

Presence

- Tangible vs. Intangible
- Extrovert vs. Introvert
- Global vs. Local

Diversity
- Group vs. Individual
- Generic vs. Personalised
- Homogeneous vs. Heterogeneous

Interaction

- Many-to-many vs. One-to-one
- Private vs. Shared
- Exclusive vs. Inclusive

Condition

- Stand-alone vs. Add-on
- Rigid vs. Flexible
- Heavy vs. Light

Time

- Flow vs. Stock
- Long-term vs. Short-term
- Slowing vs. Accelerating

Attitude

- Physical vs. Spiritual
- Rational vs. Emotional
- Serious vs. Playful

Culture

- Result vs. Process
- Easy-going vs. Disciplined
- Empathy vs. Performance

is long-term vision vs. short-term action. Each choice towards an extreme is harmful. Focusing only on long-term thinking might erode revenue and become unsustainable, and focusing on action will lead to rapid obsolescence. We can also query as to why there is a dominance towards one pole.

— Paradoxes can be used to assess and benchmark current offerings in the marketplace. Are they generic or personalised? Addressing individuals or groups? Can we do better? For example, creative resolutions for a digital offering might lead to enhancing its physical presence, like a music streaming platform embedded in physical locations, and brand-linked to live music festivals.

Level Two: Creating 'AND Solutions'

— A common belief is that we must compromise, reconciling the polarity somewhere in the middle. The art is to honour both extremes in our solution as much as possible.

— Additionally, in complexity, there are always multiple polarities influencing each other. A compromise in one pair can lead to a new imbalance in another pair, creating novel conflicts and challenges.

— Another advantage of embracing 'AND solutions' is that an offering will become future-proofed by its adaption to contexts, allowing for shifts in perspectives. For example, the paradox of global vs. local was painfully revealed by the risks of global dependency in the COVID-19 pandemic. But of course radical localism is also not a sustainable response. We might find ways in which global and local production processes are harmonised, to foster both scale and local capacities and skills.

Level Three: Creating New Growth Loops

— Discover how the paradoxes can be used to create reinforcing loops. The paradox of bottom-up vs. top-down frequently emerges. In systems, top-down and bottom-up initiatives are often disconnected, leading to frustrations at both sides (e.g. policy makers and volunteers in the healthcare sector). However, if we start looking at how they can help each other, a new solution space opens up.

— In the healthcare sector, the volunteer networks could, for example, inform the policy makers of the hurdles that they experience in the field and inspire new common practices by their innovative ways of working. The policy makers could then include this feedback in new guidelines and regulations intended for the field.

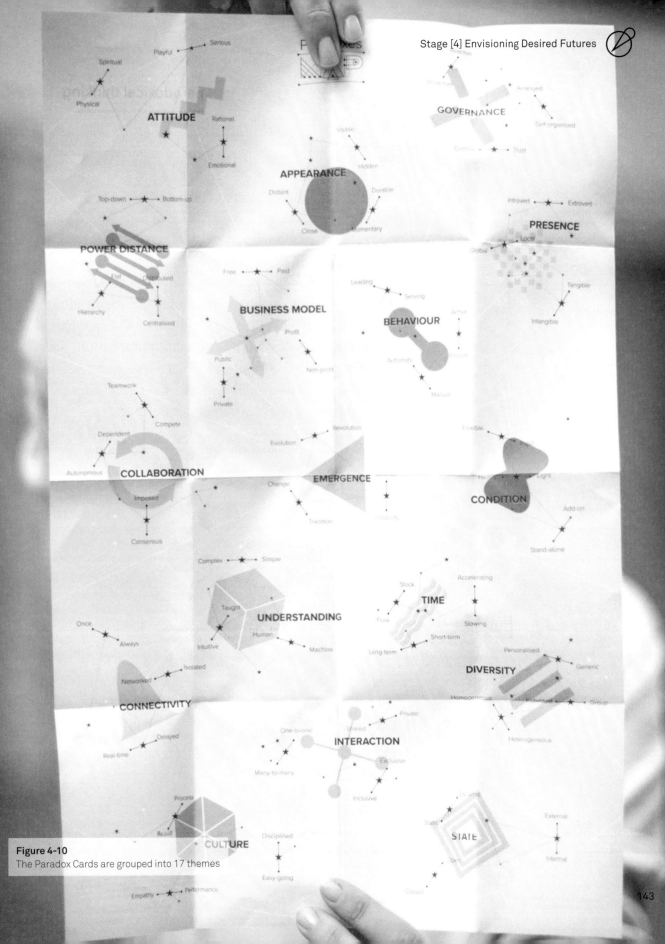

Figure 4-10
The Paradox Cards are grouped into 17 themes

Synthesis Map

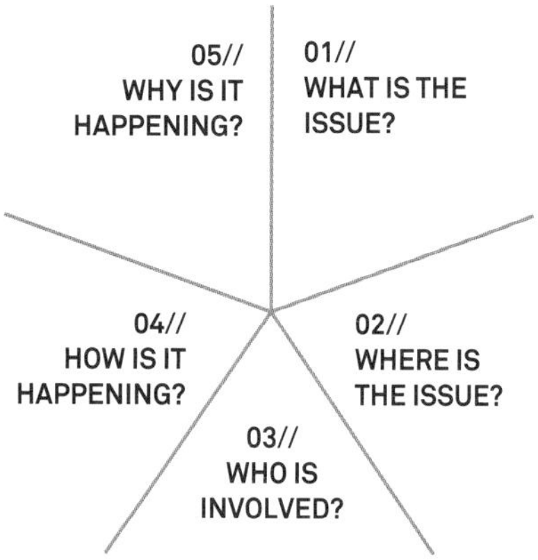

05//
WHY IS IT
HAPPENING?

01//
WHAT IS THE
ISSUE?

04//
HOW IS IT
HAPPENING?

02//
WHERE IS
THE ISSUE?

03//
WHO IS
INVOLVED?

Figure 4-11
Structure of Synthesis Map tool

— Time to Run:
2-4 hours to sketch
— Session context:
Lab & Studio
— Workshop Type:
Reframing
— Process time:
3-30 days
— Connections to:
[1] Actors Map
[1] Rich Context
[2] Causal Layered Analysis
[3] All 5 tools
[4] Three Horizons
[5] Intervention Strategy

Synthesis maps, as developed by Jones and others[7] are visualised system narratives that integrate systemic models developed from research evidence and design proposals, created for system stakeholders. They support dialogue and communication across boundaries, as well as futures perspectives and design options for complex sociotechnical systems and systems change. The visual narrative enables synthesis maps to reach broader audiences than analytical models. However their construction takes much more time, as they require prior models, and findings developed over stages of research and system modelling.

Synthesis maps were inspired and informed by Birger Sevaldson's open-modelling *Gigamapping*, a foundation design practice supported by years of insights from Systems Oriented Design.[8] Gigamaps are developed directly by teams as an expression of a collaborative design space for complex systems. They differ from the synthesis in that are not meant to be widely shared as communication products for non-involved stakeholders. The synthesis map is primarily a tool for understanding and presentation of complex system narratives. They are secondarily design proposals, as research through system modelling may not yet lead to effective solutions in this phase of work.

Synthesis maps are formulated by mixed-discipline design teams as artefacts for developing a shared understanding of highly complex sociotechnical problems. While a templated tool is provided for practitioners (Tourists), experienced mappers will also find the structured tool helpful in planning and guiding workshops. The disciplines of design, architecture, and urban planning have historically developed visual compositions and associated visual languages to frame and illustrate complex systemic problems. Mapping methods emerged from myriad visual design tools and representation frameworks to generate complex problem understanding, visual analysis, and solution finding. Synthesis maps are an evolution of what Edward Tufte[9] refers to as "design strategies for presenting information about causality and process."

[7] Peter Jones & Jeremy Bowes (2017). Rendering systems visible for design: Synthesis maps as constructivist design narratives. *She Ji: The Journal of Design, Economics, and Innovation.*
[8] Birger Sevaldson (2022). *Designing Complexity: The Methodology and Practice of Systems Oriented Design.* Common Ground.
[9] Edward Tufte (1997). *Visual Explanations: Images and Quantities, Evidence and Narrative.* Graphics Press.

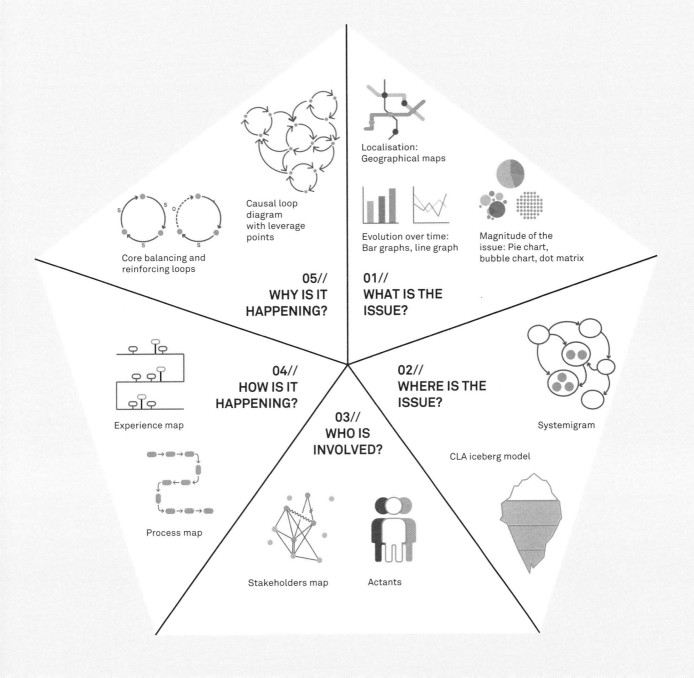

Causal loop
diagram
with leverage
points

Core balancing and
reinforcing loops

Localisation:
Geographical maps

Evolution over time:
Bar graphs, line graph

Magnitude of the
issue: Pie chart,
bubble chart, dot matrix

05//
WHY IS IT
HAPPENING?

01//
WHAT IS THE
ISSUE?

Experience map

04//
HOW IS IT
HAPPENING?

02//
WHERE IS THE
ISSUE?

Systemigram

Process map

03//
WHO IS
INVOLVED?

CLA iceberg model

Stakeholders map

Actants

Cocreating the Synthesis Map

Planning and Prep

Almost any or all models developed from Stages [1-3] will be useful in a bricolage approach to assembling the synthesis as a visually compelling narrative for a wicked problem or system change context. A synthesis map provides the basis for solutions and interventions in the stages that follow. Updates to the synthesis map from other stages can be added in to create a final presentation of problems and proposals. The canvas is useful more as a template for initial composition, but Explorers will typically take a creative, bespoke approach to designing a unique map style. Either of these approaches are supported well using interactive whiteboards. Formal interactive models can be developed using online platforms (such as Kumu or 7Vortex) and incorporated into the map. Several principles for preparation apply, whether using the tool or starting from sketches:

— A synthesis map is a qualitative system model that presents a narrative constructed through design. As a design team iteratively sketches and composes a map, frames, images and supporting information are chosen as decisions that reflect agreement and shared meaning.

— A key idea is to illustrate the complexity of a system 'as experienced' so that a sense of the complex issues as felt by people can be visualised. Structures of systems and processes can be diagrammed using formal models, or by visual composition designed for the problem.

— Synthesis mapping uses multi-scale modeling, spanning from the global scale down to small details. Maps can construct multiple layers of many types of information. Categorically separated information must be meaningfully connected by events in timelines, spatial relationships (such as geography or landscapes), and information categories.

— The synthesis map is a design artefact and can be framed as a system change blueprint. A map in formation needs only to communicate to the immediate team. This allows for a dramatic increase in information, since creating the map internalises far larger amounts of information than when approaching it as an outsider. The visualised graphic design takes shape after model synthesis.

— Many synthesis maps are formed with rich timelines or temporal models over long horizons. System mapping formalisms are used to draw attention to system behaviours and problematics in social systems. Systemigrams, causal loop diagrams, influence maps, rich pictures, process flows, panarchy cycles, and ecological models are integrated to represent discovered system relationships.

Method Mapping

For Tourists, start with the Toolkit canvas, to integrate prior models developed from framing and analysis.

1. **What** – To visualise the core issues, use graphs that reveal the magnitude of the framed problem, its evolution over time, or its local effects. Quantitative references from desk research are often available.

2. **Where** – Next, depict the locus of the issue occurring in the system. An iceberg model (CLA) can show the patterns and interfaces with the system and the location of issues.

3. **Who** – Depict who is involved and affected. This can be visualised by integrating actors and actants from the prior models, in the context of the whole system story. If personas are developed their images can be used to humanise the journeys or narrative structure.

4. **How** – Timelines and influence maps are often foregrounded as defining structures in the map to show the macro-scale evolution of system formation or cycles of growth, decline, and change. Journey maps and touchpoints situate the micro-experience of actors in the system.

5. **Why** – Underlying systemic problems are often revealed by highlighting applicable system archetypes, and visualising the core story loops with possible leverage points.

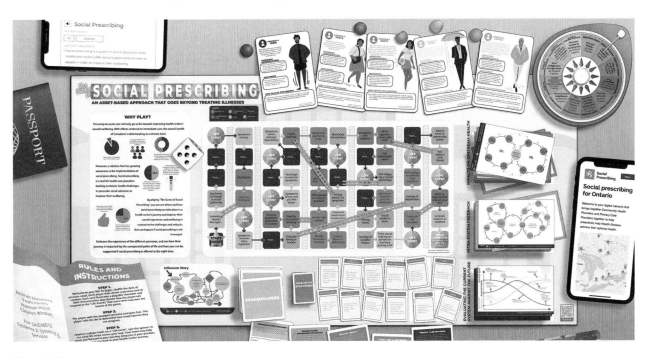

Figure 4-12
The Game of Social Prescribing. Synthesis map using a gameboard metaphor to model and propose systems for non-medical social prescription. OCAD University research team: Amirah Mahomed, Yoshi Perera, Hannah Walsh, and Clayton Windatt

Explorers might follow a more unstructured process by visualising directly from the composite models and ideas discovered in the analysis stages. With experience, we can use sketching and basic systems principles, often leading to a more integrated and coherent visual narrative.

1. Systemic problems: Express knowledge of the systemic issues and causes using an iceberg (CLA), timelines and of course, brief text. Boundaries clarifying the system in focus and its containing systems or overlaps can help to locate the issues.

2. **Temporality**: If the analysis reveals complexity evolving over time, sketch a timeline with temporal indicators to represent historical periods, cycles, and prospective futures. Use variables within the timeline to show curves for magnitude of change, key events, or multiple overlapping timelines.

3. **The social system or network**: Map organisations and actor-network relationships, to show multiple social systems. Show the connection of relationships within networks and between social systems.

4. **Stocks, flows and causality:** Stage [3] models can be recruited to show system and material flows, complex influences, and causal story loops.

5. **Influences**: Influence maps can be integrated, or layered with timelines, to show system relationships, drivers and trends, and root cause to outcomes.

6. **Identify places to intervene**: Synthesis maps use narratives and visualisation to call attention to the leverage points for change. While intervention opportunities are discovered in the analysis models, their presentation is often highlighted in list boxes, organised by category, or visually indicated according to the inherent logic of the map.

Delivery and Destination

Create a single large-scale poster of the integrated models to compose the synthesis map. A final digital image will be prepared, and a full-size printed poster can be used for high-impact client communication of design proposals and policy options. Be sure to define the final print size and resolution even in a digital-only delivery and use, if sharing the map beyond the team. Both PDF and (compressed) image files should be provided.

After the models and included information have been assembled, Explorers can compose a graphic metaphor as a visual organiser to encompass the entire mapping. The convey the essence of the issue or solution. For details and icons, draw on material and content from within the domain itself, such as clinical details in healthcare, a game metaphor (Figure 4-10), and the 'brain' metaphor (Figure 4-11). For maps that benefit from a humanised aesthetic in storytelling, hand-sketched personas can be effective.

Travel Tips

Synthesis maps can be used in numerous applications informed by systems thinking to support non-design functions in a project or organisation:

— Education: Concept mapping and storytelling scholarly knowledge and learning points
— Research: Visually organising the findings and recommendations from major research
— Management: Mapping the organisation as a complex production system, for strategy or transformation purposes
— Process and event mapping: Designing new process proposals or mapping complex events
— Complex planning: Registering, describing, and modifying complex processes
— Innovation and system change: Innovation strategies, models of diffusion, and transformation proposals

Key guidelines from practitioner experience for workshopping synthesis maps (or Gigamaps):

- Find and learn from prior maps developed for a challenge area. Review, critique, and learn from these. What opportunities are seen for expanding, for expression, for leverage points, for system change?
- Start with sketching timelines, lifecycle curves, or spatial structures as a centre – a focal armature for a system model (use a large sheet of paper early in sketching).
- Use sticky notes to define stakeholders, structures (places and organisations), and the elements of a social system. Use a flexible system mapping approach.
- Expand the boundary to contain a larger system – how does this change the whole and parts?
- Iterate between the *frame* (the challenge or question) and the boundaries, stakeholders, and processes in the larger system. For example, in a climate change planning challenge, iterate to change geographical boundaries, timeframes, and the breadth of environmental contexts.
- Show how the system is expressed as a wicked problem. Show complexity with high-density multiple interdependencies, multiple flows over time, and connected stakeholders.
- Discover a metaphor that captures the concept of the current system, such as a roadmap, landscape, cityscape, game board, networks, etc. Adapt the visual metaphor to map content and vice-versa.

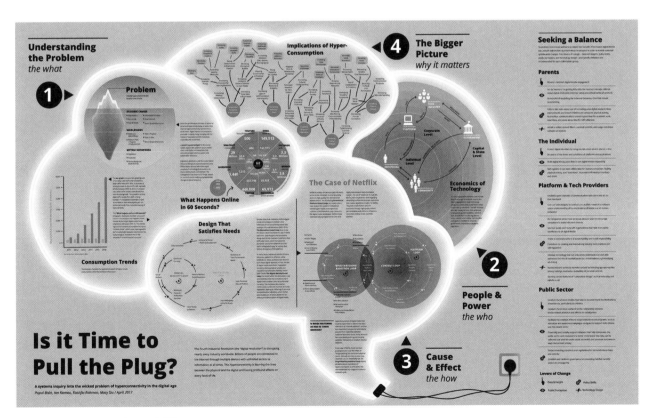

Figure 4-13
Is it Time to Pull the Plug? The Social System of Internet Hyperconnectivity. Synthesis map by OCAD University team, Pupul Bisht, Ian Prieto-McTair, Kashfia Rahman, and Macy Siu

[5] Exploring the Possibility Space
Finding strategies for system interventions

Consider the expansive range of possible design opportunities to influence change in a complex system. The influential options available in any large-scale social or transformation system are innumerable and the potential interactions among actions can be unintuitively interconnected. Systemic design tools are designed to guide convening teams with stakeholders toward the effective discovery of potential impacts. How might we learn, imagine, and map out the best fitting scenarios for future action that shape a desired future?

In [5] Exploring, we translate complex systems theory to define five tools for designing system conditions and defining options for wicked problem interventions. The tools are meant to accelerate team learning and help integrate many sources of knowledge for complex planning, meta-planning, and design. As in business strategy, a complement of strategic options can be developed to fit different scenarios as future outcomes unfold. A variety of interventions can be mapped out as a tradespace[1] of actions or options that can be designed and compared for relative efficacy to achieve transformational goals. Our ambition is to locate effective leverage points that will serve as designable options, with leverage and design opportunity. Yet these are not defined analytically by abstract reasoning in a closed office, but are imagined with others and assessed in collaboration, in dialogue with those with knowledge and experience in a complex shared terrain of interest.

Exploring the 'possibility space' here can be understood as a *search* process, driven by iterations of imaginative abductive reasoning. It is the opposite of problem solving. Problem solving assumes a 'best solution' can be reached if a situation is analysed, structured into elements, and resolved using a problem-solving method. Solutions result that solve the problem as defined, and these are quantified to identify a highest-ranking solution. *Complicated* systems (e.g., assembly lines, buildings, electronics) do have predictable, linear functions and can be decomposed into hierarchies of ordered systems. Wicked problems and complex systems are not decomposable into comparable elements, as we would lose the interactive relations between agents and processes. Complex systems cannot be problem-solved, but they can be *explored*, together, to find leverage for transformational impact.

[1] Christopher Roberts, et al. (2009). Scenario planning in dynamic multi-attribute tradespace exploration. *IEEE Systems Conference 2009*.

Searching for Leverage Strategies

This stage differs conceptually from [4] Envisioning in that we focus on defining possible impacts from the transformation strategy – through mapping scenarios, outcomes, and interventions. The Exploring mindset is that of search, searching together in codesign and co-learning to propose incremental actions as interventions with high potential for influencing system conditions. The concept of *leverage* is a chief criterion of effective intervention. A systemic design principle is defined as Leverage Impact, the function of optimising desired effects from minimal energy inputs.

The five Exploring tools provide in-depth modelling canvases that can be employed with mixed teams in facilitated codesign workshops. The Intervention Strategy is an indispensable tool, as it provides the team's intervention proposals to other, primarily roadmapping, tools. The intervention proposals are source material to compare and trade off as systemic options.

In practice, the flow of convening can move from the generative proposals in [4] Envisioning to mapping specific impacts and interventions, as a seamless series of reframing and codesign sessions. One journey leads into this stage from the System Value Proposition or Three Horizons to the Intervention Strategy. Both of these can be transduced to an Outcome Map as a strategic roadmap.

Design Journeys tools are helpful for generative team brainstorming, but they do not show how to use leverage analysis as a discovery process. While useful and potentially high-impact options can be generated in team workshops, yet the determination of relative leverage can follow as an analytic process. In their development of systemic theories of change, a method published by Murphy[2] and Jones uses principles to locate high-leverage options from causal loop diagrams (CLDs). The principles informing this approach can be summarised as an overview, as they will be helpful for the pathway facilitated by tools in Stages [5] and [6] in particular.

As in CLDs, the number of incoming and outgoing causality indicators (arrows) provides a first locus of attention to determine measures of degree, closeness or reach. Our analysis should always confirm the relative impact of these connections, as any mapping can be biased, and the flows might not be influential.

- Identify factors that might be used as fulcra, or leverage points that propagate effects across the network or relations. Remember that this network is only a model of the system and the concept is to reveal the salient fulcra for which design might produce expected benefits of change.
- Defining outcomes or a systemic theory of change can be expressed by identifying signals (primary flows), revealed opportunities (and risks), selecting key fulcra (leveraged factors), and identifying barriers that impede leverage flow.
- Murphy (2022) goes further to show that locating "local" leverage, that which can be influenced directly, will always be favoured over global, or long-trend leverage for which the design team might only have indirect influence.

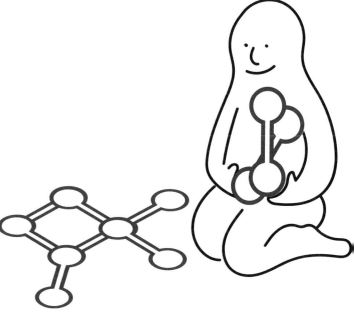

[2] Ryan Murphy & Jones (2021) Towards systemic theories of change: High-leverage strategies for managing wicked problems. Design Management Journal.

Design Journeys for Exploring

Future State Scenarios
Future State Scenarios define future contexts in which different interventions can be tested. It's a flexible tool for defining four distinct, incommensurable future scenarios in which to envision effective sets of change options. The scenarios help to define the scope and timeframe of an intervention strategy.

Intervention Strategy
The Intervention Strategy tool generates proposals for the various areas where leverage might induce significant effects in interventions, according to the relative impact of influential positions or levels. The tool provides a strategic framework for design and change decisions based on leverage impact, with these ideas contributing to many of the next steps.

Intervention Model
The Intervention Model is a technique used to translate the intervention strategy into activities, products, services, and preconditions. Because this is an extension of the Intervention Strategy, it is presented as a technique to enrich and further develop the interventions.

Contextual (Spatial) Variations
Contextual Variations provide a tool to define different placements of interventions in space, as opposed to the leverage of time. We use the intervention proposals as options. Contextual Variations can be used for the current situation, but can also be combined with the scenario possibilities for mapping interventions as options to intervene in scenario outcomes over time. This tool contributes to the Theory of Systems Change.

Outcome Map
The Outcome Map structures the influencing relationships of planned activities, leading to outcomes, strategic outcomes, and future impacts. This tool provides extensive detail of potential outcomes in a complex system plan, to define organisations, roles, and the support networks in a transition plan or theory of change. Outcome mapping develops a model that can translate directly to a Theory of Systems Change.

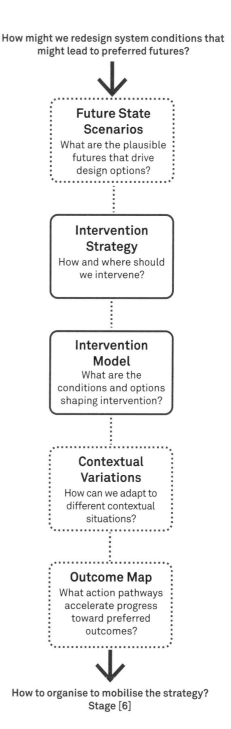

Future State Scenarios

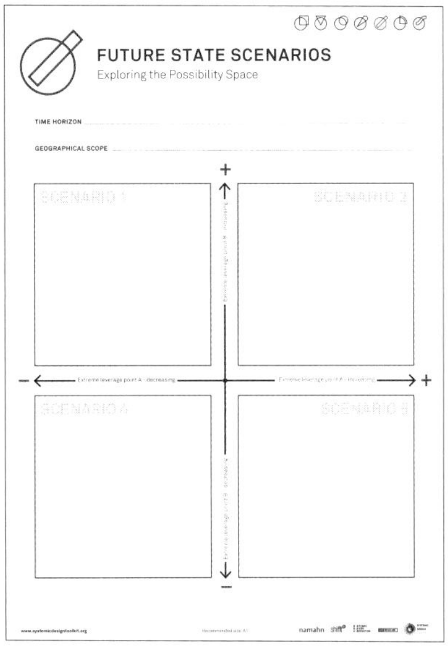

Figure 5-1
The Future State Scenarios

- Time to Run:
  2-4 hours +
- Session context:
  Studio
- Workshop Type:
  Codesign
- Process time:
  2+ days
- Connections to:
  [3] Influence Map
  [3] Story Loop Diagram
  [4] Three Horizons
  [5] Intervention Model

A complex systems perspective requires an appreciative mindset along with the embrace of uncertainty. A longer-term horizon for outcomes inspires thinking about multiple futures that might evolve given different initial and changing system conditions. A meaningful interpretation and anticipation of system changes over time involve mapping complex scenarios as thematic stories with critical variables reflecting uncertainties and possible futures.

The scenario process encourages nonlinear and dislocating change effects, made tangible through mapping and story-making so that interventions might be effective regardless of how systems will evolve in the future. The goal is to create narratives of alternative future intervention needs that can stand as a ground for the generation of ideas.

Cocreating Scenarios

Planning and Prep

Review prior work from system mapping across the journeys, especially from [4] Envisioning, to assess major trends, weak signals, and drivers for change. Analyse the thematic content to identify a set of variables that stand out as critical axes upon which the themes and trends are dependent. Sometimes these are called 'cross-cutting' variables; they must be consequential depending on their evolution toward higher or lower magnitude of impact (the 'uncertainty' refers to the fact that we do not yet have confidence in how these variables will evolve). Social variables at the level of 'economic growth,' 'social flourishing,' or 'technology acceptance' are typical, as higher or lower indicators of these variables will result in distinctly different worlds.

The possible solutions identified as interventions can be mapped to these variables, known as critical uncertainties, as some will be much more effective in one scenario versus another.

The well-known 2x2 matrix is used to cross the spectra of two critical uncertainties in a defined future time horizon. Each scenario is mapped to contribute the highest-impact options for each defined future state. The two critical uncertainties are paired in a 2x2 matrix in the tool. The team and workshop participants must also define the rich contexts for the four scenarios, including the terminal time horizon and geographical scope.

TIME HORIZON & GEOGRAPHICAL SCOPE : ....

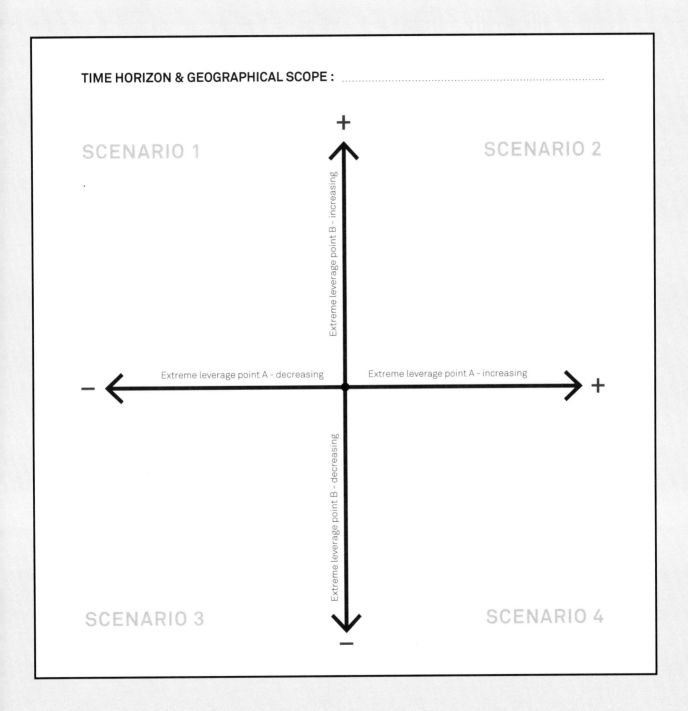

Mapping Method

1. For each of the two uncertainty axes, name the line and define the end points for the high and low ends. For example, if the axis is 'economic growth,' the poles can be stated as 'Low' and 'High,' but the team should also discuss and agree on what these positions might mean. They are not meant to be value-laden, as low growth can be a deliberate sustainability strategy and high growth can be corrupt.

2. By crossing the axes, define four distinct, alternative scenarios for the time horizon. The two lines will normally create four spaces that can be defined as More / Less or Pro / Con for the relative effects of the uncertainty variables. But do not name the quadrants until after composing their attributes.

3. Generate responses (notes) to fill each of the quadrants with trends, themes, and drivers identified in the prior systems maps. Consider how each of the four scenarios will start from different initial conditions that lead to some trends, and not others, taking shape in accordance with the two axes.

4. For each scenario quadrant, use the value system framework to expand the dimensions available in the scenario extremes at different levels (user, organisation, ecosystem, society) and from different perspectives. This also helps to ensure each scenario includes comparable systems levels and impacts, and analytical categories.

5. Be sure to identify unforeseeable or extreme outcomes ('Black Swans') in each scenario quadrant that might symbolise the unique character of that future state. Capture the conclusions in a text description that begins with the conditions of the future state and continues with their impact on the different areas of the systems map.

Delivery and Destination

After the workshop, designers can further enrich the generated scenarios with descriptions of impact that the participants might have missed. Scenarios can take some further time to develop. The goal of the tool is to generate high-quality participation to include the ideas from all team members with different perspectives. The final iterations of scenarios are the composition of compelling imaginaries that bring the scenario features to life. In a follow-up session, participants can generate ideas to intervene in each scenario as possible futures, using the Intervention Strategy canvas and leverage points for inspiration.

Embellish the narrative construction, and be sure to find or illustrate provocative imagery to bring the scenarios to life and relevance. It's especially helpful to generate memorable and even playful titles that become working themes and can travel far in discussions. Scenarios are very much like research findings and can be published, shared, and discussed within team dialogues independently of other design activities.

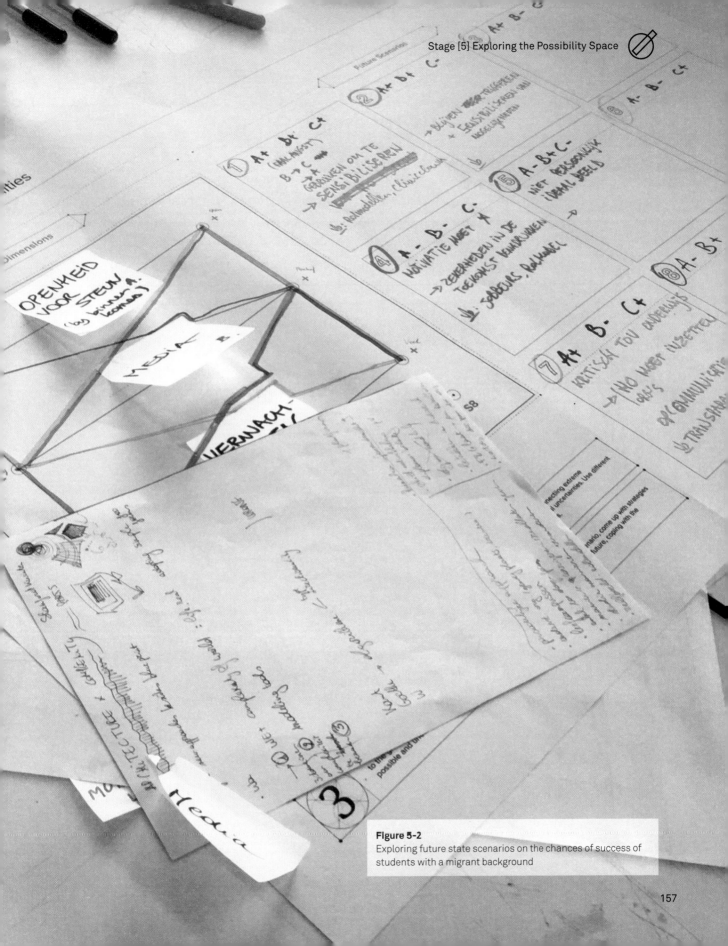

Figure 5-2
Exploring future state scenarios on the chances of success of students with a migrant background

Intervention Strategy

As several influence mapping tools across the journeys demonstrate, there are distinctly different ways to map out and define interventions in complex systems. Each mapping tool provides a unique value, but some projects might use multiple maps to triangulate (or cross-analyse) the different findings that each tool generates.

The Intervention Strategy tool helps to visualise a spectrum of possible high-impact proposals through codesign and dialogue with stakeholders. The Intervention Strategy translates the well-known twelve leverage points[3] from Donella Meadows 'places to intervene' for multiple versions of the tool canvas. These include two wheel styles of 12 leverage positions and a horizontal view that visually signifies relative impact.

This tool allows a team to construct a strategy of mixed solutions that can be selected as strategic options, using a combination of interventions. As an assessment tool, we can identify where to intervene effectively, considering the highest impact and timing.

Convening the Intervention Strategy

Planning and Prep

Organisers should prepare stakeholders to work with the concepts of leverage. Participants can read the original Meadows article as homework. Summaries of leverage points are available as cards (or images) from the Toolkit library on the *Design Journeys* site. Choose either the wheel or the horizontal tool to use in the workshop (if unsure which is best for the purpose, start with the horizontal version, as it provides more space for annotation).

Previous maps, especially Three Horizons or Synthesis Maps are critical inputs to review and set the stage for workshopping. Provide the Story Loop diagrams from [3] Understanding. Combine them into meaningful sets, and discuss the themes and findings behind them.

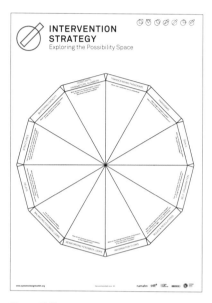

Figure 5-3
The Intervention Strategy

— Time to Run:
  2-4 hours
— Session context:
  Studio
— Workshop type:
  Codesign
— Process time:
  1+ days
— Connections to:
  [3] Story Loop Diagram
  [4] Value Proposition
  [4] Three Horizons

[3] Donella Meadows (1999). *Leverage Points: Places to Intervene in a System*. The Sustainability Institute.

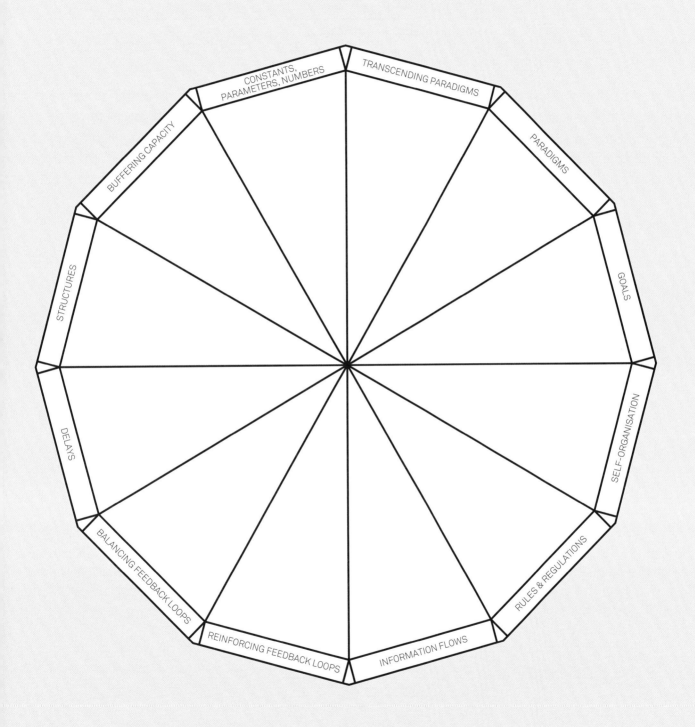

Mapping Method

Consider each of the 12 leverage point references as pathways with multiple potential system proposals that might yield many future actions toward a desired future outcome. These proposals can range from the very specific and tactical (such as measures and incentives, at the lower points of leverage) to the aspirational and visionary (with paradigms, at the highest end of the scale).

1. Use previous models to collect input sources to identify, select, or adapt ideas as inspiration for intervention proposals. Consider arranging with participants a method for selection (i.e. each member chooses their top three ideas).

2. Tourists: Place existing notes within the canvas (either style) by locating the best-fit or highest-impact leverage point for the idea, if applied. Refer to the prompt questions under each intervention level. Write new or revised ideas on virtual notes (if online), adopting different colours per theme if that fits the map.

3. Iteratively review the proposed ideas, their positions and potential for leverage on the system challenge. When the canvas is full, review ideas starting from either the lowest point (parameters) or the highest point (paradigms). The starting positions have a bias – in that the low-high direction is more of a realist pathway, and the high-low direction is more idealistic and prioritises high-impact change proposals.

4. Look for relationships between the ideas that may show connections and timing effects between outcomes to form a strategic pathway or roadmap timeline.

5. Review the product at the end of posting up the notes. Edit the populated map if needed, to narrow the focus and a Not all intervention proposals will be seen as useful or workable in a programme context.

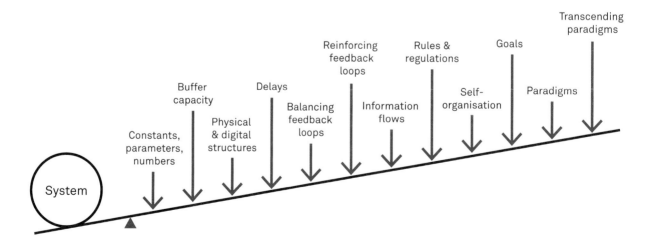

Figure 5-4
Relative system impact of leverage points

If all the ideas are posted and kept in the final diagram, the impact and readability will be enhanced by defining a number of themes (such as technological, legal, policy interventions). Decide which interventions will be selected for a final mapping, based on programme goals, organisational capacity, time horizon, feasibility, impact, momentum, and power and knowledge availability.

Delivery and Destination

After generating and thematically organising the intervention ideas, turn to a critiquing phase. Discuss and ideate ways to improve the posted approaches. Bear in mind that they should lead to an meaningful impact or benefit for all stakeholders/actors. Develop intervention strategies by writing concrete story lines (or what-if scenarios). Make the intervention more concrete by asking 'what ought to be done, by whom?'

Assign a design lead to compose a final diagram with a readable arrangement of the chosen interventions, so that it can be presented in a single poster or on a wide slide. Even if the team uses the wheel version of the canvas, the final diagram could be presented in the horizontal model, with its variable lengths of 'leverage arrows' to suggest the degree of impact.

Figure 5-5
Exploring intervention strategies for fostering intercultural connection through music sharing

Table 5-1 presents a model strategy with prompts and responses for a systemic policy approach, including guidelines for nine of twelve leverage areas that apply to policy and programme planning.

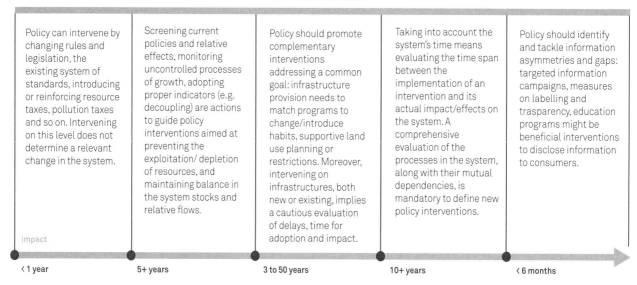

Taxes & subsidies	Buffer capacity	Digital/physical infrastructures	Timing and coordination	Information flows
Constants and parameters such as subsidies, taxes, standards, pricing schemes.	The "volumes" that the system can contain.	Digital systems or physical infrastructures, and their nodes of intersection.	The duration of changes relative to the rate at which the system changes.	The structure of who does and who does not have access to information.
Ex. Food prices, pricing schemes, minimum wage rate	Ex. Enough doctors to handle a sudden flue outbreak; enough money to be able to pay an onforseen bill	Ex. Production plants, fisheries, road network, digital network infrastructures, virtual communities	Ex. The introduction of a new technology does not correspond to its adoption: it takes a certain amount of time for people to learn to use it, and this time will cause a delay in the uptake	Ex. Do the consumers know the carbon footprint of a product? Can we intervene to provide them this information?
Can we influence behavior through incentives and restrictions?	**Can we stabilize the system by introducing some buffers?**	**Can we adapt the infrastructure in function of our goal?**	**Can we shorten the uptake?**	**Can we support access to information?**

MEANING FOR POLICY

Policy can intervene by changing rules and legislation, the existing system of standards, introducing or reinforcing resource taxes, pollution taxes and so on. Intervening on this level does not determine a relevant change in the system.	Screening current policies and relative effects, monitoring uncontrolled processes of growth, adopting proper indicators (e.g. decoupling) are actions to guide policy interventions aimed at preventing the exploitation/ depletion of resources, and maintaining balance in the system stocks and relative flows.	Policy should promote complementary interventions addressing a common goal: infrastructure provision needs to match programs to change/introduce habits, supportive land use planning or restrictions. Moreover, intervening on infrastructures, both new or existing, implies a cautious evaluation of delays, time for adoption and impact.	Taking into account the system's time means evaluating the time span between the implementation of an intervention and its actual impact/effects on the system. A comprehensive evaluation of the processes in the system, along with their mutual dependencies, is mandatory to define new policy interventions.	Policy should identify and tackle information asymmetries and gaps: targeted information campaigns, measures on labelling and transparency, education programs might be beneficial interventions to disclose information to consumers.
impact				
< 1 year	5+ years	3 to 50 years	10+ years	< 6 months

Table 5-1
Leverage points briefing for policy makers

Rules	Governance & Self-organisation	Goals	Paradigms
Incentives, punishments, constraints, regulations: the codified norms which govern the system's behaviour.	The possibility of local actors to organize by themselves so as to add, change, or evolve the system structure.	The purpose or function of the system or subsystem, which is shaped by the values, goals, worldviews of the actors.	The mindset out of which the system - its goals, structure, rules, delays, parameters - arises.
Ex. Changing mandatory standards for existing buildings or specific processes, providing incentives for the application of resources conservation methods	Ex. In neighborhood planning different actors (neighbours, major, commercial activities, ...) might join together and "self-organise", by taking collective decisions on the future neighbourhood, assigning responsibilities and rules	Ex. If the current goal is "increasing GDP", an intervention might turn it into "increasing people's wellbeing". In the same way, "efficient use of natural resources" might be turned into "conservation of natural capital stocks"	Ex. Malnutrition might be tackled by changing established taboos on specific types of food, and spreading awareness on the nutritional value of a varied diet
Can we steer the systems by changing the rules?	**How can policy makers foster this?**	**Can we attain the goal by changing the viewpoints about the purpose?**	**Can we change beliefs on how things work?**

MEANING FOR POLICY

Policy interventions should be powerful enough to change rules and legislation, create incentive programs for initiatives that advance public policy goals, or consider punishments aimed at pushing the behavioural change.	Policy support might be provided to facilitate the collaboration and communication among different actors: collaboration platforms can take various forms, including industrial symbiosis, public - private agreements, R&D clusters or voluntary initiatives.	Update the purpose of the food system, the associated objectives and indicators in all policy and strategic documents. Implement, for instance, new policies which go beyond the concept of "growth and efficiency", to embrace the principles of "consistency" and "sufficiency".	Promote and support visionary leadership, or plan long-term interventions aimed at spreading information and raising awareness on specific topics.

impact

5+ years   3 to 10 years   20+ years   30+ years

163

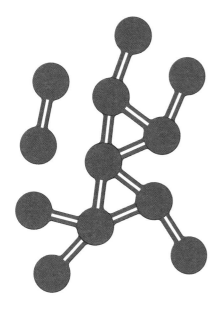

Intervention Model

The Intervention Model follows the Intervention Strategy tool to define and map relations among core functions of the interventions, to simulate the evolution of change within the next system. The tool develops a more complete strategy and supports the team's progress by defining options, principles, actions, and evaluation criteria that activate system change, or to structure a complex service.

At this stage of design, people often tend to focus on each intervention as a separate option. The technique positions connectors and visible linkages that stimulate workshop participants to reimagine how interventions connect and reinforce each other and envision a more effective strategy for change.

Cocreating the Intervention Model

Planning and Prep

In a physical workshop, printed connectors are used as props to lay over printed posters on tables or the wall. Online, the digital version employs hexagon images to represent the intervention and smaller square notes to write up and describe their interactions. The codesign approach to mapping involves spreading out the intervention proposals as options, and defining the composite activities and preconditions that trigger their selection. Touchpoints between activities or interventions are indicated by the connectors.

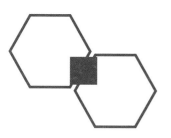

Figure 5-6
Physical and digital props as used
in the Intervention Model

- Time to Run:
  2-4 hours
- Session context:
  Studio
- Workshop type:
  Codesign
- Process time:
  3+ days
- Connections to:
  [4] Paradoxing
  [5] Intervention Strategy
  [5] Contextual Variations
  [5] Outcome Map

Mapping Method

1. Review the ideas from the Intervention Strategy and revise their definition as more concrete activities (e.g. provide online courses to increase capacity, contact members of parliament to promote a change in policy). Transcribe the ideas on notes, if using connectors, or directly on the hexagon images.

2. Connect propositions to build a networked map of interconnected interventions. Discuss how they could reinforce each other – write how they so influence in the middle section (on the white stroke).

3. Discuss how boundary conditions could be changed to achieve the desired impact (e.g., engage government instead of NGOs).

Figure 5-7
Intervention Modelling with props and Paradox Cards

4. Also use the Paradox Cards to inspire variations of the proposals in the model.

5. Conduct a walkthrough to simulate the actions and outcomes from the perspective of the actors involved.

Delivery and Destination

The Intervention Model is a staged refinement of the Intervention Strategy, with its initial proposals of leverage points. A final version would be visualised to present a readable, presentable visual composition, which can be done effectively using the online whiteboard and tool materials.

The purpose of this tool is to encourage deeper thinking about the actions and functional relationships of and between the interventions. Once set up, further adaptations can be constricted with variations in time and space (future state scenarios and contextual variations). Further detail of the strategic roadmap can be defined in the model or in the Outcome Map, defining sequential steps of action, locations, and resources required (e.g. skills, money, motivation, information, etc.).

Travel Tip

In a Studio or Lab (internal) setting, the team can flexibly bypass this tool and move directly to the Outcome Map. This is more helpful when engaging with knowledgeable stakeholders who would be able to develop an outcome-based strategic roadmap at this point.

Figure 5-8
Intervention Modelling, connecting the interventions
with the props at RSD7 (Torino)

Contextual Variations

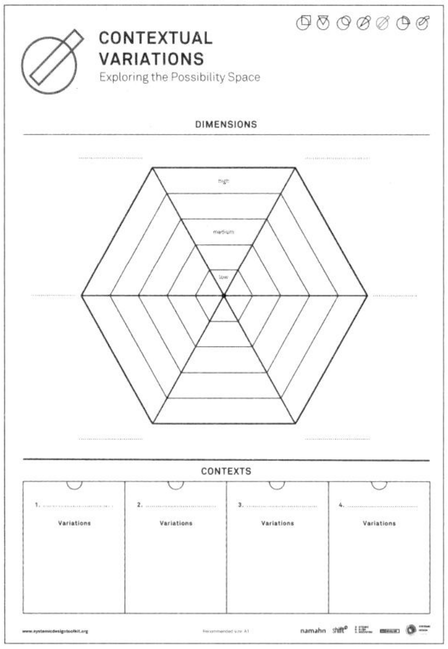

Figure 5-9
The Contextual Variations

- Time to Run:
  1-3 hours
- Session context:
  Studio
- Workshop type:
  Codesign
- Process time:
  1+ days
- Connections to:
  [2] Stakeholder Discovery
  [4] System Value Proposition
  [5] Intervention Model
  [5] Outcome Map

Contextual Variations is our name for a technique for further expressing the assumptions and conditions for the environments wherein our expected interventions take place. Contextual variations can be any aspects of the context that might vary due to geography or place, culture, politics, demographics, time of year, or so forth. The codesign approach activates this tool with the prompt question of 'how well will the intervention strategy work in these different circumstances?' Workshops can be staged by continuing to build upon the Intervention Strategy and Model from the previous steps on this journey. The tool can also be used as a way to generate and critique our assumptions that determine whether interventions are successful – a helpful technique for the TOSCA theory of systems change in [6] Planning.

Cocreating Contextual Variations

Planning and Prep

With the core team, discuss and determine the contextual differences and variables that would influence or vary by context in the problem or intervention. Develop trends or background on these factors from desk research or experts that might inform or participate in the workshop.

Mapping Method

1. Brainstorm and generate contextual factors that are most likely to influence how the interventions will be implemented or received in their settings. Assign each factor to a vertex edge in the tool template (See Fig 5-11).

2. Assess how these factors are met in the different contexts that influence the interventions (quantitatively as Low, Medium, High, qualitatively as a cultural or age-based variation, etc.).

3. It is typical to profile each context in the radar diagram, using a colour for each. Provide a name for each profile at the bottom part of the poster.

4. Now for each profile, look back to the Intervention Model and Outcome

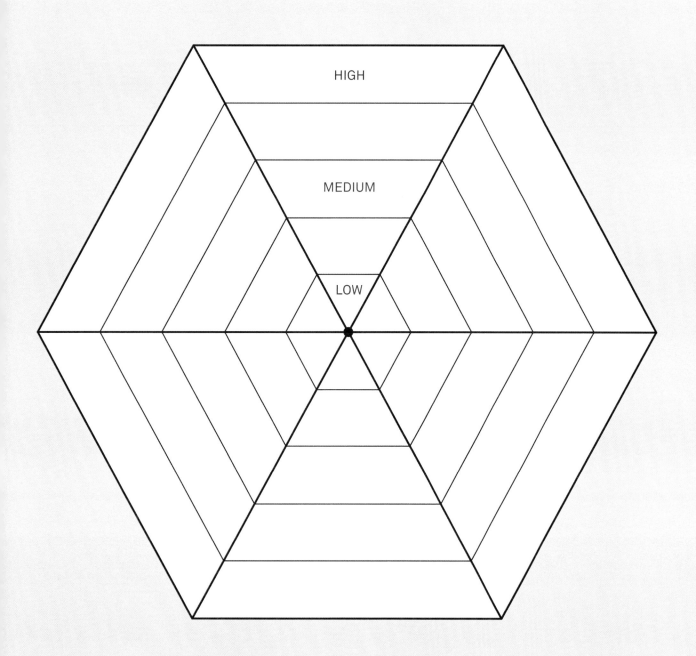

Map. Rethink the activities and preconditions to make them work across contexts or propose variations to accommodate the differences.

Delivery and Destination

Contextual Variations contributes a deepening of the assumptions and applications of the interventions in the developing strategy. As contextual scenarios are proposed and considered, these updates will strengthen the Outcome Map and the TOSCA theory of change by defining assumptions under which the strategy is more or less effective.

Travel Tips

Consider contextual variations as a coherent system function like DNA in living beings, which contains a variety of possibilities from which a particular instance generates. The illustration below[4] (Figure 5-10) shows how the DNA of a type of tree can generate different leaves adapted to the context.

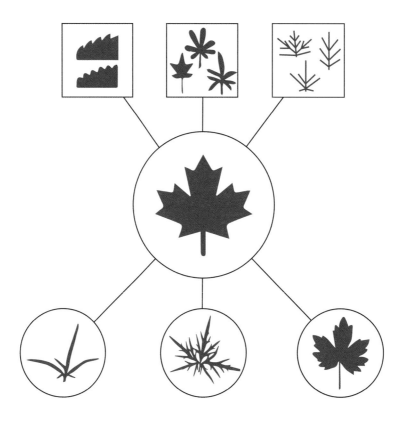

Figure 5-10
The DNA of a tree leading to different leaf shapes depending on the context

---

[4] Inspired by: JW von Goethe (1790). *The Metamorphosis of Plants*.

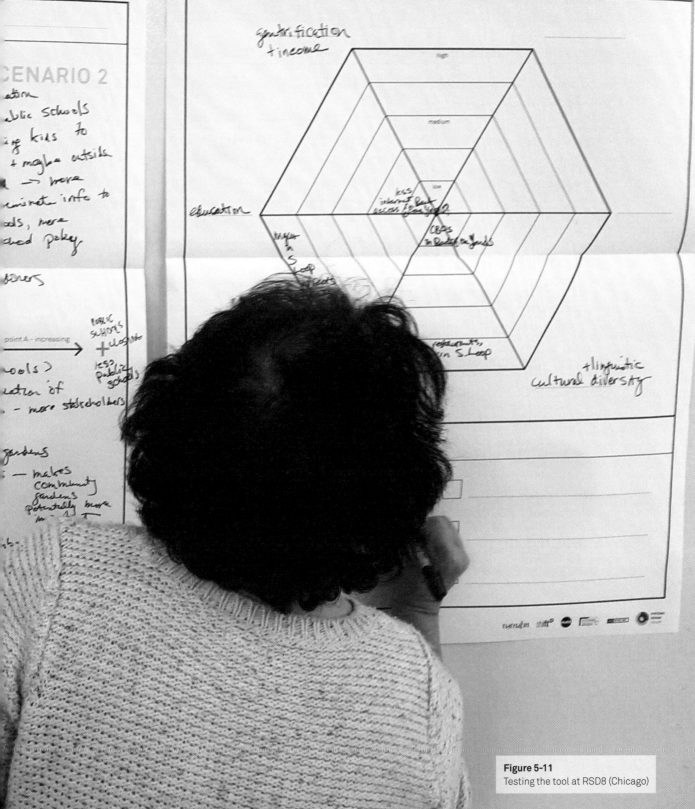

Figure 5-11
Testing the tool at RSD8 (Chicago)

Outcome Map

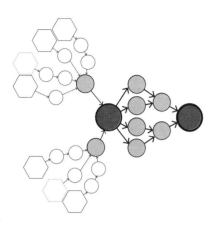

Figure 5-12
The Outcome Map structure

- Time to Run:
  2-4 hours
- Session context:
  Lab, revise with Studio
- Workshop type:
  Codesign
- Process time:
  3+ days
- Connections to:
  [3] Multicapitals Model
  [3] Influence Map
  [3] Story Loop Diagram
  [4] System Value Proposition
  [4] Three Horizons
  [5] Intervention Model
  [6] Theory of Systems Change

Outcome mapping[5] defines and visualises the major activities and outcomes of a change programme to the intended strategy and desired system impacts.

An Outcome Map incorporates interventions and the intended or desired outcomes from [4] Envisioning into a single integrated transition roadmap. We show one of several different known techniques for creating outcome maps (sometimes called *impact* maps). All of these use the logical transitive relations as used in influence maps, and the outcome map uses a similar style of a theory of change.

The Outcome Map tool depicts:

- Purposive intentions (sustaining purposes) and indirect (strategic impact) strategic outcomes of the programme. These are indicated by the two large circles in the middle and to the right.
- The smaller circles throughout the map are intermediate outcomes that are seen as enabling the strategic goal.
- Activities and near-term actions needed to create these outcomes are shown as hexagons in the canvas, often rectangles in other models..
- Arrowed lines connect related outcomes to indicate their influence on each other and overall progress.

Cocreating the Outcome Map

Planning and Prep

The Outcome Map tool builds upon the System Value Proposition, leverage points in the Intervention Strategy, and assumptions learned in Contextual Variations. These contributions can be formulated in a codesign workshop collaboration. Constructing a well-defined Outcome Map requires at least several major reviews and iterations, so a series of 3-4 short workshops could be planned, or at least as review phases with the team. It could be used to define, or be used as or instead of a theory of change.

[5] Peter Tsasis, et al. (2013). Outcome mapping for health system integration. *Journal of Multidisciplinary Healthcare.*

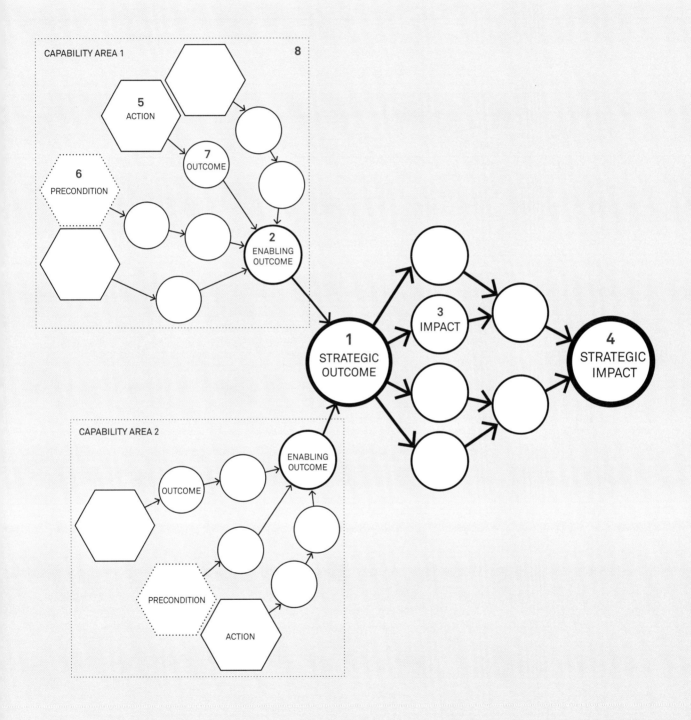

Mapping Method

Outcome maps follow an abductive logic like influence maps. They can be cocreated by backcasting (start from the end and work back) or forward chaining, or a mix of both. The following steps are a mixed progression that will facilitate an iterative map-building approach.

1. Start with the desired **Strategic Impact** – this is usually a well-defined idea. This bubble names the goal of the programme or intervention. There may be just one goal, or several (such as SDGs).

2. Identify the significant **Strategic Outcomes** – these "bubbles" are high-level subgoals that are final outcomes of a chain (these can be outcomes of interventions and their loops).

3. The strategic outcomes enable an intermediate impact, that of a **Sustaining Purpose**. For an SDG programme, for example, this could be the ongoing purpose that leads to the SDG results. This is a purpose being fulfilled by the outcomes, such as 'community resilience' as a necessary stage before an SDG target is accomplished.

4. With these anchors in place, either **Outcomes or Impacts** can be defined. The Outcomes on the left side result from the programme activities and connect the results of activities to strategic outcomes.

5. Describe the **Impacts** (on the right) realised from the sustaining purpose. They will contribute to the ultimate strategic impact. (Hint, these might be drawn from the System Value Proposition).

6. Detail major **Activities** associated with and leading to each outcome. These are more near-term projects that team members will be responsible for.

7. Identify the **Preconditions** needed to make the activities/action successful (e.g. a law should be changed, or major financing is required).

8. Group the outcome chains and related activities and capacities by drawing a background area and naming it as a potential project area (see Fig. 5-13).

Optional

– Describe the challenges and assumption for the actors to contribute to the activities. They are typically linked to resources, organisational structures, roles/mandates, skills, and mindsets.

– Define how the project activities can support the team and its partners (e.g. set up a training programme and a knowledge repository).

Delivery and Destination

The final product is a refined visualisation of the Outcome Map created from the tool, and a summary description of the programme. This can serve as a blueprint for implementation and stakeholder alignment.

Figure 5-13 shows a final outcome map for the HealthNest programme. HealthNest is a coalition of concerned professionals and organisations committed to improving health literacy in Belgium. In 2021, HealthNest created alongside its board, a dedicated task force. Its role is to first bring clarity to the complex issue of health literacy, which lies at the crossroads of health and communication. The outcome map was a main deliverable that defined the most important intervention areas for fostering health literacy in Belgium.

The mapping was constructed by first creating a system map, based on scholarly research and insight from stakeholders during workshops. The leverage points on the system map were further investigated through the value proposition and intervention strategy exercises. In this map, the activities were left out as this map was made to provide a frame for submitting projects.

Through this systems thinking and systemic design exercise, HealthNest expressed interest to ensure the projects it supports reach their successful completion with a measurable impact on health wisdom. It also wants to accelerate sensitisation around health literacy.

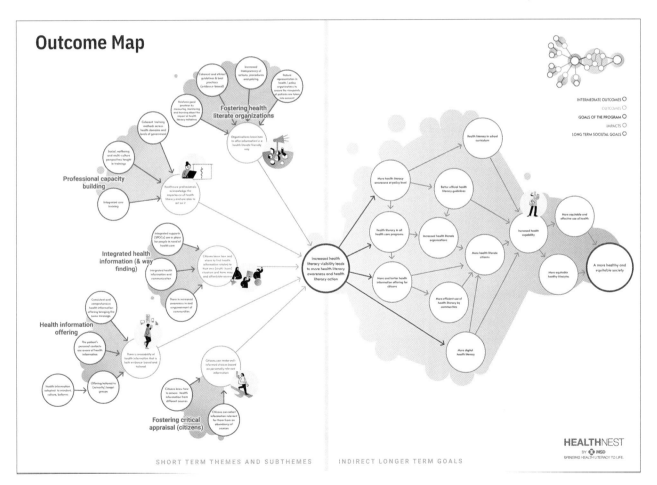

Figure 5-13
Outcome Map for HealthNest

[6] Planning the Change Process
Organising to mobilise systems change

In transformation work we often hear the term 'leading change', but what does it mean exactly to lead or design for change in complex systems? Systems are, by definition, a complex outcome of the evolution of many interconnected parts that self-organise over time. They are not designed directly and resist being de-designed directly. And likewise for complex sociotechnical systems, such as transportation or healthcare – what counts as 'leading change' in a design process, or is design itself the process of change? We believe systemic design facilitates these different design contexts relatively well with the same toolkit, as a process of *meta-planning*. Design Journeys provides a tested set of novel tools for meta-planning that help teams and organisations organise and plan transformation and complex design.

Up to this point, Design Journeys tools have facilitated framing, research, system mapping, the cocreation of a vision for system value and potential interventions for complex design or system change. The net effectiveness of the methodology, of adapting these semi-structured tools for collaboration, will be realised in the ability to propose and implement a strategy. Roadmapping tools in this chapter and in Stage [7] provide management innovations for strategic, organisational, or transition planning.

The interventions defined in [5] Exploring push on critical points where leverage has been located, creating opportunities believed by the team to result in a confluence of positive effects. After defining interventions in the different forms of cooperative governance, the collaborative team is now organised to promote the recommendations

from the preceding design work. Uniquely provided in this journey are innovations for designing organisational identity, process, and roles. These might not be required in every programme, but every major project ought to assess whether they have the best-fit organisational structures in place to lead the transition or system change.

Practical transformation planning is done by mixed-discipline design teams and (usually) a sponsoring organisation of stakeholders. Organisational transformation (Design 3.0) is not always a complementary goal in systemic design. Rather, the aim is to form a change organisation as a coalition or 'fractal team' that represents system leaders and can self-organise to lead the way. All organisation-building activates at the micro-system level, the team unit.

Facilitating Change Planning

Planning for transformation is an iterative process of managing complexity, which is itself a paradox. Traditional planning methods analyse tasks and normalise scheduling so that activities and outcomes can be coordinated over long periods of time to achieve a well-specified goal. However, no two transformation projects are alike, and the goals of systems change are always underconceptualised at first. In every organisation a demand is made on future capabilities that may not even yet exist, and success depends on the orchestrated performance of these nascent capabilities.

Design Journeys presents a simplified course that follows a methodology with tools for collaborative strategy making, but there will always be gaps in any process. These gaps provide the opportunity for learning, extension of these methods, and organically integrating with local practices. Many teams, especially in consulting and policy work, will have the research and analytical skills to use these tools to adapt them well to their style of planning. However, in Planning, fellow travellers in the team are called to decide, to organise and take action beyond the 'design.' How will your team or organisation proceed with the change interventions? Is the team prepared and ready for the journey ahead to propose, fund, and implement the programme or perhaps an entirely new organisation?

Where many of the systemic tools model cyclic and nonlinear processes, plans are often more linear by intent. All of these meta-planning methods adapt to a nonlinear temporality (as opposed to typical timeline roadmaps).

A strong human-centred focus is taken in Planning, as in Stage [2] Listening. Meta-planning and organisational development are always conducted by collaborative teams, as these are essentially social system design activities. These tools are not typical analytical processes conducted for management approval.

Four tools follow for convening collaborative design and co-developing organisational plans. Two of these are adaptations from original systemic management innovations, the TOSCA theory of change and the framework to construct the Process Enneagram, a management cybernetics approach to organisational design. The other two, Readiness Assessment and Ecosystem Governance, are new tools designed specifically for *Design Journeys*, to address recognised demands that occur in planning engagements.

Design Journeys
for Organisational Change

Theory of Systems Change and Action
The Theory of Systems Change and Action (TOSCA) constructs complex change logics supporting a programme's prospective vision for system-level change, tracing the causal chains of actions, to outcomes and impacts in order to achieve a desired strategic impact.

Process Enneagram
This tool provides a canvas for facilitating the Process Enneagram within an organisation, to explore and design a model for self-organising leadership from a complex adaptive systems (CAS) perspective. This process initiates the self-organising process that complements and supports strategic and operational leadership.

Change Readiness Assessment
The Change Readiness tool provides an assessment process as an organisational checkpoint to help determine the team's readiness to act on the systemic design proposal or systems change project.

Ecosystem Governance
Ecosystem Governance is a framework that facilitates an ecosystem analysis, similar to a social network, to define connections among networks within and across social systems and allied change programmes. The tool is useful for clarifying relationships, identifying gaps in relational support and complementary strengths, and for finding and leveraging leadership across the value constellation.

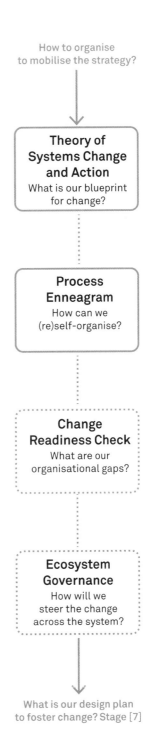

How to organise
to mobilise the strategy?

Theory of Systems Change and Action
What is our blueprint for change?

Process Enneagram
How can we (re)self-organise?

Change Readiness Check
What are our organisational gaps?

Ecosystem Governance
How will we steer the change across the system?

What is our design plan to foster change? Stage [7]

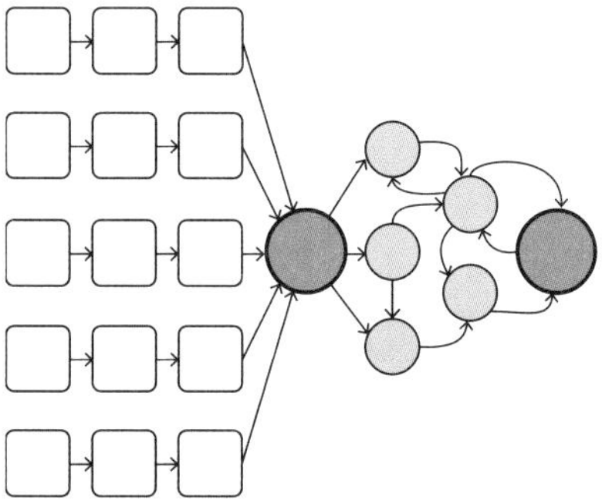

Figure 6-1
The Theory of Systems Change structure

- Time to Run:
  2-4 hours
- Session context:
  Studio
- Workshop Type:
  Roadmap
- Process time: 3+ days
- Connections to:
  [3] Influence Map
  [4] Three Horizons
  [5] Outcome Map
  [7] Transition by Design
  [7] Adaptive Cycle

Theory of Systems Change

A Theory of Change (ToC) is a structure used in large-scale social change and philanthropy programmes to present a simplified story about the planning team's model of impact for sponsors, funders and stakeholders. Over more than 30 years, the ToC has become a well-developed management innovation used to construct narratives supporting a programme's proposition for changemaking, based on a so-called logic model. A theory of change is summarised at a storyline level to show how our planned action-outcomes are expected to enact changes that lead to desired ultimate transformation goals.

Theories of change are useful to present arguments for a causal logic of impact, as well as to reveal risks and assumptions that might interfere with progress. Once developed, a ToC is referred to throughout the lifespan of a programme. It becomes a commonly-held mental model for strategic alignment across the constellation of programme participants, as a visual plan for enacting value cocreation. They are often used as frameworks for evaluation of programme effectiveness.

The ToC graphic (often represented by a simplified logic model) is a tool used to build and agree on a collective theory of change. For change at the system level, or a Theory of Systems Change, a more complex graphic is necessary to accommodate the variety of possibilities, and to reveal leverage and loops in the system model as change occurs.

A theory of change model typically consists of chains of outcomes, beginning with strategic activities and ending with the ultimate results they aim to achieve. ToCs may have any number of outcomes in between these activities and the ultimate strategic impact or goal. The basic ToC is based on a logic model, or the structure known as a *logic frame* (logframe). This structure presents three or four pathways from activities through outcomes to a single goal, usually bottom-up. The ToC can be visually defined as a simple structure for coordinating members of a project to reach consensus on the conditions and actions necessary to achieve proposed system change.

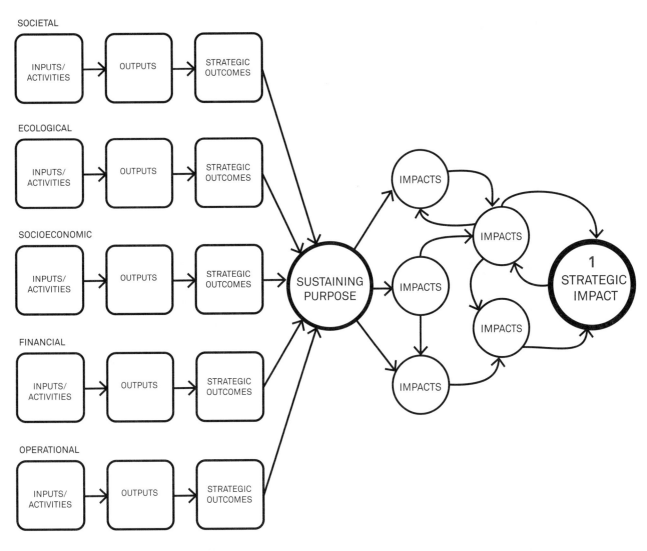

SOCIETAL

ECOLOGICAL

SOCIOECONOMIC

FINANCIAL

OPERATIONAL

... OTHER CATEGORY

STRATEGIC ASSUMPTIONS	EXPECTED RISKS	TAIL RISKS

The Theory of Systems Change is an emerging perspective developed through research into leverage analysis[1] for large-scale systems change. It has been particularly applied to the UN Sustainable Development Goals (SDGs) and promotes a more realistic consideration of complexity by defining the systems value logic of a programme's change proposal. A Theory of Systems Change answers the question: How will plans to transform the system interact with a complex environment to deliver on the promise of impact? It defines the causal structure of activities and outcomes that manifest the change in plain terms. A new modelling tool, the Theory for Systems Change and Action (TOSCA), has been developed for representing theories of change of a system (showing the causal chains of actions to desired impacts).

To retain its continuity and understanding from the logframe, there are some structural similarities to the language in the well-known ToC logic models used in social innovation and philanthropy. The TOSCA method is used here and extends several dimensions of the ToC to allow for more complex representations, including the significance of action. The 'theory of action' defines how activities in the near term are necessary to achieve outcomes. Future actions (boxes) and influences (arrows or directed arcs) show the pathways of reinforcing influence from the conditions created by successive actions over a series of stages, named as follows from the lowest to highest level:

- Assumptions and systemic risks
- Programme actions or activities that enact initial conditions
- Outputs or intermediate outcomes
- Outcomes or effects
- Strategic impact or goal

Cocreating the TOSCA

Planning and Prep

The TOSCA is prepared more like a narrative than a system map, where the product is a structured model of outcomes that produce a desired major change in a complex social system. Prior work done with causal loops, system mapping, outcome mapping, and interventions can all be used for candidate outputs and outcomes.

For the TOSCA to portray a systemic model of change, we must account for the complexity in the world in which change happens, as well as the relations between conditions and outcomes under the control of the programme leadership. In most social and systems change, we are modelling a series of action-outcomes leading to interrelated long-term goals, each of which should be specified as precisely as possible. Starting from the goals or strategic impacts, we *backcast* (build pathways backward from the goals) to define the outcomes that are necessary preconditions for enabling the change process.

The timeframe selected for a systemic theory of change is dependent on the scale of the programme logic, as well as the use and audience. A macro-ToC shows a model in which a broad

---

[1] Ryan Murphy & Peter Jones (2021). Towards systemic theories of change: High-leverage strategies for managing wicked problems. *Design Management Journal*.

sweep of major envisioned outcomes for future change might occur. The long-term impact for economic change programmes can realistically be 20 years – therefore the macro-ToC covers the project's longest-term vision and may take the form of a known frame such as Three Horizons, Crossing the Chasm, or the Berkana 'Two Loops.'

A meso-level ToC builds on outcomes aligned to proposed programme actions. Often funders and partners want to understand the project's ToC within the range of time that they might directly support. If the funding model is a necessary part of the change strategy, funding might be included as a precondition, an assumption, and possibly an outcome. A micro-level ToC can be shorter term, and expresses the methods and necessary actions supporting the other scales of change. The TOSCA can be used to model all three levels. It's recommended to maintain their separation into coherent diagrams presented at the same level of rationale for the purposes of communication and mental model clarity.

Any theory of change process provides a significant learning opportunity for a design team. Plan and convene a core team of 5-10 participants who have real-world and historical understanding of the programme and the strategy. Gather and review supporting materials in advance of the construction. Provide an overview of the expected activity and supporting materials, and like any of the tools, set up a printout or whiteboard image of the TOSCA and workshop tools. Be prepared to lead the instructions as a facilitator, attending to the ability of every participant to understand the objectives and to add propositions. Stop and check their understanding, and provide guidance on the quality of proposed outcomes and their position.

Mapping Method

1. Start with a general agreement as to the **overall timeframe** for positioning impact – as this is typically a constraint of the funder or a proposal.

2. Define and agree on the **strategic impact** that represents the qualitative system change (at the end point, the far-right of the timeline). What is the desired or necessary resulting impact? This is not always a simple process, as even small cohesive groups will have difficulty reaching consensus, often having different ideas, priorities, and language for the outcomes.

3. **Use a backcasting process to envision the necessary outcomes** that precede the ultimate goal, by tracing them back from the desired impact. What outcomes are necessary that lead to the change goal? Even though we use different terms for the near and longer-term outcomes, essentially all the noun phrases on the pathway are outcomes or **preconditions for other outcomes.** Following the strategic impact, at each step backward, generate with the team the outcomes necessary to achieve these impacts at that level. A typical prompt is 'what are the necessary preconditions for these outcomes at this stage?'

4. Often the middle ground of causal connections will seem fuzzy and undefined, and it will be tempting to make linear connections to connect the map. At this point, it is helpful to **work from the present forward** (the left), making multiple connections to the pathways.

5. **List initial outputs, one per box**, aligned to programme functions if these are used (and listed on the left column). Outcomes result from major programme activities. Chains of outcomes are

the result of actions, and action-outcomes define pathways from the starting point. Generate short outcome phrases (with sticky notes or the same with an online whiteboard) to propose the intermediate outcomes.

6. **Assumptions and systemic risks** can be defined at the start of the exercise and listed in a foundations zone where they can apply anywhere in the model, as they evolve and are changed by future events. Assumptions are often discovered through the exercise of mapping out the steps of system change. Capture (on the side) suggestions that are assumptions for the process to be successful, and risks to the outcomes, if they are not part of the change logic.

7. The final TOSCA model is tested by reading from the start to finish carefully, assessing the steps associated with each level. Indicators for evaluation for key outcomes can be identified and agreed as proposed markers for system evaluation.

Delivery and Destination

Completing a final theory of change can take time as a learning and developmental process. A ToC is commonly defined for an organisational mission or funding proposals, and the activity leads to a commonly held narrative structure that aligns with key activities and programme evaluation. The workshop designer should plan for such a series of iterations to proceed from longer and more complex TOSCA diagrams (or even full influence maps) toward simpler and more concise narratives, with more concrete language and fewer 'boxes and bubbles' with each turn.

For groups new to the theory of change process, the tool will be useful as a template from which to start. It is helpful to construct the TOSCA on an interactive whiteboard accessible to all team members (or a printed poster for a Studio session). Consider the template a 'training wheels' approach as the iterations will inevitably lead to a customised diagram, and of course, a final version that can be rendered into slide decks for proposal pitches or sharing. The discussions associated with each iteration will disclose increasingly more mental models, and will require attaining agreement among core members of a planning team on impacts and assumptions, and the progressive influences of outcomes. The point is to align team commitments to a complex change proposal, a proposal that will essentially become a plan and a shared mental model for future action.

Travel Tips

Planning for complex systems or change campaigns is no more linear than the resulting models. As we act on behalf of organisations for future change initiatives, a shared understanding of intractable complexity and messy guesswork emerges. We risk biasing programme planning with assumptions and the linear logic of first-order causality. The TOSCA provides for several unique system descriptions not explicitly included in other ToCs:

— Nonlinear influence pathways resulting in outcomes
— Indications of leverage to suggest the strongest points of influence across the network
— Feedback loops from outcomes and impacts, reinforcing initial influences
— Multiple initial conditions are indicated (STEEP categories)
— Inclusion of environmental complexity and systems

It can be challenging to construct a ToC, or the TOSCA, as a collaborative process. The TOSCA is not a simple logic-style theory of change. It was designed to address complex, big-picture systems change proposals such as country-level SDG programmes or social movements with major change outcomes and complex causality. Yet, too much generative ideation can overwhelm the creation process. Involving too many 'possible' outcomes will instead necessitate commitment to a plausible model of causation. The TOSCA is formed by careful assessment of the probability of real outcomes effected over different temporal periods of activity. Defining this logic is best done as an analytical task with 2-3 people developing the model on a whiteboard and sharing in iterative discussions.

When mapping changes in a complex system, outcomes in distinct functional domains can be identified as the different constituencies in the system are affected by the change. Several categories are suggested in the model (Societal, Ecological, Socioeconomic, Financial, Operational) for assigning outcomes within these expected domains. Each domain might show lags in outcome from others, as typical of system effects. Societal (and ecological) outcomes take time and will not manifest for at least an intermediate time period, after several other developmental processes have proceeded in the other domains. Outputs in these domains will continue to cause a chain of outcomes toward the impact goal.

In the middle of the TOSCA, intermediate outcomes will develop. These are considered evolutionary – not directly action-related as these outcomes evolve from the effects of prior outcomes through the system environment. These may be enabled by outcomes from other programmes that develop around the region or context of the system change (e.g. allied programmes or social movements).

There are two other critical factors to developing and using a systemic theory of change, and those are a) assumptions, and b) evaluation. These represent entire discourses within professional evaluation practice and cannot be adequately developed in a handbook style. Yet, some brief points might assist fellow travellers in seeking appropriate resources to continue with systemic planning and evaluation.

Evaluation Process

Design Journeys offers only minimal guidance for evaluation, by design. The seven-stage design process ends with transition or launch – thereby evaluations within the Journeys are feedbacks to update and iterate maps and plans. However, in Planning, we define indicators for assessment of future value or successful outcomes. A workable theory of change should be defined so that the action-outcomes are directly useful in evaluation. If a developmental evaluation process (such as Principles-Focused Evaluation[2]) is contemplated for the programme during implementation, the formation of initial qualitative principles might be drawn from the values and themes developed in Stages [4] through [7], and especially in the Theory of Systems Change.

---

[2] Michael Quinn Patton (2017). *Principles-Focused Evaluation: The Guide*. Guilford Publications.

Case Study – Bounce Beyond Theory of Transformation

Bounce Beyond is an organisation started by a core team of systems practitioners and change leaders in the UK and North America that spun-off from an academic ecological economics research programme. It was formed to curate and enable promising bioregional and industry initiatives that demonstrate real progress toward alternative, wellbeing or flourishing economies. Bounce Beyond defines these initiatives as 'transformation catalysts' that have the potential to grow into leading alternative models while creating significant localised value.

As with many social innovation programmes, several theories of change were advanced and considered. An early-stage influence map, connecting over 100 outcomes, was originally cocreated along with a macro-level Theory of Change to guide planning. As macro ToCs are typically high-level stories of long-term change, a meso-level theory of systems change was developed to define nearer-term change logic and impacts in social-economic change.

The following narrative describes a story logic pattern for the TOSCA graphic in Figure 6-2. This is a typical prose structure that should accompany any theory of change, but is important to show when using a more nonlinear model such as the TOSCA.

The ultimate impact of Bounce Beyond (BB) is "A world where people have mobilised their communities, organisations and countries to shift from exploitative economies to move toward regenerative, life-valuing economies that benefit all."

This is achieved over time by successful accomplishment of outcomes that include:

1. Building regional and global knowledge and action networks
   – So that BB influences change makers, researchers, networks, institutions
   – And that BB recruits and partners with 5-7 next economy initiatives

2. These actions support a powerful convergence of stakeholders to convene a next economy platform for dialogues to connect and sustain global learning
   – BB initiatives influence social/economics research
   – Flourishing economy narratives become widely adopted
   – Social infrastructures are catalysed by initiatives for flourishing economies
     These demonstrate emerging economic harmony with people & planet

3. The selection and development of high-impact initiatives
   – Demonstrate the initial evolutionary potential of regenerative economic innovation
   – Demonstrate the impact of transformation catalysts as they are evolved
   – BB becomes a transformation engine to build a larger network and lead adoption
   – So that, initiatives will achieve envisioned impacts in their contexts
   – And BB validates the intent and manifests the transformation system

So that we will see the groundwork for a world where people have mobilised their communities, organisations and countries to move toward regenerative, wellbeing economies that benefit all.

The TOSCA model for the Bounce Beyond programme, its Theory of Transformation, is fairly complex, and for presentation purposes, a next step of simplification has been done. The model of change outcomes is predicated on the success of its cadre of Collaborative Next Economies initiatives. Each of these initiatives are developed as unique economic change models, as change catalysts for their own contexts, and each holds its own theory of change and vision for regional or industry economic transformation. Bounce Beyond employs systems methods and a consultative design process to facilitate their programme development, as well as their engagement in broader research and deliberations to change economic values at regional and national levels.

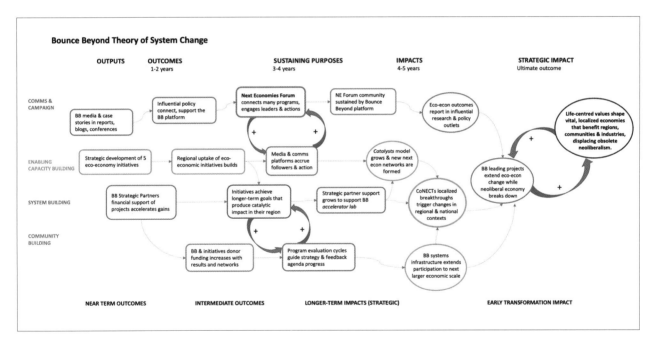

Figure 6-2
TOSCA model defining Bounce Beyond's theory of economic change

Process Enneagram

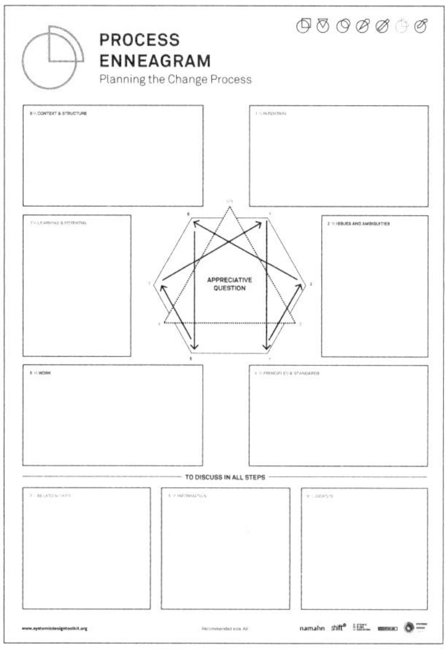

Figure 6-3
The Process Enneagram

— Time to Run:
  2-4 hours
— Session context:
  Lab or Studio
— Workshop Type:
  Codesign
— Process time:
  3+ days
— Connections to:
  [3] Social Ecosystem Map
  [6] Future State Scenarios
  [6] Theory of Systems Change
  [6] Ecosystem Governance
  [7] Collaboration Model

The Process Enneagram[3] is a complete system of organisational definition and structuring, based on a second order cybernetics approach to complexity. Developed since 1990 by Richard Knowles, the Process Enneagram uses the well-known Enneagram framework as a collective model of social qualities and performance commitments. It is not based on the popular personality model – it is a different process adapted to the same figuration.

Organisations are self-organising processes, and like many of the tools and processes in systemic design, a process cocreated by the stakeholders themselves. In systems theory, organisations function as open systems, as *dissipative* (kept coherent by constant energy flows to sustain) and *metastable* (a stable identity over time) systems. The self-organisation of complexity involves several processes: patterns (clues to invisible functions), uncertainty (inability to predict the future), and fractals (similar configurations at multiple levels of scale). The process is designed to facilitate organisations in moving up – from organisations focused on problems and problem-solving to a dynamic social system moving up its self-organising criticality. This notion derives from complexity theory, where high-functioning teams operate at the 'edge of chaos,' and maintain coherence and meta-stability by organising around a core purpose and shared identity.

The use of the Process Enneagram is a focused, disciplined, and dialogical process in which an organisation gains crucial insights about the needed organisational change, guide by a series of questions around the nine perspectives of the enneagram. The dialogue releases the emotional energy and commitment to do the work quicky and well. The tool is used by core teams within organisations to map out and enhance purposeful work together, and thus collaborate much more effectively to achieve the intended goal.

The elements on the right of the Process Enneagram help to co-create a shared value system, and an open and stimulating environment. The elements on the left side guide thinking around activities needed to accomplish the goal.

---

[3] Richard Knowles (2002). *The Leadership Dance: Pathways to Extraordinary Organizational Effectiveness.* The Center for Self-Organizing Leadership.

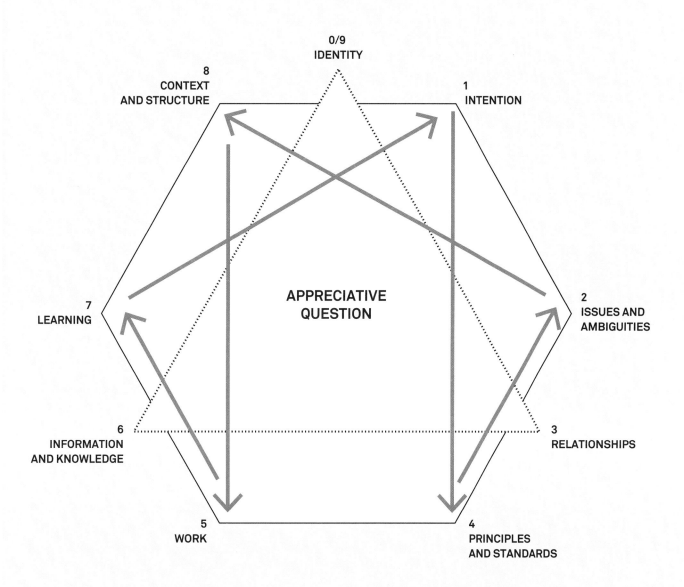

Cocreating the Process Enneagram

Planning and Prep

The Process Enneagram diagram represents an entire organisational process for defining a complex, adaptive, self-organising network of people in a working collaboration within a single diagram. The method is run in a three-phase process of 'Plan – Cocreate – Deliver.' The Process Enneagram is not merely a modelling tool, it drives a whole-organisation inquiry, where the canvas model is used as a guideline.

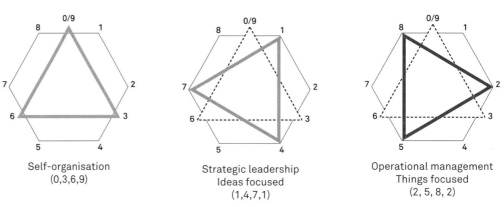

Self-organisation
(0,3,6,9)

Strategic leadership
Ideas focused
(1,4,7,1)

Operational management
Things focused
(2, 5, 8, 2)

Figure 6-4
The Process Enneagram triangles

The three phases of the process are as follows:

1. Set up the context for the exercise. For the proposals to be taken seriously as guidance for the organisation, everyone must understand how the results will be used. Start the workshop with a full core team. Use a short presentation to explain the concepts. The Process Enneagram starts as an open circle, the 'crucible' in which the organisation is contained.

2. Run the tool as a full process as in the steps below. Place the tool as a canvas or image on the group whiteboard. Cocreate inputs for all the steps and questions following the numbered order. Refer to the three colours of the labels and reflect those in the answers. These refer to the three components (triangles) of Identity (green), Strategy (blue), and Operation (red).

3. Discuss the meaning of the completed model. Walk through the diagram following the Enneagram pattern (by the arrows connecting the pattern, not by the numbered order). Discuss the three triangles (Figure 6-4): *Self-Organising, Strategic, Operational* as these summarise the three composite models of the organisation.

Mapping Method

In each step, the facilitator guides participants to generate responses to the questions pertaining to the Enneagram points. Each point might require from as few as 5 minutes to as much as 20 minutes of ideation and discussion. Because the main objective is to construct a model of the organisation and agree on its purposes and functions, dialogue is necessary in each step. All responses to each question can be consolidated into patterns that reflect the meaning of the participants. The tool template can be filled either by notes posted up by participants, or by direct text entries by the facilitator in a verbal discussion.

Start the workshop with developing the compelling, complex, 'opening question.' This provides the focus and the container for the dialogue going forward. Create questions of an Appreciative Inquiry[4] nature, which assumes a positive shared context and are oriented toward an idealised possible future by asking 'what is our common dream and why do we want to make it happen?' All the dialogue that follows, and the creation of the Process Enneagram, is related to this opening question.

Steps following the numbered points on the Enneagram:

1. Start at **Identity** (0/9) and declare identity as a group, as a social system. Who are the members of the team cocreating the circle? List everyone. What are we standing for? Where do we come from, how did our identity evolve? How is our goal linked to our identity? How does each step above strengthens or threatens our identity? How are we individually relating to the team/organisational identity?

2. The group moves to (1), **Intention**, by asking the following questions: Why are we together? What are the ultimate outcomes we intend to achieve? Is our intent clear to everyone involved or anyone affected? What value do we want to create for the multiple levels and perspectives (see also the value proposition)?

3. At (2), what are the **Issues and Ambiguities** we expect to encounter? Think about both internal as external challenges – e.g. internal: capacity and time; and external: acceptance by stakeholders. Are there paradoxes at play? Do we see tensions or even potential conflicts? Do we understand sufficiently the underlying causes of the tensions? What do we not want to happen? Most teams know the problematic issues being faced in the organisation well. Look over material from the Actors and Activity Maps to inform this step, if they apply to the organisation.

4. List and describe the nature of (3) **Relationships**. What are your relationships like? How do we engage with each other? How are we connected to others in the system (e.g. cross departmental or with internal organisations)? What is the quality of these connections? Are there enough or too little connection? Is there trust and interdependence? How can we improve our relationships for each step above?

5. Next, discuss the underpinning (4) **Principles and Standards** of behaviour, action, and decision-making (e.g. trust, accountability, sharing, etc.). How different is this from the current principles and standards? There is a need to bring the espoused values and values-in-use together to close the gap. This gap is often the cause of major trouble in groups coming together.

6. What is the nature and the tasks of (5) **Work** to be done? What are the activities that define the organisation today? What capacities do we already have and could build upon? How might we

[4] David Cooperrider developed Appreciative Inquiry for his PhD dissertation (1986), with a body of accessible work following this methodology for whole-system organisational flourishing.

(re)organise our work to achieve the goals?

7. How is (6) **Information and Knowledge** produced and shared? Does everyone involved know what is going on? What mechanisms are in place to make sure everybody understands and can contribute to the steps above? What are the key touchpoints to make the information flow across the system? Should we improve the current touchpoints?

8. Next, cocreate the (7) **Learning and Potential possibilities**. What do we want to learn from the change process? How can we measure failure and success? How can we create multiple learning loops in our organisation? What type of mechanisms should we have in place to adapt the process?

9. Finally, define the (8) **Context and Structure**. What is happening around us? How is our work domain evolving? What are others doing? How should we reorganise to cope with challenges? How should we organise ourselves to do the work? Should the overall strategy be changed? What is our change strategy?

Hold a dialogue that navigates the perimeter of the nine points to cohere the group's mental picture, and to affirm commitments, as well as the 'who and what' of the social system. The inner patterns tell us 'how and why' things happen as they do. The *Self-Organising* pattern (0, 3, 6, 9) defines the organisational identity and brings life into the process. The *Doing* pattern (which includes *Strategic* (1, 4, 7, 1) and *Operational* (2, 5, 8, 2)) shows the cycle used to answer the opening question and inform the production of work.

Delivery and Destination

The Process Enneagram is designed as a core stimulant for appreciative discussion to generate consensus on commitments, organisational decisions, and direction setting.

The diagram produced by the total set of contributions can be reviewed and revised immediately after the exercise, and/or be refined for presentation in a single slide (with details in an accompanying document). The completed image of the Process Enneagram (with the crucible or bowl), including summary lists for each point, can be provided as a fractal model of the organisational concept and goals. This image or presentation can be used in plans and organisational strategies. In discussions following the workshop, it can be raised as a touchstone and as guidelines to be reminded of commitments and core values.

Travel Tips

It is important to keep this living, strategic organisational plan current and in circulation, especially during times of changing conditions or successful progress. Revisit it to remind everyone of the plan and agreements, add content to reflect new information and delete goals or commitments that have been completed. Write the changes onto the chart and when it gets too messy, construct a new chart to show the current state.

One good practice is to begin each team meeting with 10 minutes of reflection with the framework to recreate commitments to needed changes and as a presencing activity to revitalise the shared image of the organisational identity.

8 \\ CONTEXT & STRUCTURE

- World is in crisis, societies need this alternative
- Geographies, Societies, Industries
- Self-organized teams
- Core team of Stewards
- Advisory Board
- Active Partnerships

1 \\ INTENTION

- Bring to life new economic paradigms
- Demonstrate a transformative way of working
- Connect, Cohere and Amplify
- Tell new stories about what's possible for the future
- Transform ourselves to embody the new stories
- Find examples of the New Economies—Cohere
- Exemplify the transformation catalyst concept
- Working towards a flourishing future for all

7 \\ LEARNING & POTENTIAL

- Participative re-patterning
- Personal growth
- New transformational pathways being created
- Making the Implicit Explicit
- Helping people see what's possible
- Learning about Next Economies context
- Develop transdisciplinary expertise
- Reflect on learnings

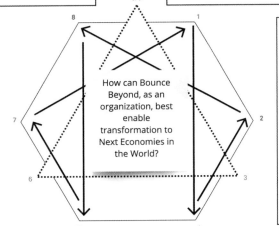

How can Bounce Beyond, as an organization, best enable transformation to Next Economies in the World?

2 \\ ISSUES AND AMBIGUITIES

- Funding & cash flow
- Individual capacity (and time)
- Explaining our work & its value
- Positioning in the larger system
- Working as a team
- Different mental models
- Is anyone listening?
- A sense of urgency

5 \\ WORK

- Develop relationships w/ sponsors & partners
- Identify & implement for value
- Co-create programs with partners
- Learn & grow ourselves & with communities
- We work on our own evolution as individuals
- Find models to transform economies
- Be in transformative dialogue with communities

4 \\ PRINCIPLES & STANDARDS

- Respect, Authenticity, Trust
- Humility
- Acknowledging mistakes
- Accountability
- Telling the truth
- as you see it
- Listening for
- understanding
- Active participation
- Taking responsibility
- Empathy
- Seek reconciliation
- Willingness to learn
- Share all information
- Seek diversity & appreciate it
- Passion & commitment
- Feedback to whole group

--- **TO DISCUSS IN ALL STEPS** ---

3 \\ RELATIONSHIPS

- Trust is developing
- Interdependence needs development
- Roles are emerging
- Respect for each others' approaches

6 \\ INFORMATION

- Website. media & online presence
- Zoom + Some F2F meetings
- Academic publishing, conferences
- Online training
- Webinars
- Community platform

9 \\ IDENTITY

- Diverse group of pioneer thinkers
- Deep context backgrounds
- Virtual & Self-organized group
- Passion & commitment
- Transdisciplinary experts

Figure 6-5
The Process Enneagram results of the Bounce Beyond project

Change Readiness Assessment

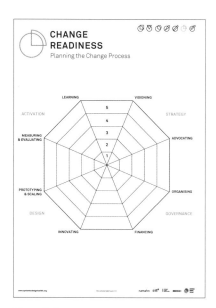

Figure 6-6
The Change Readiness Assessment

— Time to Run:
.5-1 hour
— Session context:
Studio
— Workshop type:
Sensemaking
— Connections to:
[4] System Value Proposition
[5] Outcome Map
[6] Theory of Systems Change
[6] Process Enneagram

The third tool in this Journey is the Organisational Readiness Assessment, designed as a novel tool to fill a gap perceived in the continuity of systemic design for change. The assessment can be used as a quick internal evaluation of capabilities, organisational readiness, innovation capacity, and team development. The tool provides a critical determination for which a team must be honest – if a systemic design (and proposal) team is not the right group to staff and lead the systems change initiative, a transparent self-reflection should be made. The checklist format will help guide this assessment and provide feedback to the organisation about steps to be taken for progress on readiness and team confidence.

Checking Change Team Readiness

Planning and Prep

The purpose of the Change Readiness tool is to assess the development capacity, functional readiness, and maturity of a team, organisation, or multistakeholder coalition. The tool is designed as a radar diagram, which can be posted or printed and annotated with responses by a workshop facilitator. The radar is structured around eight dimensions, cross-sectioned by five levels of concentric octagons within the diagram boundary.

The eight dimensions are nominally defined as follows (drawn from Steve Waddell's model[5] of societal transformation systems):

1. Visioning
2. Organising
3. Financing
4. Learning
5. Measuring & evaluating
6. Advocating
7. Innovation process capacity
8. Prototyping & scaling

---

[5] Steve Waddell (2016). Societal change systems: A framework to address wicked problems. *The Journal of Applied Behavioral Science.*

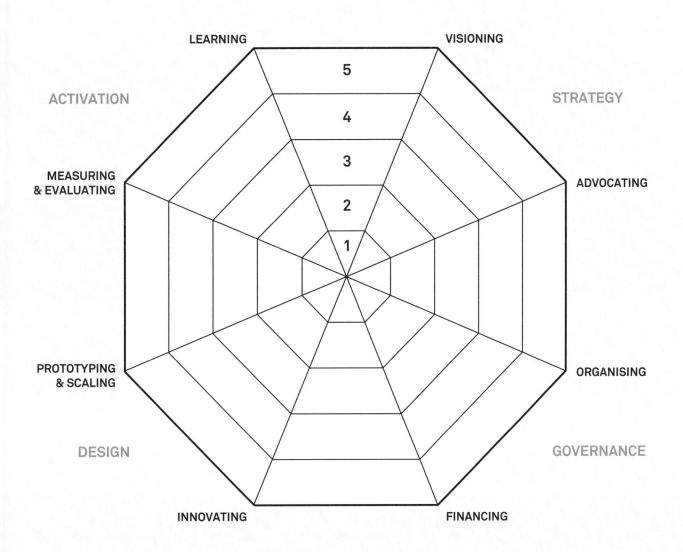

These are paired into four clusters of capability areas: Strategy, Governance, Design, and Activation.

The relative scores marked at each point in the radar scale can be referenced by the maturity of each dimension as developed in the organisation. An evaluation can be done by checking-off the relative maturity level at the time of review.

— Level 1: Ad hoc level, no process
— Level 2: Initial level of process in place
— Level 3: Defined processes in place at a project level
— Level 4: Alignment between projects and organisational management
— Level 5: Capability is defined at a strategic level with continuous improvement

Mapping Method

The Change Readiness tool can be convened by a small group or a full team. Set up the evaluation criteria for the tool and instruct participants to score each dimension with an indicated level or number according to the assessed readiness level. Decide on the organisational scale to be assessed: team, organisation, or a multi-member coalition. Assess the following dimensions:

Strategy
1. **Visioning**: What is the level of shared purpose and direction? Is a common mission narrative emerging and communicated both internally and externally?
2. **Advocating**: What level of programme advocacy or diffusion is currently demonstrated? Does the team have a realistic change strategy that generates pressure and energy for change?

Governance
3. **Organising**: What level of organisational structure is in place or being developed? What degree of internal development (process and practices) and external (advisories and constellation network) is being coordinated?
4. **Financing**: What financial resources are available and continuing for the initial phases of implementation? How well-developed are plans and support for attracting funding in later phases?

Design
5. **Innovation**: Score the level of skill and multidisciplinarity of the implementation team. What level of innovation experience is assessed for team leads? Do the available team competencies represent a complementary mix of skills?
6. **Prototyping and scaling**: What is the capacity for rapid prototyping of sociotechnical services? How well prepared is the core team at team organising, policy development, communications, and service design? How well developed is the capacity to scale to larger social systems?

Activation
7. **Measuring and evaluating**: Does the programme have an evaluation process in place to assess the programme outcomes and impacts? At project, programme, and societal level (see also outcomes in Outcome Map of [5] Exploring)?
8. **Learning**: Does the whole organisation have the knowledge and capacity to implement transformation? What processes and tools are in place to share and build knowledge?

A score can be derived from the assessments of each dimension, relative to general progress over time. With eight dimensions and five levels to be scored from 1-5, the highest possible single score is 40, and the lowest is 8. However, single number scores might only be of value for determining the magnitude of change over time.

The best measure of readiness would be adapted to the readiness of selected dimensions critical to the performance of a given change programme or project. Scores associated with each of the four summary themes might be more valued for these purposes, between 2-10. For the early stages of a new project, Strategy and Design might be more critical to success than Governance or Activation. Immediately preceding implementation, the emphasis might be switched, requiring further development of management and evaluation practices.

Delivery and Destination

The Change Readiness tool provides an important reference model for comparison of programme and team development over time, and for use in proposals and funding discussions to demonstrate capacity level associated with programme management. The completed diagram can be rendered as an image from an online whiteboard to be circulated in presentations or reports. Figure 6-7 shows a completed map for the Bounce Beyond case, which can be used as a baseline for facilitating this tool.

There is insufficient data on the use of the model in this tool form. Organisations using this might determine their criteria for the level of readiness necessary for a project greenlight, funding pitch, or stage-gate decision based on an agreed level of performance readiness.

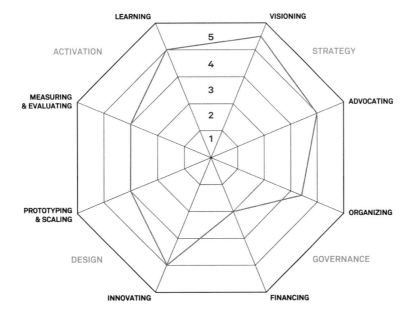

Figure 6-7
The Change Readiness results of the Bounce Beyond project

Ecosystem Governance

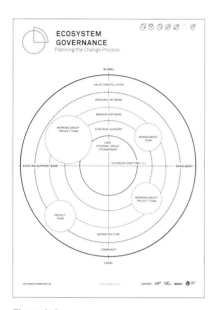

Figure 6-8
The Ecosystem Governance

- Time to Run:
  2-4 hours
- Session context:
  Studio
- Workshop Type:
  Roadmap
- Process time:
  1+ day
- Connections to:
  [6] Theory of Systems Change
  [6] Change Readiness
  [7] Transition by Design

The Ecosystem Governance tool provides a uniquely designed, fit-to-purpose framework for the planning stage of the Journeys. Its purpose is to analyse and map out a programme's organisational networks to confirm agreement about their contribution to the mission. The tool adapts concepts of the Social Ecosystem from [3] Understanding. Ecosystem Governance maps the relations among networks and actors in system-wide network governance. The tool is found useful for clarifying relationships, identifying gaps in relational support and complementary strengths, and finding and leveraging leadership across the value constellation.

The Ecosystem Governance framework was inspired by Stafford Beer's Viable System Model (VSM),[6] a foundation of management cybernetics structured as a whole-system model of organisational coordination (itself inspired by the communications functions of the nervous system). The VSM models the distribution of management functions from strategy and governance to line-level operations. But the VSM model also has no generally accepted multi-organisational model that might apply in a true network or ecosystem context, in a non-market-facing non-profit or mixed-stakeholder mission team.

Based more on the Social Ecosystem model than VSM directly, the Ecosystem Governance tool was adapted for the mission-based network organisation. It can be used to define leadership, influence, and relations among networks within and across social systems and allied change programmes. Activities and strategies coordinated across multiple organisation teams and groups, rather than a firm or single-purpose team, is useful for task and role clarification, emergent leadership formation, and governance across the network or programme ecosystem.

Mapping Ecosystem Governance

Planning and Prep

Ecosystem Governance can be used in transformation system planning as a mapping tool to plan and communicate programme governance roles and leadership. A baseline model of the current social ecosystem can be mapped

---

[6] Stafford Beer (1984). The Viable System Model: Its provenance, development, methodology and pathology. *Journal of the Operational Research Society*.

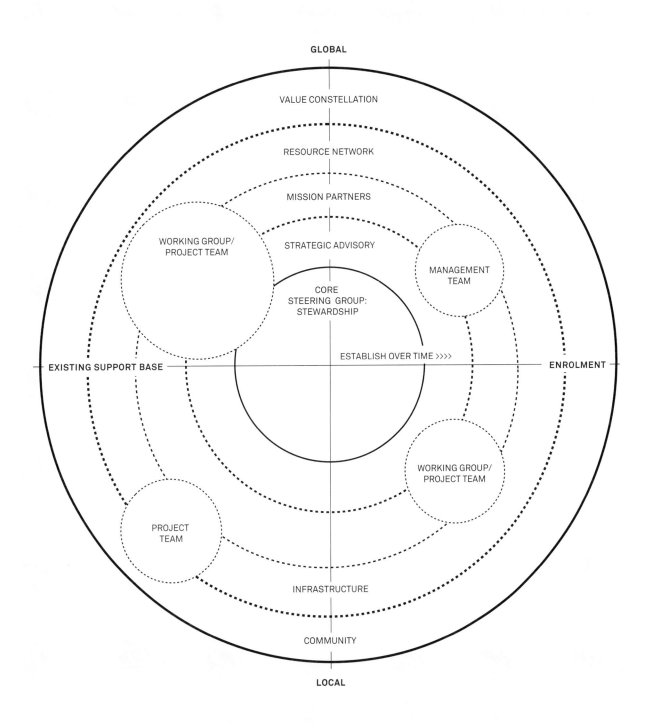

GLOBAL

VALUE CONSTELLATION

RESOURCE NETWORK

MISSION PARTNERS

STRATEGIC ADVISORY

WORKING GROUP/
PROJECT TEAM

MANAGEMENT
TEAM

CORE
STEERING GROUP:
STEWARDSHIP

ESTABLISH OVER TIME >>>>

EXISTING SUPPORT BASE

ENROLMENT

WORKING GROUP/
PROJECT TEAM

PROJECT
TEAM

INFRASTRUCTURE

COMMUNITY

LOCAL

as a network analysis of the current networks and organisations that support the mission. This baseline can be updated as players change and can show gaps and opportunities across the levels of the ecosystem. A further gap analysis can be done to compare the current ecosystem baseline and capabilities, and the intended future ecosystem. A second map can be made to develop future complementary initiatives outside the current ecosystem.

Mapping Method

The model is defined by ecosystem level (circles), relative time (X), and collaboration scale (Y). As with other tools, entries can be generated by individual responses within the levels, followed by analysis and clustering of common content. Entries do not have to be entered in the sequence shown here, as they can be nonlinear as with many tools. This sequence can be considered a strategist's view, from the core group perspective, to develop the working teams for action in the ecosystem.

1. Start by defining the **Core/Steering Group** in the centre. This would typically be the planning group defining the map. As system planners, the core group steers the common purpose, defines and adjusts strategic direction, builds partnerships, and determines success indicators. The core group is complemented by representatives of the partners in the ecosystem to increase endorsement advocacy for the programme.

2. Locate and list **Strategic Advisors**, the trusted experts and colleagues closest to the organisation that help inform the programme. This circle is most helpful for external advising on disciplinary expertise, to review work in progress, and for leveraging their networks to recruit power competencies as the programme progresses.

3. Plot **Mission Partners** who are connected to other networks and organisations. These might be direct funders or those that can help locate funding streams. Located outside the organisation, they have valuable information about significant changes and consequently, how the programme should adapt to stay viable and relevant. They will also be very valuable in the scale-up phase, helping to implement and spread the new practices.

4. Map out the **Resource Network** (and/or coordinating infrastructure) necessary to support expansion and to execute the strategy. Depending on the programme, this might require a project management office, communications teams, financial administration, monitoring and evaluation, event coordination, resource management, online community building, cross-group relationship management, and knowledge building (e.g. learning networks).

5. Define the **Communities and/or Constellations** to be engaged. This can include civil society, but also government or academic groups that can be drawn in as allies. Having multiple communities in the social ecosystem enables the recruitment of experts, leaders, or special interest groups – often under-represented or otherwise not engaged in an initiative without such a specialised effort.

6. Define the **Management and Working Groups/Teams** that are tasked to implement the primary activities. These can be intact multidisciplinary teams working towards intended outcomes, which is typical of an established organisation. For a new programme, a single working group

starting up in pilot mode is typical, and one of the goals of this mapping is to ensure the planners have ecosystem capacity to recruit from and support the development of the working group into a functioning startup team.

Tool Tips

The template shows circles for four Team locations that are indicated as possible inclusions. This size of the bubble is defined to cover the different levels of ecosystem that team is drawn from and has responsibility for. These examples may not be needed, depending on the teams in a given programme. The position of the team bubble is indicated to cover the circles at the levels of engagement in the ecosystem. The placement is also a finding, as well as a judgement to be determined by the organisation. Also note the X-axis placement, where an intact team might be placed to the left and new or planned teams 'in progress' can be placed the right of the timeline (Enrolment).

Delivery and Destination

The Ecosystem Governance tool should be used iteratively and as a complement with other organisational strategy tools in this stage. It will best be updated over time as a living model, as a map of the social context of complementary relationships. Updates to the Process Enneagram might lead to updates of the social ecosystem, but the Ecosystem Governance map will not directly influence the Enneagram, as the organisational identity defines its role in the ecosystem.

This tool also provides a helpful reference for programme development over time, and for use in proposals and evaluation. The completed diagram can be rendered as an image from an online whiteboard to be circulated in presentations or reports.

Travel Tips

This tool can be used concurrently with, or to guide organisational decision-making for social system design. The form and relationship of core planning groups, partners, and working teams require some iteration and feedback from members of these groups. Team formation can be either management-defined or self-organising, or even improvised collaborations that become teams.

There will typically be several inputs available from the other tools preceding it, not only in this stage but even from minimal versions of the Intervention Model and the capability areas of the Outcome Map in Stage [5] Exploring.

Case Example

The Ecosystem Governance tool is depicted in Figure 6-9 as a model representing a current case, defined to show sufficient representations of the governance concepts of a working research institute involved in transformation programmes. While the tool looks conceptually similar to the Social Ecosystem in Figure 3-2 (including the timeline of a chronosystem) the ecosystem of the transformation organisation is very different than the social ecosystem of social actors and system participants. The multilevel nested system is adapted here to show the range of social support, resource networks, and other organisations that contribute to the mission and projects of the change team.

The presented model is a simplified case and has been edited to present salient aspects useful for understanding its. application. In many cases the transformation team will be created as a group within a larger network, or will be a leadership team within a non-profit or institute such as in the case. The names and assignments associated with the groups are dynamic and subject to change. The use of this tool is meant to show the significance of multiple relationships and advising and support functions across a dynamic network. In most cases of systemic design or transformation projects, programme teams will be constructed for their relevance and relationships to the extended social systems of action and support.

The case shows the Flourishing Enterprise Institute (FEI)[7] as an active research organisation based on a network model with relationships across North America and Europe. The FEI was formed with a small core team of leadership, who also are consultancy owners or professors. Depicted in the map, the FEI shows a research working group for a programme known as MARC (Municipalities Adapting in Response to Complexity) and this larger research team includes members from all levels of network as suggested by its placement.

The FEI leads various internal and collaborative projects, and a single project team is dedicated to manage grants and communications as shown. While these teams draw from the core team members, they are all different compositions of members. Actors within the model are not exclusive to a single assignment. The management team is in a state of formation, with some core team leaders also moving into programme and organisational management. Several universities, consultancies, and other partners are involved in the FEI network as active members of the resource network, and some more directly in value cocreation (service provision or direct work).

[7] The Flourishing Enterprise Institute was co-founded in 2019 with the assistance of a Connection Grant from the Social Science and Humanities Research Council (SSHRC) of Canada, by Peter Jones and Antony Upward, with Manuel Reimer of Wilfrid Laurier University and Randy Sa'd of REFOCUS. flourishingenterpriseinstitute.org

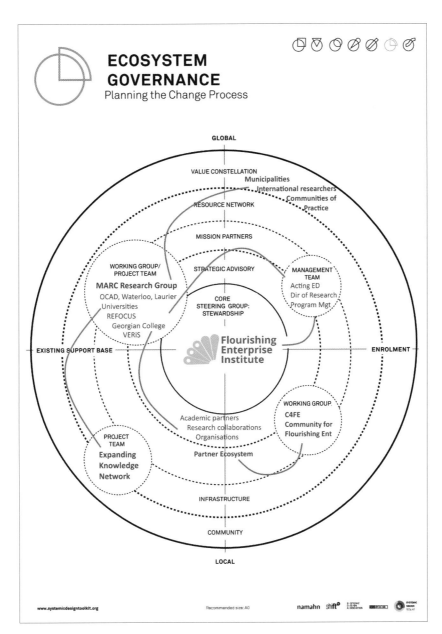

Figure 6-9.
Ecosystem Governance model for the Flourishing Enterprise Institute.

[7] Fostering the Transition
Preparing the transition to transformation

We might observe that a major weakness of design methodologies (not to mention systems practices) is the lack of positive guidance for implementation. In many well-known five-stage design processes, we find 'delivery' given as the conclusion of an intensive design programme. Implementation is left to the client organisation. Even if the leading functions of a systemic design project are imagining, prototyping, and validating innovations, we can offer much from experience in leading successful transition.

In [7] Fostering the Transition we do not fully redeem this shortcoming. The primary rationale for this step is to prepare and advise an implementation team, whether the same as the design team or not, for the execution of audacious strategies promising long-term value in a complex system or transformation programme. Transition, more than the other stages, requires a core team to lead from their own practical knowledge and ethical understanding. Moving into coordinated action draws upon skills of *phronesis,* one of Aristotle's three forms of knowledge. The majority of *Design Journeys* embeds two learned forms of knowledge in the tools – the theoretical frameworks of *episteme* and the technical practice of *techné.* A selection of complementary systems theories and models for system change and design have been developed based on their epistemic value. As tools, we have reduced the cognitive workload of learning and translating these methods for each application. Their

techné is demonstrated by their validity (in our experience) as practical techniques that fulfil complex requirements, and are reusable and teachable as well. Moving from planning to doing demands practical knowledge, that blends experience, ethics and judgment. Flyvbjerg's[1] work on planning for complex megaprojects emphasises phronesis as pragmatic and realist, a problem-driven orientation for which tools can only be supportive. Flyvbjerg focuses on issues of purpose and direction, of desirability, of power and benefit, of gains and risks – all with practical ethical import.

We cannot embed phronesis into the tools. We can only point out how to take a pragmatic approach, and help to develop social wisdom, repertoires of skilled experience, and practical ethical insight within the team. These qualities can only be suggested by the tools; they are not defined as a series of steps.

---

[1] Bent Flyvbjerg (2004). Phronetic planning research: Theoretical and methodological reflections. *Planning Theory & Practice.*

A Transition to Action

The Fostering Transition journey orients visioning, planning, and coalition building toward a practical implementation of the preceding stages. While this journey presents a final set of four systemic design tools, they might be considered complements to a full programme strategy. Most organisations that have mobilised a serious proposal and project team will have other successful management strategies to which these contribute.

The 'transition' of this journey signifies a shift from the metaplanning mindset and skillset from collaborative systemic design to the pragmatic execution of the plans as a transformation project. It represents the transition to implementation and project teamwork. This stage might be seen as complementing a Transition Design[2] approach, which also integrates systemic methods in multistakeholder design for complex sociotechnical systems. Many of the methodologies and tools (techné) used differ, but these processual methods can achieve similar end goals.

Transition Design promotes a living systems perspective and is informed by several compatible schools of practice, including transition management (Geels and Loorbach[3]), Futuring (Tony Fry), and multistakeholder engagement. Both Transition Design and Design Journeys (as a systemic design approach) provide guidance for affirmative design leadership of stakeholder teams in convening projects for complex system change and large-scale wicked problems.

Two tools in this chapter are crossovers between these philosophies, the Transition by Design (based on ecological succession) and the Adaptive Cycle tool (an ecological succession model). Both of these tools (and transition approaches) address and design for the long duration periods of development that may be necessary with programmes dealing with multiple scales of economic change or energy-mix transition. The adaptation to massive variations of scale uniquely characterises these practices.

The primary purpose of journeys in Transition is to move the design process into action by roadmapping the implementation of a systemic design transformation programme. As with other stages, we designed or enhanced tools found useful in our own work and experience.

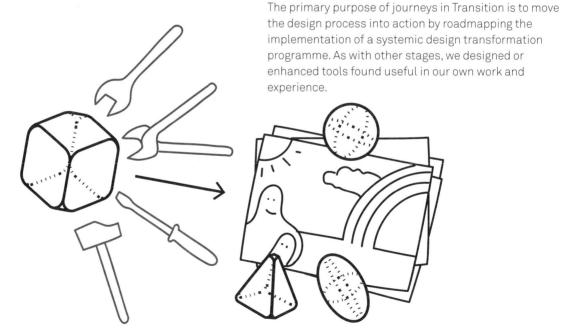

[2] Terry Irwin, Gideon Kossoff & Cameron Tonkinwise (2015). Transition design provocation. *Design Philosophy Papers*.
[3] Derk Loorbach (2007). Transition management. New mode of governance for sustainable development. Utrecht: International Books.

Design Journeys
for Transition

Stakeholder Mobilisation
Stakeholder Mobilisation facilitates strategies
for effective engagement with stakeholder groups
in the ecosystem, across system transition and
implementation.

Transition by Design
Transition by Design defines a three-stage roadmap tool
for scaling, enabling teams to map out transformation
strategies from niche innovation to scale-level impact of
a social ecosystem or enterprise launch.

Collaboration Model
The Collaboration Model provides a novel tool for defining
the makeup and concept of the new social system,
cocreating agreements on the team principles and
guidelines that will best advance the change plan.

Adaptive Cycle
The Adaptive Cycle tool translates the Panarchy
ecological cycle to an organisational change model,
useful for aligning theories of change or launch strategies
to larger ecosystem trends and dynamics. Even when all
other plans are in place, the cycle dynamics are critical to
timing the advancement of proposals for major change
initiatives.

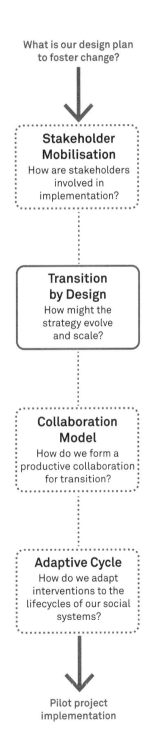

What is our design plan
to foster change?

**Stakeholder
Mobilisation**
How are stakeholders
involved in
implementation?

**Transition
by Design**
How might the
strategy evolve
and scale?

**Collaboration
Model**
How do we form a
productive collaboration
for transition?

Adaptive Cycle
How do we adapt
interventions to the
lifecycles of our social
systems?

Pilot project
implementation

Stakeholder Mobilisation

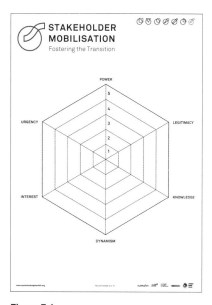

Figure 7-1
The Stakeholder Mobilisation

- Time to Run:
  1-2 hours
- Session context:
  Studio
- Workshop Type:
  Roadmap
- Process time:
  1-2 days
- Connections to:
  [5] Intervention Model
  [5] Outcome Map
  [7] Theory of Systems Change
  [7] Collaboration Model

As suggested by the title, *Stakeholder Mobilisation* supports strategies for orchestrating stakeholders in different degrees of participation. The tool is useful to construct a basic outline of the position and roles of stakeholders committed to the change programme, starting with the pilot phase.

The Change Readiness and Ecosystem Governance methods from [6] Planning are tools for assessing the organisational preparedness to move into action. In this stage, the focus is on power tools for initiating action.

Build Pilot, Learning Tests, Network Promotion

In the pilot phase, the intervention model remains flexible and vulnerable, and it's important to involve stakeholder actors who can contribute pertinent insights to the transition. Especially in the initial pilot, there should be a strong mix of connective power, urgency, interest, dynamism, knowledge, and legitimacy. To assess and maximise these qualities in the team, the following tool can be adopted.

Mapping Stakeholder Mobilisation

Planning and Prep

Start by defining the goals and desired outcomes to be achieved with developing and mobilising stakeholder groups, such as:

- Including more stakeholders in implementation
- Better understanding of stakeholder drivers and issues
- Addressing initial conditions for intervention strategies
- Collaborating during the transition phase
- Connecting to policymakers

Drawing on the Ecosystem Governance tool, review and cluster stakeholders according to the criteria of power, urgency, interest, dynamism, knowledge, and legitimacy.

- **Power (or Influence)** is about the power position of a stakeholder toward the other stakeholders, the influence on others to get things done.
- **Legitimacy** is the generalised perception or assumption that the actions of a stakeholder or entity are desirable, proper, or appropriate within some socially constructed system of norms, values, beliefs, and definitions.

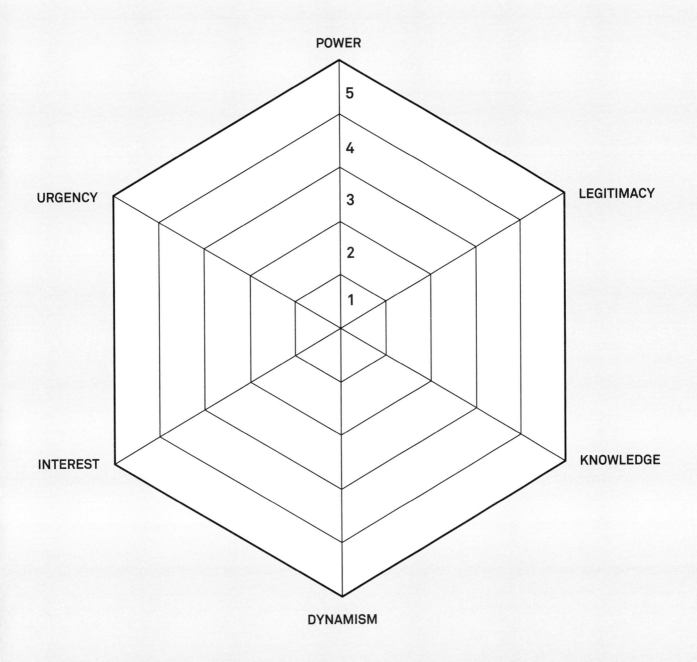

- **Knowledge** is about facts, information, and skills acquired through experience or education related to the issue, and the theoretical and practical understanding of the issue.
- **Dynamism** is the capacity of the stakeholder to change opinion, perception, or stance.
- **Interest (investment)** has to do with the stakeholder's engagement with the issue or project. How much is the issue a concern for him/her? How much does it affect the stakeholder?
- **Urgency** is the degree to which stakeholder claims call for immediate attention. It can be perceived as time sensitivity or criticality based on ownership, sentiment, expectation, or attached importance.

Mapping Method

A separate map can be constructed for each stakeholder group being assessed, and of course, they can be compared and iterated on to reflect differences that emerge in discussion. Similar to the Change Readiness tool, the spider diagram is scored by assigning points at relative positions from 1 (initial or minimal) at the inner ring to 5 (full capacity) at the outer ring.

1. Start by assessing the core team and planning organisation: What level of power, urgency, interest, dynamism, knowledge, and legitimacy are currently prevalent? Indicate the levels on the spider map.

2. Score the levels associated with other stakeholder organisations in the programme or partnering in the project. Add their names to the correspondent scorings

3. Assess the gaps between the maps. The practical ideal is that complementarity can be found across the groups, to achieve close to full capacity on all levels. If this is not the case, consider how to address the missing capability or to engage or add other participants to fill the gaps.

Delivery and Destination

The tool is best used as an assessment of multi-team capability and as a checkpoint for determining the level of readiness for action. A separate assessment can be done by and for each distinct stakeholder group, and these can be aggregated into a combined model (overlaying the radar graphs, with each team or group in a different line colour). Create an action plan to define the roles and relationships for each stakeholder or group. Get agreement on common near-term and end goals and develop appropriate communications routines for each participating group. Determine the type and frequency of communications best suited to each group, relative to their centrality and responsibility. Engagement might include project management emails, newsletters, weekly check-in calls, monthly onsite or other formal meetings, scheduled workshops, or more formal reports.

Travel Tips

Stakeholder Mobilisation can also be used to map individual stakeholder capacities. For example, a deputy minister sponsor would have significant power and interest, but perhaps much less knowledge, requiring balance with more technical experts. The participation of the civil service organisation will be necessary in this case for legitimacy and perceived urgency.

As with other stakeholder tools, these models can be used to plan for recruitment in cocreation workshops. In this case, recruiting those with high levels in at least two dimensions, e.g. high power and interest, or high urgency and dynamism, or high knowledge and legitimacy.

Figure 7 2
An alternative way to map stakeholder mobilisation using a 2x2 matrix (prosaic/visionary – reformist/radical). Depending on the ambition of the project one might want to engage at first with the visionaries/radicals or visionaries/reformists

Transition by Design

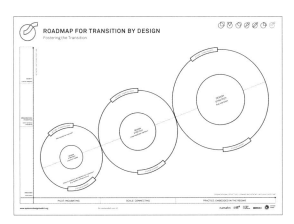

Figure 7-3
The Transition by Design tool

— Time to Run:
2-4 hours
— Session context:
Studio or Arena
— Workshop Type:
Roadmap
— Process time:
3+ days
— Connections to:
[1] Actors Map
[1] Rich Context
[1] Niche Discovery
[4] System Value Proposition
[5] Intervention Model
[5] Outcome Map
[6] Theory of Systems Change
[7] Collaboration Model

Transition by Design has emerged as one of the most widely-used tools in the Systemic Design Toolkit. Visualised by the familiar model of succession — from niche, to regime, to landscape levels of system scale — the transition tool supports all types of innovation planning, from social tech startups, to system change initiatives, to policy innovations. The transition roadmap provides a simple strategy map to envision scale shifts working from the micro to macro levels.

When a new system or process innovation is introduced within an existing institutionalised system, it often fails or becomes submerged into the dominant system due to any system's resistance to change. Earlier, we touched on contrarian systems rules (i.e. John Gall's Systemantics) that explain in parable form the real-world systemic effects of system capture and breakdown. Most of the system archetypes represent well-meaning systems gone wrong. 'Better design' through systemic design is not necessarily sufficient to deal with this constant issue, but we believe a self-aware collaboration of people using the Journeys Toolkit offers a significant advantage to long-term success.

The visual tool for Transition by Design, based on Geels' Multi-Level Perspective, can be used to collectively think through the implementation stages of a new system concept to facilitate change through stages of organisational design. The transitions are mapped towards a desired (macro) outcome by defining and adding design interventions in time and space.

Roadmapping Transition by Design

Planning and Prep

The Transition tool is a roadmap-style planning model and can be convened as a collaborative roadmapping workshop. In preparation for the workshop, the organisers can draw upon several previous models, if available:

— Rich Context
— Niche Discovery
— Intervention Model
— Theory of System Change

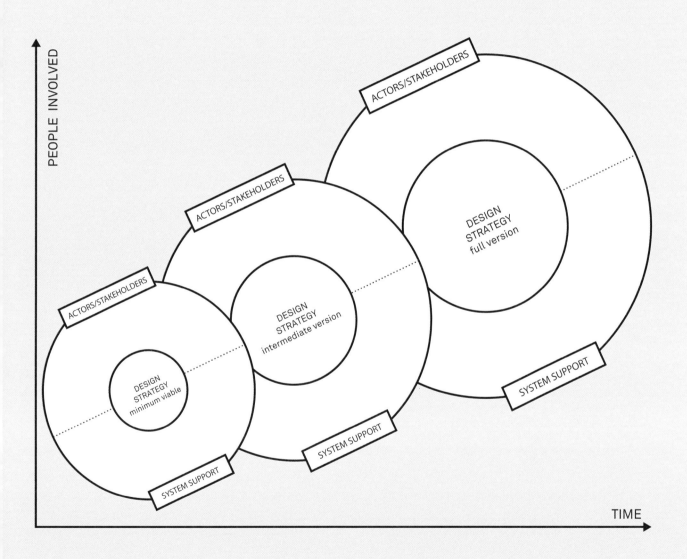

Preparation for team participation is largely framed toward an implementation mindset. The preceding tools are useful planning and design models that suggest alternatives. The Transition by Design is meant to be a simple roadmap for defining organisational strategy toward scaling and growing the innovation or intervention.

Mapping Method

This roadmapping tool represents the growth or diffusion of a systems change programme from the micro (niche actors), to meso (expanding the system to larger networks or organisations), and to the macro landscape (where transformation reaches broader society). The new system is pictured as emerging within the old regime and eventually replaces it.

1. **Start with the Micro** – Pilot or niche innovation. What is the core 'engine' representing value creation in the emerging system? Identify the engine (in the centre) as a transformation pilot or service launch, implemented in an initial form. Annotate flows and outcomes from the engine that can be implemented independently, without any links to or help from the current system elements or processes. List the main actors involved and the necessary support to empower them – typically knowledge and capabilities.

2. **Grow to reach the Meso** – Regime level. Describe the transformation engine that has grown to multiple networks. Identity the capital and influence flows connecting partners, stakeholders, and customers through actor-networks. Identify transformation catalysts[4] that might expand from the niche level to grow significantly in a well-supported network or geography. Identify fellow-traveller collaborating organisations that share outcome goals and values. If available, indicate how this transition is supported to develop experiments, self-organising capabilities, and learning networks.

3. **Scale to Macro** – Landscape. Map out the elements that require involvement from society (e.g. where policies or social perspectives should be changed). Identify the key policymakers and citizen groups that might be involved. Define how the transition is empowered with support such as major funding partners, industry support, media coverage, and popular endorsements.

Delivery and Destination

The result of the Transition by Design is a classic strategic roadmap, unfolding from near-term innovation toward longer-term transformation, with the implicit concept of cycles of emergent growth, rather than linear development. The rendering of the final version can be visualised for use in presentations and continuing strategy and planning discussion, and it can of course be iteratively updated.

Travel Tips

Transition by Design implies a scaling-out strategy for large-scale impact, by its use of the Multi-Level Perspective model. This model can be applied in sociotechnical transitions and social

---

[4] Sandra Waddock, Waddell, Jones, & Kendrick. (2022). Convening transformation systems to achieve system transformation. *Journal of Awareness-Based Systems Change*.

innovation for systems change. If a 'scaling-in' or internal-institutional programme is envisioned, the Adaptive Cycle would provide a more suitable roadmapping model.

The Transformation Catalyst (TC) concept noted previously is an emerging model of societal-level innovation impact based on the concept that niche-level social experiments have the potential to more rapidly evolve and diffuse transformative outcomes to regime and landscape levels. The Bounce Beyond theory of change leverages this concept, selecting and developing the capacity of pilot initiatives cultivated for their long-term transformation potential. The catalytic effect is envisioned as the focused impact that ecologically-attuned initiatives can achieve in a specific context, rather than a large-scale general purpose programme that must function similarly across many locales or niches. While the TC model fits the Transition by Design roadmap in particular, it also has relevance to the TOSCA theory of change model, the Outcome Map, and Intervention Strategy.

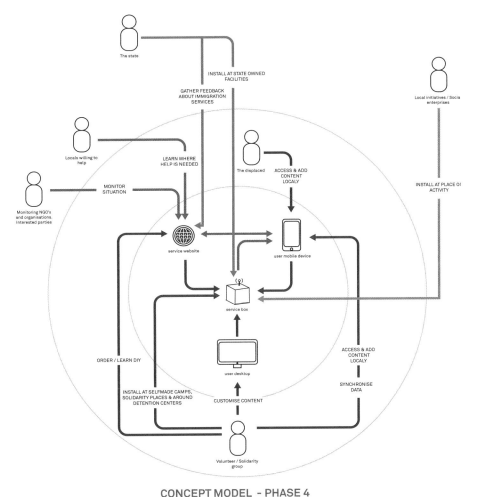

CONCEPT MODEL - PHASE 4

Figure 7-4
Schematic depiction of the expanding stakeholder engagement for a service assisting safe migration

Collaboration Model

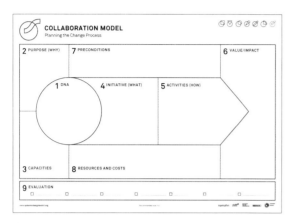

Figure 7-5
The Collaboration Model

- Time to Run:
  .5-2 hours
- Session context:
  Studio or Arena
- Workshop type:
  Codesign
- Process time:
  1+ days
- Connections to:
  [5] Outcome Map
  [6] Theory of Systems Change
  [7] Transition by Design

The Collaboration Model provides a framework for a team to design their organisational collaboration for the common purpose of a sociotechnical project or system change. The tool is convened with a team workshop to compose the structures of an enduring collaboration, such as those needed for a social innovation coalition or an organisational effort of service system design project.

This is a socially-creative tool that can be used in different stages of team development, although it is most useful in the final stages of the methodology. In practice, the team-level definition of the Collaboration Model follows the Process Enneagram. It can be used as an early definition of the programme's business model or operations strategy. Definition of transformation catalyst initiatives can be modelled as collaborations with shared impact goals. The entries and thought processes in the discussion contribute directly to that of the Flourishing Business Model[5] canvas, or other business definition frameworks. The Flourishing Enterprise Canvas requires a business model to be defined from core business purpose and system value cocreation.

Cocreating the Collaboration Model

Planning and Prep

Prework is helpful to gather information about participating organisations and the team context. If the tool is to be used with an intact working group with shared experience and values, no prior informing may be necessary. If the team involves either new members or a high level of seniority, 3-4 interviews might be conducted in advance of the collaboration workshop.

Invite the core team members of the collaboration or multistakeholder team to a scheduled workshop (at least one hour). Ensure all understand and agree

---

[5] See Antony Upward & Peter Jones' Flourishing Enterprise Model: http://flourishingbusiness.org. The Flourishing Enterprise Toolkit is recommended for its ability to represent integrated social-ecosystemic business models for any business or policy, and due to its rigorous development and support in the literature as the first 'strongly sustainable' business model for organisations to define future value for societal, ecological, and financially prosperous outcomes.

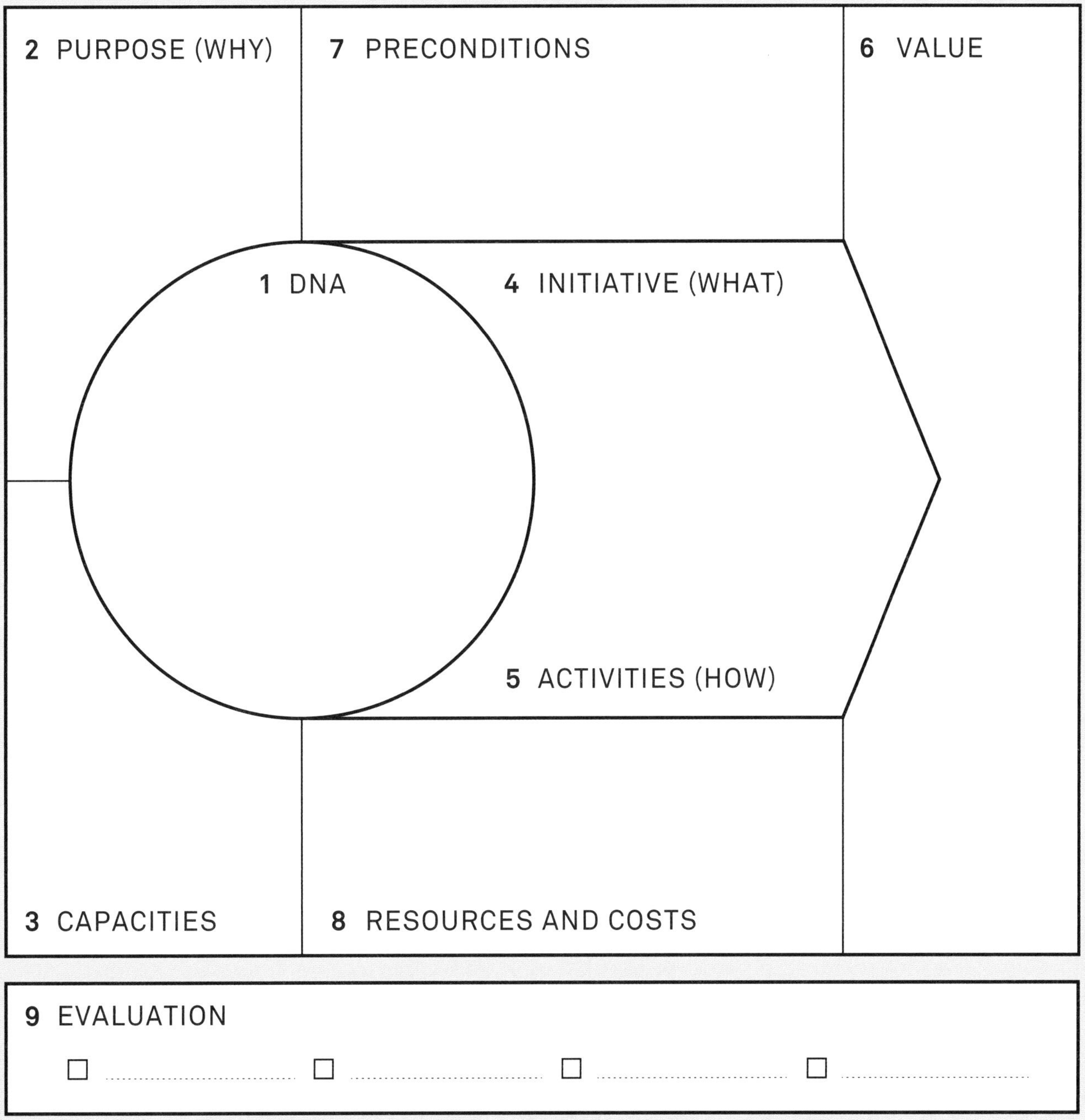

2 PURPOSE (WHY)

7 PRECONDITIONS

6 VALUE

1 DNA

4 INITIATIVE (WHAT)

5 ACTIVITIES (HOW)

3 CAPACITIES

8 RESOURCES AND COSTS

9 EVALUATION

☐ .... ☐ .... ☐ .... ☐ ....

upon the desired future (scope, purpose, and DNA). Provide access to the tool in print or online whiteboard and use a simple Generate-Dialogue-Select model to facilitate the contributions.

With this workshop, it is essential for participants to hold a trusted space for sharing authentically with others. Have members share their personal vision for the team – there are exercises from organisational development (such as the Team Spirit[6] mandala) that can create a 'clearing' or space of disclosure. Individual mandalas (hand-drawn shapes forming a personal expression of values and vision) can also be constructed as a team mandala in this exercise.

Following the opening exercise, have members present their ideas of purpose and role to each other.

Mapping Method

1. Start with **the organisation's 'DNA'** as the first step. This could be the team vision or essence. What are the key characteristics of the team that might inspire the collaboration going forward?

2. Discuss and define the central **Purpose** of the collaboration. What is the continuing purpose, what is the ultimate goal to be achieved together?

3. Identify **Capacities** – define the necessary roles, skills, and competencies. What roles will each member or partner contribute?

4. Generate the ideas and titles for the main **Initiative(s)** to be pursued by the collaboration. What are the major projects that will meet the purpose?

5. Develop a list of near-term **Activities**. What activities (building a website, hosting learning events, a workshops series) will be done to engage collaboration and launch the initiatives?

6. An 'arrow' that joins 1 (DNA) to 4 (Initiative) to 5 (Activities) points to step 6, **Value Impact**. Here, the expected value cocreated in the programme, short and long-term, for all stakeholders is listed and refined. Consider how to measure value cocreation when naming the points of the value proposition.

7. List the **Preconditions** (or assumptions, from the Theory of System Change). What regulations, policies, processes, dispositions in the team are preconditions for the initiative? What should change to make the initiative possible or more impactful?

8. Estimate **Resources and Costs** for the collaborative project. What does the team believe is required for the near and long-term sustainability of the programme? What fixed or one-time costs are known? What major issues require budgeting? How will you finance the initiative?

9. **Evaluation** is the final component, placed at the bottom of the panel. For a new organisation,

---

[6] Barry Heermann (1997). *Building Team Spirit: Activities for Inspiring and Energizing Teams*. McGraw-Hill.

there will be no concrete actions to assess, but rather, there will only be the criteria and principles to be used in future evaluation by agreement from team members. Define the fit to purpose, vision, and mission. Define criteria for assessing programme diffusion (or connection), the quality or production of innovation, expected economic and social impact, ecological improvement, or scalability (involvement of partners over time).

Delivery and Destination

The Collaboration Model draws from across the foundation methods used up to this point, but it is not duplicative. This stage is the first point at which the design team will be focusing inward on the organisation and stakeholder team itself. Most teams would not have a sufficiently developed plan to build the appropriate organisational system until this point.

There are numerous social adjacencies that deliver real value within the team or multi-stakeholder engagement. The Collaboration Model provides the opportunity for a dialogue on team purpose, and to explore possible strategies for coordinating (as well as funding) a complex project. The entries in this tool reflect choices and identities of the organisation planning the systemic design work. The consensus reached goes well beyond the material representation of the tool and provides a durable mental model of the organisational agreement. Of course, the results of the tool can be represented differently in a final presentation, to present the findings back to the large organisation or the stakeholders.

Figure 7-6
Exploring collaborations to foster embracing diversity

Adaptive Cycle Strategy

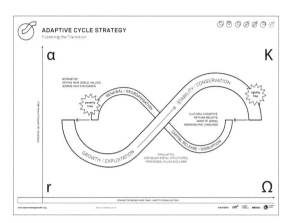

Figure 7-7
The Adaptive Cycle Strategy

— Time to Run:
2-4 hours
— Session context:
Studio
— Workshop Type:
Roadmap
— Process time:
1-2 days to review and revise
— Connections to:
[5] Outcome Map
[5] Contextual Variations
[6] Theory of Systems Change
[7] Transition by Design

The adaptive cycle, based on ecological systems theory, has become a staple of sustainability transition planning and has been smartly applied to organisational strategy. The adaptive cycle loop describes a recurring series of transformations of living systems as they adapt to natural phases of growth and collapse, drawn from principles of ecological succession. A powerful insight of Holling and Gunderson's Panarchy[7] theory was the extension of the ecological cycle to organisational and social systems that can also be observed to grow and release through a canonical series of four adaptations.

Before moving forward with high-risk programs with long-term aims, it helps to observe the relative position of a social-ecological system (or organisation) within its adaptive cycle and its next-higher panarchy cycle. This helps to understand when and how a social system is capable of absorbing change productively and when it is vulnerable or resistant to system changes in their nested or containing systems.

The Adaptive Cycle Strategy tool helps identify the phase of growth or re-organisation of any social system in the planning context, whether it's the system of change interest, or the ecosystem in which a mobilised organisation is situated. The selection and effective timing of interventions are often highly sensitive to the 'readiness' or accessibility of a system's current conditions.

The four phases of the loops in the adaptive cycle include:

1. Growth/exploitation
2. Stability/conservation
3. Release/disruption
4. Renewal/reorganisation

The 'front loop' of growth and conservation represents a longer cycle of a sustained period of development, while release and renewal (the back loop) together are often relatively short. These are visually indicated in the tool to help new users with the model.

---

[7] Lance Gunderson & C.S. 'Buzz' Holling (2002). *Panarchy: Understanding Transformations in Human and Natural Systems.*

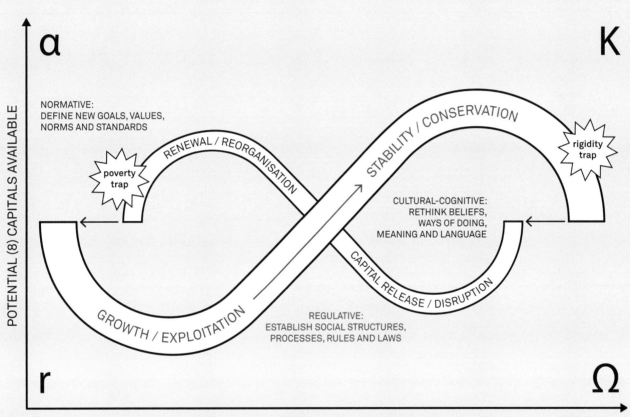

α

K

NORMATIVE:
DEFINE NEW GOALS, VALUES,
NORMS AND STANDARDS

RENEWAL / REORGANISATION

STABILITY / CONSERVATION

poverty
trap

rigidity
trap

CULTURAL-COGNITIVE:
RETHINK BELIEFS,
WAYS OF DOING,
MEANING AND LANGUAGE

CAPITAL RELEASE / DISRUPTION

GROWTH / EXPLOITATION

REGULATIVE:
ESTABLISH SOCIAL STRUCTURES,
PROCESSES, RULES AND LAWS

POTENTIAL (8) CAPITALS AVAILABLE

r

Ω

CONNECTEDNESS OVER TIME / INSTITUTIONALISATION

Roadmapping the Adaptive Cycle Strategy

Planning and Prep

The Adaptive Cycle is visually defined to support a tool for mapping organisational and transformation strategies. For at least a decade, leading practitioners have already adapted panarchy as a model for facilitating adaptive strategy for organisational change. In essence, the panarchy cycle invokes a theory of change, suggesting that change is most probably at points of extended conservation or reorganisation (in the containing or next-larger cycle). We have attempted to structure the basic form to improve its accessibility for new uses and adaptation, and specifically for strategic roadmapping of change initiatives.

As preparation, the design team should collect or arrange on a whiteboard the several system roadmaps produced to this point. The primary inputs might include the Three Horizons, Outcome Map, Theory of System Change, Intervention Strategy, and the Transition by Design. What these are all missing is a theory of prospective timing, in which the intervention has stronger leverage due to institutional or ecosystem propensity.

Mapping Method

There are numerous versions of practice for workshopping the adaptive cycle as a model for a dynamic strategy. The following steps can be used as a starting point for learning and sharing this tool as a type of living system planning roadmap.

1. Where is the intervention project situated in the cycle? Determine the phase of the cycle the organisational process system is currently in by observing the dominant trend activities. Annotate the activities on the tool to show where and how the current strategy took shape (in early formation or following reorganisation). If the current process or innovation is currently growing, indicate the observations on the 'r' curve that support this finding.

2. Annotate these observations on the cycle as a systemic timeline, up to the point of a recognised current state. List notes that indicate the qualities of connectedness and growth/potential.

3. Annotate the map to indicate trends or proposed activities consistent with the cycle:

    —   **Renewal/reorganisation**: A focus on new project formation, and promoting novel practices and inventive approaches introduced into the organisation.

    —   **Growth/exploitation**: There is financial growth, high productivity, organisational support, significant adoption of programmes and a clear formation of developed networks (e.g. funded partnerships, alliances, associations).

    —   **Stability/conservation**: Leaders and programmes are sustaining gains and managing productive processes. The organisation holds to planned strategies, markets and positions, and established policies and rules.

- **Collapse/release**: Programmes are dissolving, significant trend change toward drawing down growth or positions, an internalised focus replaces external development; established foundations are released.

4. What is the foreseeable availability of the larger, slower systems for the proposed design intervention? Prepare a second adaptive cycle map to represent the social system in which the programme or intervention is primarily situated. Follow the same instructions as above to locate trends and issues to determine the relative stability or tension, closure or readiness to change.

Delivery and Destination

The Adaptive Cycle tool provides insight into the timing and impact of strategic planning and interventions. All the roadmapping tools might be iteratively updated from panarchy insights. The adaptive cycle image can be rendered as another optional presentation, but in some ways, the results of this strategic tool can be better integrated into one of the other roadmaps that include a cyclic timeline. The TOSCA or Three Horizons can be modified to show the organisational propensities or trends drawn from the adaptive cycle analysis. Consider the intervention model to determine which interventions have the most leverage within the current or upcoming turns of the adaptive cycle.

Travel Tips

The adaptive cycle is represented in the tool as a lemniscate laid out within two dimensions indicated by the X and Y-axis. The X-axis shows the degree of connectedness or the degree of institutionalisation of organisational evolution. The Y-axis shows the potential for renewal and growth, due to the recruitment of underused (novel or adapted) capitals available in the ecosystem.

On the loops in the lemniscate image, the dominant directions for strategic interventions are proposed:

- In the **Renewal** phase, innovation is prioritised, with the creation of new practices and projects of high potential and few resources to reshape goals, values, norms, and standards at the working levels of an existing social system.

- In the **Growth & Stability** phase, the goal is to sustain and exploit earned gains by establishing and maintaining resilient social structures, best practices, processes, rules, and laws. Toward the end of the phase, often a *rigidity trap* appears. At this late stage of the cycle, the system becomes so structured and inflexible that the organisation finds it inexpedient to respond to emergence or contextual change.

  To overcome the rigidity trap, the organisation is forced to rethink beliefs, established practices, obsolete meanings, and positions. However, because the rigidity trap occurs toward the end of the conservation phase, most systems are unable to change sufficiently and the commitment to an obsolete system triggers the release of capitals associated with system collapse.

The *poverty trap*, indicated at the point of reorganisation, suggests the opposite of the rigidity trap presaging collapse. Here, the willingness is high, but available resources are insufficiently available to build and sustain innovations or lead new projects.

These three directions are always present together, but depending on what phase the system is in, they will be more or less effective. In any case, shifts in each of the directions should be mutually reinforcing.

Light on the Path

Nested Adaptive Cycles (Panarchy)

In large organisations and societal systems, there is never one adaptive cycle, but multiple adaptive cycles nested in each other. These nested cycles, or the 'panarchy' as referenced in the title, are organised into a hierarchy which connects adaptive cycles at small scales to adaptive cycles at large scales. While 'hierarchy' is generally used to describe a system in which power, influence, or authority originate at the top and travel down to the bottom, in panarchy theory, 'hierarchy' is defined more broadly as the overall structure of the scales where systems operate.

The panarchy concept is defined by a dynamic system hierarchy typically nested as three containing loops. The loops are interconnected so that faster patterns (such as organisational processes) are proposed to intervene in slower normative social structures that are themselves constrained by slow-cycle institutional or signification patterns. They are in constant parallel, unfolding mutually, and constraining and influencing each other.

If two systems' structure and processes occur at the same temporal or spatial scale, then they are at the same scale of the panarchy. However, this does not mean system effects only travel one way (from large scales at the top to small scales at the bottom). Instead, influence can travel from top (slower) to bottom (faster cycles), or from bottom to top since self-organised, smaller scales also affect larger scales (this is through the mechanism of the 'revolt' of a faster-moving cycle having effective influence on the next level cycle).

Finally, the Adaptive Cycle model should be considered as a three-dimensional dynamic process, with constant gain or decline in a) connectedness (x-axis, increasing over time), b) potential (y-axis, with potential gaining with growth, up to a point of exhaustion), and c) resilience (z-axis). Resilience, the third dimension, decreases as the system extends into (K) conservation, and increases on the back loop as the system recovers resources. In two-dimensional models such as the Adaptive Cycle tool, the full model is generally flattened for simplicity of learning and use.

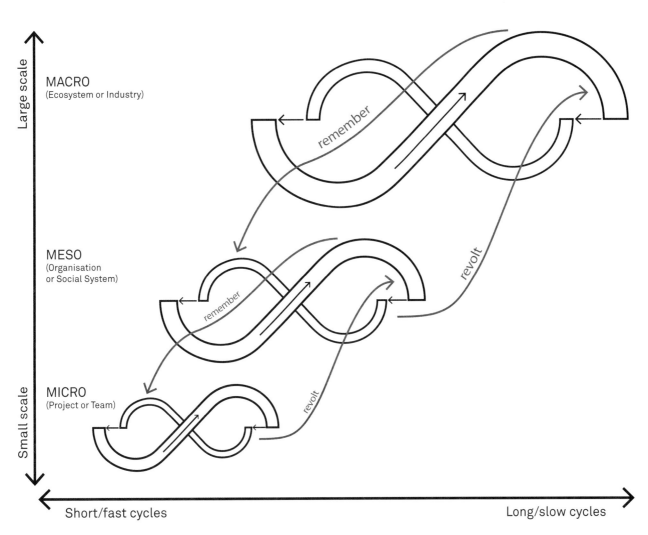

Figure 7-8
Panarchy: nested adaptive cycles

The Return Home

Reflecting on the roads taken, and the pathways less taken

The overarching context motivating *Design Journeys* could not be more consequential. The societal and civilisational crises emerging in the 21st century require an paradigmatic shift in the means of organising, designing, and leading complex projects that promise social betterment with ecological balance. Systemic design makes no exclusive claim to efficacy - we advise the systems principle of *equifinality*, that in open systems there are many viable pathways to satisfy a goal. Yet, following in the footsteps of industrial and service design disciplines before it, the continuing demand for radically improved and purpose-fit systems drives new practices into use.

Forward-looking leaders and organisations are starting to seriously regard the systemic impacts of complexity. Our work with the Systemic Design Toolkit and training has revealed increasing interest in learning to effectively lead transformation. We provide an integrated approach to systemic design, based on a systems theory canon for design applications, building on social systems as the primary unit of design. The Journeys toolkit selects from systemic management innovations we have tested in consulting and training, for transformation programmes, policy design, strategic planning, and design futuring for societal transition.

Design Journeys advances the fit of design-shaped systems tools for complex, long-term transformation efforts for organisations pursuing the challenges of societal wicked problems. We have attempted to create an accessible packaging of the best-fit methods that create high-quality observations and outcomes, and

resolve known concerns that arise in systemic design projects with clients and stakeholders. Observations and testing across dozens of teams and use cases have ensured a good level of practice usability. If the tools can be designed any simpler to provide high-quality insight into contextual complexity, we will continue to evolve them.

The Journeys methodology is one of many serious development over the last 50 years to translate systems thinking to a form and language accessible to organisations and design practices. We are now past the 50-year anniversary of the first Club of Rome meeting, at which Hasan Özbekhan presented the prospectus, *The Predicament of Mankind*.[1] Özbekhan had analysed the range of unfolding future crises, called the *Global Problematique*, comprising 49 Continuous Critical Problems (CCPs) ranging from increasing population to ecosystem degradation, from inadequate education to obsolete political institutions. He predicted that their continuous interaction and overlaps would soon emerge as a single megacrisis (the problematique), now often called the 'polycrisis.' He anticipated that future generations would, in effect, be coping with all 49 CCPs and their interactions, all at once.

Two proposals were offered to address the *Predicament*, and Özbekhan's own proposal was not selected for funding by the Club of Rome. The Meadows and Forrester proposal to run system dynamics modelling scenarios on the near-future sustainability crisis was chosen instead. Their findings from running the World3 system dynamics simulations led to the famous book, *The Limits to Growth*.

---

[1] Hasan Özbekhan (1970). *The Predicament of Mankind: A Quest for Structured Responses to Growing World-Wide Complexities and Uncertainties.* Club of Rome.

The Özbekhan proposal had advanced ideas perhaps 50 years ahead of its time, but at the time the methodology was underdeveloped. Now, we have better methodologies and conceptual framework - but yet the Global Problematique has metastasised over the decades.

Özbekhan was correct that these specifiable CCPs would become entangled into an inseparable mess, and inaccessible to technological amelioration or problem-solving. The societal or global problematique drives the necessity for a creative design-led practice convening a series of collaborations for stakeholder-inspired cocreation – a developmental approach to interventions informed by multiple perspectives on complex systems.

Even today, most system change initiatives advocate a problem-specific focus, as educational and advocacy groups are formed to address the constituent concerns of the megacrisis. The authors have experience with emerging transformation programmes, including environmental and climate planning, social policy, community health, and the subject of several cases in the book, new ecological economies (e.g., Bounce Beyond, FEI). These issues overlap considerably, and we can now visually map how these different problem systems emerge from the outcomes of common root causes identified in the original Global Problematique. These causal drivers include the corporate control of the government, corruption of democratic rule, hegemonic misinforming media, obsolete policy institutions, and the influence of global financial interests, among others. However, we rarely address these root issues directly, as our projects usually do not allow for relevant accessible leverage to ameliorate them. Typically, system change programmes are formed according to social movement logic rather than service logics, marshalling dedicated leaders, stakeholders, and local or networked community action networks toward problem-specific outcomes consistent with the shared values bringing these groups together.

Dealing with these problem contexts in systems change programmes invites considerable uncertainty, complications in decision-making, and ambiguity in determining effective strategies. However, with the power to analyse multiple perspectives and influences over iterative journeys and methodologies, design teams will discover the inherent capability of identifying ever-deeper, higher-leverage drivers of behaviour, and will design powerful strategies that finally address these roots, in the interaction of deeply-connected systemic drivers.

The Other Promise – Designing Better Systems

The other major design practice of *Design Journeys* applies to complex sociotechnical systems, inclusive of a wide array of complex systems from healthcare service, complex municipal planning, cybersecurity, or digital service platforms. Systemic design has been criticised for its apparent reliance on mapping and methodology, which are visible referents. Yet systemic design is a relatively new discipline, the equivalent of the 1960's if compared to the development of systems science. The design practices being formed in the field are pragmatic and results-oriented, and not based on strongly-held or proprietary methodologies.

Methodology provides a platform for a powerful learning process, and a concrete basis for training and development. Methods offer clearly-marked, pragmatic pathways for structured process and democratisation of stakeholder participatory design. And we can design effective action without methodology. Yet often these actions will fall short of aims due to the very issues resolved by these tools: misunderstanding the nature of complexity or interconnected problem contexts, or the interdependencies of small actions on each other, the path-dependency of initial conditions, or the initial decisions taken within a frame.

Non-methodological schools of theory and practice have much to offer to a learning journey. Philosophical and theory-led approaches, such as pluriversal design,[2] ontological design,[3] redirective design,[4] and the transition design school have much to offer systemic design practice. Richly-informed theory inspires imaginative solutions and reframing. These schools may avoid the use of structured methods, but without proposed pathways to learn a type of practice, their theoretical value will be harder to adopt. Philosophical schools of design require significantly more personal investment in training and experience to become a credible or effective practitioner. A 'Tourist' or early-career designer will not become productive with these approaches within the urgent timeframes of practical project performance.

Systemic design has within it a pragmatic direction and not inherently positioned with or against design methods. Recognising the value of deep scholarship and practice legacies that are often overlooked by advancing trends and brands of practice, the tools in *Design Journeys* account for the advancement of knowledge not just broadly across systems theory and practice, but specifically from sociotechnical systems, social complexity, ecological design, design science, system evaluation, and systems change.

Are We Designing Systems?

Does the question matter? We will not argue here the systems thinkers' dilemma of whether systems, as defined as whole contexts constructed by agreement in language, can be 'designed.' We can state several positions in favour and against, but it might be clear to those inspecting the epistemological commitment that *Design Journeys* integrates both constructivism and critical realism. We would agree with Buckminster Fuller that net-new systems can in fact be wholly designed – the institutional problem of their implementation and replacement remains the sticking point.

After all, few if any articles refer to systemic design practices in terms of 'system design.' Yet this puzzle, the heart of the issue, is not resolved by clever definitions of what it means to design, or whether a 'system' exists in objective reality or not. Here, we might say that the constructivist design of system functions (yes, through language as well as virtual sticky notes) results in real processes and services that are as objectively designed as a product or service.

In fact, we cannot advocate for these tools and practices without holding a deep and serious affirmative outlook (i.e. 'optimism') that such significant transformation is possible. If organised well and convened with systemic principles and social awareness, a small group of dedicated practitioners can indeed design interventions that emerge to displace social and institutional practices intended for change. The outcomes of these intentional forms are in the social proof of their adoption as 'new systems.'

Design Journeys equally facilitates design for socio-technological infrastructures that require stakeholder knowledge in the design process, such as organisational processes or public policy. The tools, and their collaborative convening approach to stakeholder design engagement, are better suited to these decisions than, for example, system engineering teams in Lab contexts.

Years of experience and case studies show how social/system change, sociotechnical systems, and complex policy can be effectively addressed with similar tools developed from validated systems theory. While their resolution logics are very different, these domains of action all require convening developmental learning processes with stakeholder engagement, incrementally evolved through an ethical selection by requisite variety. This philosophy also has roots in the era of normative planning and social system design championed by first-generation systems thinking, a school of thought also developed by Özbekhan. He was also an early proponent of systemic design planning and democratic, values-based, stakeholder-informed decision-making, which he called 'normative planning.'

[2] Arturo Escobar (2017). *Designs for the Pluriverse: Radical interdependence, autonomy, and the making of worlds*. Duke.
[3] Charles Spinosa, Fernando Flores, & Hubert Dreyfus (1999). *Disclosing New Worlds: Entrepreneurship, democratic action, and the cultivation of solidarity*. MIT Press.
[4] Tony Fry (2009). *Design Futuring*. University of New South Wales Press.

The social system design school of systems emerged from these forays into societal system problems, with early methodologies developed by Özbekhan's colleagues Erich Jantsch, Alexander Christakis, and John Warfield, as well as West Churchman and Russell Ackoff, who advanced social systems practice in the early 1970's. While the dominant school of systems thinking developed from the 'hard' system dynamics methods for many years, systemic design followed soft systems and social systems. Many of the tools in the *Journeys* Toolkit are inspired by their design principles and systems methods. While their original methods were well-conceived, they were rarely inspired by the learned experiences of actual designerly practice. In nearly all cases, across the schools of systems thinking, the idea of 'design' was considered a generic practice of developmental improvement, which reflected Herbert Simon's notion of "changing existing situations into preferred ones." Systemic design has further integrated research, theory, and methodology to facilitate stakeholder collaboration capable of addressing, to the best of any discipline's capability, the most complex issues of our time.

Design as a Social, Systemic Practice

One aim of Design Journeys was to accelerate the learning curve for training and leading systemic design methods for primary design practitioners. The practice of design, at all levels of complexity, takes a creative stance toward a preferred future, whether that is a future for users, for people, or an ecosystem. In designing 'with and for complexity,'[5] the intent is not to model and understand complexity per se, but to produce a satisfying and sustainable overall experience in any design context – whether an end-to-end service, sustainable consumer products, or the production and experience of multifunctional complex industrial products such as electric cars.

The envisioned future of the design process for industrial and service design involves the balance between an optimised customer experience and the capabilities of the underlying system being designed, packaged, and revealed.

Can systemic design through methodology engender a viable, usable engagement of systems thinking for complex systems that shows up as a better design experience? After all, to new readers and Explorers, a daunting footprint of theory underpins all the methods. Do we expect practitioners to become well-versed in the theory in order to perform the tools well, let alone lead competent outcomes in highly-complex projects?

An initial reading of *Design Journeys* reveals every citation to theories in the book refers to a systems thinking framework that suggested a practice prior to our development. Whether Geels or Klein in [1] Framing, or Irwin or Holling in [7] Transition, the reader will find a systems thinker (and systems theory) behind every reference. We affirm our respect and debt, as it were, to these original thinkers and forerunners on the paths that join up in the Design Journeys. We are not just reframing or translating these practices for a new practice community. As scholar-designers, we have learned, adapted, and iteratively tested all these models or ideas in one project or another, even those we invented as wholly new.

We also hope to transfuse a deeper meaning and usage of these foundational ideas in the Journey tools. The purpose of the Toolkit is not just to simplify and popularise well-formed models for a broader audience, although that might be a helpful side-effect of good design. A deeper purpose is to integrate what we believe are many leading practices that deserve continuity as active legacies. All of these practices and research frameworks were developed over many years of trial and testing; of study and peer-review; in sociotechnical systems, ecological planning, social innovation, and policy development. We do not seek to improve upon these theories but to integrate them into an innovation process that raises each one to an appropriate and ready stage of learning-in-action.

---

[5] Don Norman, *Living with Complexity* (2011) and *Design for a Better World* (2023), MIT Press. Don Norman's latest book deals with the most complex problems of our time - design for sustainable development, sociotechnical systems, social change – and includes systemic design and its disciplinary community offering as a leading approach.

The tools, including the canvas images with guidelines and concise instructions, have been designed for incremental learning in practice, to provide scaffolds for designers and facilitators to safely build upon our prior development and testing. All the source models are deeply reasoned and sophisticated processes. Rather than replicated or enhanced, they have been translated – most of them for the first time ever – into practice guides and tools. We know the canvases and tools work, and they are as simple as possible, but no simpler.

Schools and Tools of Practice

Systemic design has grown from an integration of systems thinking theory to inform and expand the practical methods of design planning within an expanding field of research, practice experimentation, new methodologies, and engagement approaches. As an interdisciplinary field, it integrates systems thinking and systems methods for human-centred design in complex, sociotechnical and multi-stakeholder systems. With a developing body of applications in strategic planning, urban design, healthcare, public policy, and digital innovation, systemic design draws upon theory and knowledge from systems and social sciences, cybernetics, applied research, organisational and management studies, ecology, media studies, and anthropology.

Systemic design has grown from a research-led design discipline to a field of advanced design practice with numerous methods and frameworks for tasks such as framing the design space in a complex system, mapping stakeholders and activities, modelling services and system dynamics, and mapping leverage points for intervention. The Systemic Design Toolkit translates systems thinking methods into pragmatic collaborative design tools. It has gained adoption for its new forms of strategic design planning for complex sociotechnical systems and transformation. Yet, there has never been a widely accepted comprehensive methodology, and

we do not presume the Toolkit to become a canonical methodology, as that might limit creativity or discovery of better methods.

The development of for-purpose systemic design tools and methods has proceeded for over a decade. A range of methodologies have developed along various stages of maturity, and each methodology that follows has its own standards of practice within its community. The diamond model in Figure 1 shows a wide range of contributing practices or disciplines that have informed the Journeys methodology, with methods or epistemology. It shows a sample of schools that are mapped as either closer to sociotechnical systems or living systems, as well as either toward participatory or consultative approaches. The Journeys design approach has blended these distinctions somewhat, to provide all methods with potential for stakeholder participation.

At least six areas have contributed significantly to systemic design and have influenced methods in *Design Journeys*.

- **Systems-Oriented Design (SOD)** – SOD is one of the established systemic design methodologies, developed at Oslo School of Architecture and Design (AHO) by Birger Sevaldson and colleagues for over a decade. His recent book *Designing for Complexity* brings SOD methodology up to date with current cases and cutting-edge theory.[6] SOD has dozens of case studies to show, with numerous implementations of whole system design proposals, typically through sponsored research through design collaborations.

- **Gigamapping and Synthesis Mapping** – At least three published approaches to systemic design mapping are found in the practice, as designing frameworks for visualisation of complex social systems with and by stakeholders. *Gigamapping* developed from SOD practice is a methodology for codesign of effective new systems in continuing collaborations with stakeholders. *Synthesis Maps* serve the need to present visualisations of whole complex systems and

---

[6] A collection of SOD case studies and Gigamaps can be found at systemsorienteddesign.net.

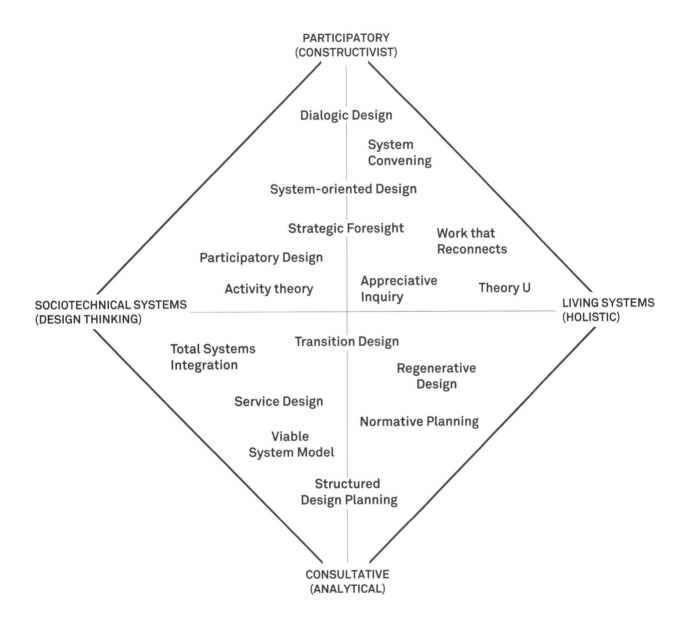

Figure 1
Design and systems approaches contributing to Journeys

systems-oriented research to broader stakeholder groups and the public. The National Institute of Design (Ahmedabad, India) also continues a history and pedagogy for complex system mapping, which continues today from the founding days of M.P. Ranjan.

– Systems Dialogues and Participatory Design – The systems field shows a long history of dialogue practices, but with only a small number developing prominence – as systemic approaches to dialogue use strong theory and facilitated methods to manage inherent complexity. Systems approaches include

Christakis' Dialogic Design and Stafford Beer's Team Syntegrity.[7] Organisational development practices include David Cooperrider's Appreciative inquiry and Open Space.[8] These deliberative practices emerged from systems science, as well-documented practices integrate formal methods for deliberation with defined system stakeholders, infusing democratic dialogue as a necessary modality of collective participation. Participatory Design practices are highly influential in the style of codesign workshops in design practice. The integration of formal deliberative practices with creative design convening continues to offer a rich opportunity space for future practice.

— **Systems Change and Transformation Design** – Early systemic design methodology can be traced back to Transformation Design, a movement (2005-2010) that led to the development of new practices to address critical social and economic challenges. After a period of intensive development, Transformation Design failed to garner institutional support, and new design practices shifted toward service design, social innovation, and systemic design. Recently, the systems change movement in new philanthropy has built support for transformational programmes, with comparable goals and competencies in systems thinking for large-scale societal challenges.
Socioecological Systems – A growing and broad area of research and practice in systemic design, with studies and engagement that involve stakeholders and system planning for social-ecological outcomes. Important developmental studies have been done by AHO, Politecnico di Torino (RETRACE programme), ETH Zurich, National Institute of Design India, and others. Mixed methods and stakeholder planning approaches are used for bioregional agroecology, integrated municipal planning, design studies for architecture and eco-tourism in sensitive ecologies, water management, and other projects to foster flourishing ecosystems.

— **Social Systems and Organisational Networks** – A growing area of practice has developed for enterprise transformation (Design 3.0 Organisational Design) in corporate, small business, and public sector organisations. The broader movement toward humane organisations and technologies has been deeply informed by the vision for social betterment and ecological sustainability of all businesses. Systemic design has influenced the creation of tools for eco-design, flourishing business models, and ecological economics.

— **Sociotechnical Service Design** – Sociotechnical service systems integrate complex work routines for high-reliability services, such as in healthcare, information service platforms, and product-service systems such as electric vehicle providers. Unlike social systems, these complex services are delivery systems comprised of dynamic value co-creation between human and automated tasks, integrated information technology, organisational networks, and integrated databases. Systemic design has co-evolved with complex sociotechnical services to provide tools and approaches to address these complex (and complicated) technical system challenges.

📍 **Also visit**: For more on systemic design methodologies and all modern systems practices, the recent *Handbook of Systems Sciences*[9] includes a series of new references of systemic design in healthcare, policy, and deliberation applications.

From the Territory Back to the Map

For decades we have seen cycles of converging and diverging between systems methods and the creative design disciplines. Systems thinking and design have an unsteady long-term relationship, but each field can credibly claim knowledge of the other. Practitioners in both fields have attempted to adopt (and exploit) the more effective models and techniques from the other field, but usually in piecemeal fashion, and only

[7] Stafford Beer (1994). *Beyond Dispute: The Invention of Team Syntegrity*.
[8] Harrison Owen (2000). *The Power of Spirit: How Organizations Transform.*
[9] Peter Jones (2020). Systemic Design: Design for complex, social, and sociotechnical systems. *Handbook of Systems Sciences*. Springer Japan.

if a problem was so suited. Two examples include the principles of biomimicry – as developed in environmental design, and the systematic application of design thinking as a method – popularised to the point of a management fad.

Relevant principles and relationships between systems theory and design methodology are called for, independent of method. Contemporary systems theory has evolved to a stable set of preferred theories for system description (or explanation), prediction (or control), and intervention (change). Michael Jackson[10] mapped the predominant schools of systems thinking as hard systems, soft systems, system dynamics, and the more recent emancipatory, critical, and postmodern schools of systems thinking. Three other branches are drawn from complexity science – complexity theory, network science, and organisational cybernetics. Most acknowledged schools do not promote a clear function of design or a relationship to design thinking, but rather identify methods and conditions for *intervention* in a given system.

The very notion of 'intervention' admits an objectification of systems, wherein we agree that a real system exists in the world, in which we can intervene. This position allows that interventions can be 'better or worse,' which drives the necessity for collaborative design (as the stakeholders will determine 'what's better'). From this perspective, design emerges as a practical epistemology for collaborative problem-solving. This idea is supported by the increasingly popular belief that 'all people are designers,' at least in Ezio Manzini's[11] sense of people intentionally constructing their work and lives toward social betterment.

The seven stages of the Journeys methodology offer 30 systemic design tools and techniques, at least half of which can be employed by new practitioners with immediate effectiveness, if thoughtfully planned. The Journeys pathway in each chapter indicates tools are recommended for Tourists or Explorers. Not all Tourists will be new practitioners, of course, and we recognise experienced designers learning these tools may be new

to systemic design, or systems thinking.

The Toolkit also does not preclude or exclude other methodologies in current use. Many readers may be skilled and trained in service design, and many designers in general have a rich variety of skilled practices. Many of the Explorers on the path will have experience in other methodologies, and prior workable approaches for which compatibility may be sought. Methodology and skills from industrial design, interaction design, environmental design, and service design will find good matches to the tools.

Reframing Sensemaking in Complexity

Designing with and for the system requires that we include those with the most relevant knowledge of their systems to inform appropriate design decisions in context. While we can deeply integrate their contributions through approaches such as structured deliberation, we can also get to the heart of matters by facilitating better ways of sensemaking. We consider sensemaking here as a practice, as the shared construction of meaning through critical inquiry among participants in their organisational or practice context.

Making sense of complexity is a creative and judgmental activity. No single expert or manager can understand an entire complex system. The approach we have taken is to create sensemaking tools for groups, for multiple stakeholders to construct their knowledge together to reach wise resolutions.

All sensemaking methodologies appear to be based on abductive reasoning, as design itself is theorized. By this we draw on observations shared with others to infer plausible conclusions from comparison and judgment. Design abduction is similarly the intuitive process of iterative ideation, such as in evaluating prototypes, wherein a design concept is hypothesised and evaluated for its fit to envisioned use.

[10] Michael Jackson (2004). *Systems Thinking: Creative Holism for Managers*. John Wiley.
[11] Ezio Manzini (2015). *Design, When Everybody Designs: An Introduction to Design for Social Innovation*. MIT Press.

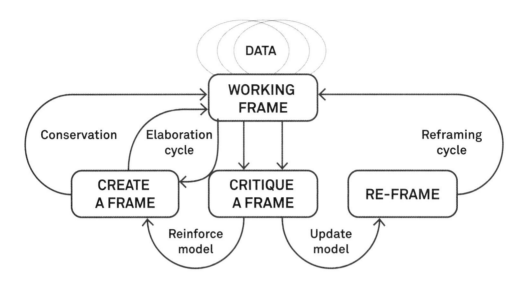

Figure 2
Data-Frame Sensemaking model (Adapted from Klein, et al, 2007)

Framing as Sensemaking

Framing draws on a variety of sensemaking skills. Framing is a process of revealing individual and collective mental models, and cultivating better-fit, explicit models about a shared problematic situation. Sensemaking seeks and tests new frames of reference and results in updating mental models to better reflect the collective understanding of risks and potentials of a situation. Updated mental models serve as positions for new frames, respecting complexity and ambiguity, and help us interpret data.

Sensemaking assimilates multiple signals and sources of knowledge, drawing on experience and intuition to resolve gaps in situational understanding. It accommodates (but does not necessarily resolve) ambiguity and uncertainty. From a design perspective, sensemaking attempts to inform and effectively respond to the possibilities and constraints in an emerging situation. In system sensemaking, as we might call it, we can lead a team to identify cues and trends from a complex situation by drawing on a rich repertoire of patterns, mentally testing alternatives, and identifying possible actions. Because there is no 'method' for conducting such sensemaking, we encourage the use of different tools and practices that can enable a collective framing process.

The sensemaking process changes one's mental models about a situation, and as such, should yield better frames, and therefore better resolutions in a design process. Mental models are referenced in the literature as under the more common term 'mindset,' and mental models are elaborated in the research of many fields: systems thinking, human factors, behavioural economics, and policy studies. The main tool provided in Journeys that elicits mental models is the Causal Layered Analysis (CLA) in Research Questions of Stage [2] Listening. However, it is indicated for stakeholder interviews and not necessarily the design research team.

The leading sensemaking theorists reveal how we make sense in different levels of system and human experience through the units of analysis describing sensemaking in their studies. As represented in the well-known model of Integral Theory,[12] the five sensemaking theories address individual or collective locations of sensemaking, across internalised or external applications or focus.[13]

Gary Klein's[14] research develops an individual's mental model (frame) as applied to a complex external context or activity, in which observations are assessed for guiding decisions. Karl Weick's focus is on organisational activity (collective), and the location of sensemaking is internalised as a representation of meaning understood through retrospection about past patterns in relation to a current problem. Brenda Dervin's methodology locates sensemaking within the individual's experience, a situational unit of sensemaking. Dervin's theory is critical, hermeneutic, and systemic; taking a deeply person-centred orientation to a situation motivated by an internalised subjective experience and their drive for help or resolution of problems or 'gaps.' Russell and colleagues developed an information theoretic model locating sensemaking in a collective context (an information world), focused on the interpretation of external data, or "making sense of external information." Dave Snowden's evolutionary 'multi-ontology' model considers sensemaking a knowledge production activity, using data toward a shared understanding of problem areas. All of these models have contributions to understanding systems and behaviour, but here we draw on Klein's model to illustrate the cognitive style of design framing, through mental model formation.

Klein's Data-Frame Sensemaking model in Figure 2 shows a nonlinear process of frame making, frame testing, and reframing. Start with a working frame or a current model about the data (data of any situation). There will always be a current frame; while it might not be explicated, some mental construct will be formed as an image of a system. The framing process can proceed to create a common frame, which can conserve an existing frame, or elaborate or change a working concept. The critique process represents the activity of re-imagining and evaluating the fit of the frame to interpretations

of the data. A reframing cycle is relevant to update the common frame when new data, or rethinking the data, demands a reframing of the perspective on its meaning.

Klein's theory was tested in high-complexity, naturalistic system contexts (such as clinical and military decisionmaking) as a mode of *macrocognition*. Macrocognition is a metatheory of distributed and reflective cognitive dispositions in complex situations, oriented to effective decision-making in context. Sensemaking and situation assessment are primary functions of macrocognitive reflection. (Klein also includes problem finding, planning, adaptation, and coordination – all of which are skills in which Journeys anticipates with collaborative tools). Mental simulation, storybuilding, and establishing common ground are all macrocognitive sensemaking strategies for critical system decisions. Klein emphasises that macrocognitive functions cannot be separated from action and decision-making in naturalistic settings. There is not a sensemaking 'stage,' a decision stage, a coordination phase, etc., as these functions all happen together in a naturalistic context.

> "Everything can be connected to everything. This makes any attempt at depicting a flow diagram either ad hoc or useless because cognition, as it occurs in the world, can't be 'frozen.'"[15]

Klein's model shows a reciprocal, recursive process of inducing from data to shape a meaningful frame and using the available frame to determine what counts as data. This account differs from standard information processing descriptions of how data are patterned into information representations, then structured as knowledge, resulting in understanding. There is an endpoint to sensemaking, which results in agreement on a suitable frame that then becomes a mental model and common ground.

The frame 'enframes' the data, such as the way in which media soundbites prime expectations about data

[12] Ken Wilber (1997). An Integral theory of consciousness. *Journal of Consciousness Studies*.
[13] Peter Jones (2015). Sensemaking Methodology: A liberation theory of communicative agency. *EPIC Perspectives*.
[14] Gary Klein, et al (2007). A data–frame theory of sensemaking. *Expertise Out of Context*. All the other references are listed in the Bibliography.
[15] Gary Klein, et al (2003). Macrocognition. *IEEE Intelligent Systems*.

presented in current events. The first frames imposed on a situation may be difficult to dislodge due to social diffusion of the meme that results from the framing. The social maintenance of first-order framing ensures that a narrative about events is controlled. For example, mass media holds immense power to maintain or change publicly held frames, and second-order questioning of public frames is rarely observed. In policy making, the change to an established frame can be slow, even if the data changes. If anomalous data questions a frame, potentially causing surprise or confusion, the first-order response is usually to 'conserve' the frame by explaining away the anomaly.

All of these framing actions can be viewed as individual or collective cognitive tasks. Therefore, a powerful strategy in convening framing journeys, whether in a 'stage' or on an ongoing engagement, is to use a sensemaking reference as a heuristic to intervene in an unproductive design or decision process. This enables one to actively rethink a frame context using new data (e.g. research findings) or an updated point of view on the data.

Making Sense of System Data

We have described sensemaking as an abductive reasoning process of synthesising observations, experiential understanding, and knowledge to form plausible meaning about complexity. While many of the tools in Journeys, perhaps most of them, are constructed through *synthesis*, we also recognise an equal-but-different role for analysis. The DIKW (Data-Information-Knowledge-Wisdom) framework defined by Russell Ackoff[16] expresses a structure to facilitate the formation of high-quality observations from sources of data, whether from desk research, ethnographic research, or the original annotations generated by workshop participants. The model in Figure 3 uses a pyramid to indicate the breadth of data observations at the base, stepping up into categories by refinement, all the way to the apex of 'wisdom.' Wisdom suggests an overview perspective across all levels, and the ability to resolve a small number of powerful insights from this data.

The DIKW framework analyses data by transforming its meanings through a hierarchy of units of analysis.

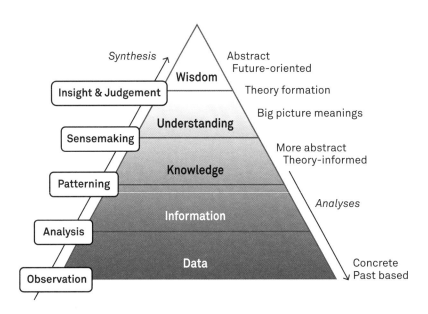

Figure 3
A DIKW model for analysis and synthesis, with a view to integrate sensemaking at the Understanding level

[16] Russell Ackoff (1989). From data to wisdom. *Journal of Applied Systems Analysis.*

Between the concrete references to data and the abstract level of wisdom, three gradations of analysis are shown – Information, Knowledge, and Understanding (a stage later added by Ackoff that affords collective sensemaking). Two arrows indicate vectors for *synthesis* (upward from data, creating theory and categories) and *analysis* (from knowledge downward, applying theory to information). Ackoff believed systems thinking was characterised by a reversal of mechanistic thinking – by synthesis first to understand the function of the whole, followed by analysis to define the parts.

DIKW is applicable to systems analysis, knowledge translation, complex sensemaking, and design research. Sanders and Stappers[17] thoughtfully translated the DIKW process for the analysis of design research. A key idea of theirs, reflected on the right side of Figure 3, is the ability to extend abstraction from theory-informed patterns of information, up to theory-formation in wisdom. They further define a *bridging* process from the power of abstraction to inform novel design proposals, future outcomes, and the ability to translate proposals into different stakeholder terms.

The DIKW can step through this synthesis for research data and most of the systemic design tools:

— **Data** is captured as the recording of phenomena as observations, whether in ethnographic interviews or sticky notes. Categories can be predefined, as most tools provide, or inductively assigned through affinity clustering.

— **Information** is the translation of data into structured representations. The labelling of categories is a simple transformation that builds information structures. Information is defined by distinctions, the differentiation of one factor or variable versus another. Distinctions can be assigned by a coding scheme used to tag the data and to summarise findings across multiple observations.

— The translation to **knowledge** is much more interpretive. For a system synthesis, we define

recurring patterns, causal relationships among factors, and the significance of meanings. Knowledge formation is iterative – often known theories will be applied and tested, assessed, and replaced with others until better explanations for the findings are discovered.

— Ackoff believed the goal of the DIKW process was to achieve an **understanding** that empowers the ability to design or change systems. We can consider understanding as a shared sensemaking, extending knowledge and learning with stakeholders.

— **Wisdom** in DIKW is the ability to make good decisions based on the learning, to creatively define theories about the underlying systems behaviour, and to propose empowering futures.

[17] Liz Sanders & Pieter Jan Stappers (2012). *Convivial Toolbox: Generative research for the front end of design*. BIS Publishers.

Navigating by Principles

Design principles, if followed as first principles, help guide the practitioner (as a 'North Star effect') to assess and make decisions in novel situations. Design principles provide a systematic process for system making, as a powerful 'kit of parts.' As Christopher Alexander[18] distinguished many years ago, the difference between a system as a whole entity and a system as a generative process is a toolkit for constructing new systems. Principles can be part of such a toolkit.

For nearly a decade, a published set of systemic design principles[19] – shared equally between systems and design theory – have been widely used to define and evaluate solutions and interventions. As *Design Journeys* is more of a practice handbook than a scholarly reference, the 11 principles are summarised in the back pages – presented after the tools and applications.

The principles are defined from the literature and iterative development, following the general criterion of being informed by primary theory and use cases equally across both systems theory and design thinking, making a summary of mutual guiding principles shared by the fields. Systemic design principles also provide a basis for designing consistently with relevant systems theory and epistemology. They can help resolve perceived differences between the fields for collaborative engagement and research.

The following summary describe the principles in brief:

1. **Idealisation** is an ideal state or set of conditions that compels action toward a desirable outcome or signifies the value of a future system or practice. Idealisation sets a high-level ideal or vision as an attractor for which a future system or system change can be designed and articulated. The idealisation is used as a future system model to inspire design, without making the ideal a goal, but as a target for design process.

2. **Appreciating Complexity** acknowledges the dynamic complexity of multi-causal (wicked) problems, their mutual interdependence and interconnection, and the limitations of problem-solving approaches. The appreciative aspect balances cognitive factors such as sensemaking, anticipation, simulation, and imagination involved in understanding and intervening in complex relationships.

3. **Purpose Finding** expresses the process of discovering primary drivers in a system, the function that determines the output of a system. Purpose seeking or finding is an iterative process of testing propositions with stakeholders in language constructed interdependently and determined by agreement as to their relevance. In design, as in systems, the purpose is expressed by its major effects, by 'what it does.'

4. **Boundary Framing** is the principle of determining the most effective fit between a concept and its target environment, considered as both concept framing and boundary critique. A boundary judgement determines the scope of a system of interest. Framing as design determines the services and features included or excluded in a proposal, as well as perspectives, values, and stakeholders.

5. **Requisite Variety** in a system is an assessment of the external variety to be controlled by an observer, and its value allocates the functions necessary to

[18] Christopher Alexander (1968). Systems generating systems. *Systemat*.
[19] Peter Jones (2014). Systemic design principles for complex social systems. In G.S. Metcalf (Ed.), *Social Systems and Design*. Springer.

control or absorb variety. In design, whether for a social system or information system, the functions of a given proposal must be calibrated to and provide sufficient options for interacting with the social and functional factors of a target environment's complexity.

6. **Feedback Coordination** describes the identification and regulation of all feedback types and relationships (first-*n* order) in social and technological systems for coordinating the dynamic fit to environmental and contextual functions.

7. **System Ordering** is a design process of defining and constructing an ordered formation of options, including information, technological functions, or social systems, in meaningful ways for human use. Designers define useful structures that facilitate visibility of affordances and salience of options within complex situations.

8. **Leverage Impact** in *Design Journeys* is a function of achieving maximal desired effects from minimal inputs. Leverage at critical points of intervention is a fundamental principle of systems and cybernetics, but its expression in design is less clearly developed. Design does not primarily seek to optimise *efficiency* – a hallmark of leverage, but is more concerned with *effectiveness*. Design leverage can be defined in several aspects: design that anticipates future system outcomes (such as a developing platform that becomes more useful with growth), the most appropriate fit of design to achieve results for a use case, and the strategic leverage of highly targeted design features.

9. **Generative Emergence** describes the selection of emergent manifestations for design signification. *Compositional* emergence in design activity is an outcome of ordering, of artificial micro-systems that adapt an artefact to environments. *Created* emergence manifests from organising systems, which include physical connections, designed forms, organising processes, and the synergies that emerge from among these functions.

10. **Continuous Adaptation** is maintaining a preferred system purpose through adaptation and objectives (or desiderata) throughout the lifecycle of conformance to environmental demands and related system changes.

11. **Self-organising** is a core principle for facilitating any size or type of group as a social system. In design, we enable actions that increase awareness and motivations to accelerate self-organising. Higher complexity social projects require cooperative organisation among multiple actors that are not regulatable through coordination, due to social complexity. Creative processes can break through system boundaries, and through self-transcendence, reach higher states of organisation.

Explorers can further investigate the principles as guidelines to extend other methods to the stages. For example, self-organising is indicated in [6] Planning, but clearly has relevance to the transition work in [7] Transition, suggesting a role for deeper team organising here.

Mapping Design Journeys' Fit to Purpose

Having followed the chapters of the book to this point, it will be evident that the Journeys are based on the structures of seven stages and 30 tools. Journeys are the unique pathways a practitioner selects and connects within these structures to best fit their own applications and complexities. The Journeys are intended as constructive processes linking one tool to another for intentionally effective results. The tools, and their data collected in each context, build upon one another. Most of the tools have defined relationships with each other, as the Figure 4 diagram portrays. Some of the primary tool relationships are described, but the reader can also follow the diagram to develop their own sense of the magnitude and reach of these connections across tools.

[1] Framing the System
The Iterative Inquiry defines boundaries, framing the scope for discovering and mapping actors, and the relevant practices of the current system in the Rich Context. This boundary critique later helps define system levels for Story Loops in [3] Understanding. The Actors Map and Rich Context shape the research samples for [2] Listening and reveal emerging niche initiatives referenced in other stages.

[2] Listening to the System
The research journey in [2] Listening is an essential stage, and its process resonates and influences the entire design process. Stakeholder Dimensions analyses and builds on the actors (and niches) to inform research planning. The Research Question (CLA) tool sets the scope and framing for ethnographic research, which results in input for the Actants Map and the tools in [3] Understanding. Remember, the tools in Listening are a kind of starter kit for Tourists and to inspire Explorers. Many organisations will have fully-developed user research practices that can be adapted to systemic design projects.

[3] Understanding the System
Several system models are developed for the first foray into functional system analysis. The Social Ecosystem and Story Loops construct working models of the social system used to locate, leverage, and assess design interventions.

The Influence Map feeds all the roadmap models that follow in later stages, especially the Theory of Systems Change and Action.

[4] Envisioning Desired Futures
Maps in [4] Envisioning create a guiding future vision for the project and system change potentials. In domains where the desired future is already well-defined (e.g., green buildings for resilient cities), start with the System Value Proposition as a first exercise in reframing. If desired futures are contested or ambiguous, the Story Loops and Influence Map from [3] Understanding can be integrated into the system story of a synthesis map. Three Horizons develops a temporal roadmap of the transition to the next regime, showing how sociotechnical innovations enable transition toward desired futures.

[5] Exploring the Possibility Space
The Intervention Strategy forms an armature that fits leverage proposals for all change strategies and roadmaps into a usable structure. All the tools in [5] Exploring provide insight and work together to locate and propose effective points of intervention. The Outcome Map defines a strategic roadmap style for stakeholders to chart actions and outcomes that follow the Intervention Strategy.

[6] Planning the Change Process
Several unique tools in [6] Planning develop and assess the organisational capability to lead complex change design. The Theory of Systems Change and Action translates the Outcome Map and interventions into a programmatic rationale used for communications, evaluation, and funding. The Process Enneagram provides an organisational design tool useful for any team or firm to define its purpose and operating model.

[7] Fostering the Transition
Design Journeys closes with tools guiding the rollout to implementation. The Stakeholder Activation defines how stakeholder leaders, coalitions, and roles are best formed. Transition by Design aligns the change strategy to the environment of action. The Adaptive Cycle Strategy informs the timing and force of the strategy.

As the final figure illustrates, all the tools can work together to lead and inform design, strategy, and implementation.

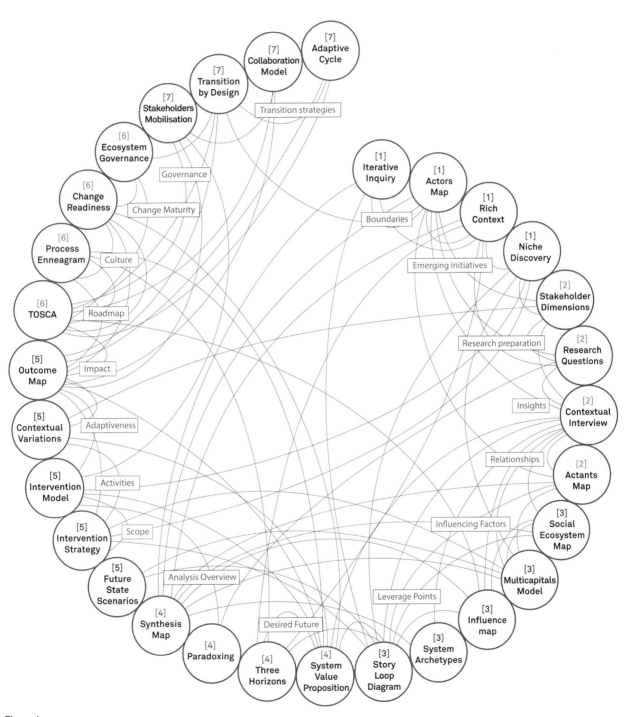

Figure 4
How the tools are linked (non-exhaustive)

Bibliography

References in the book

Ackoff, R. L. (1981). The art and science of mess management. *Interfaces, 11*(1), 20-26.

Ackoff, R. L. (1989). From data to wisdom. *Journal of Applied Systems Analysis, 16*(1), 3-9.

Adnan, I. (2021). *The Politics of Waking Up: Power and Possibility in the Fractal Age*. Perspectiva Press.

Alexander, C. (1968). Systems generating systems. *Systemat, 1*.

Alfonso, S., Benson, C., Claude, V., Kamalmaz, S., Ng, E., & Prakash, P. (2021). *Policy Framework for Green Building*. OCAD University, Toronto.

Banathy, B. (1996). *Designing Social Systems in a Changing World*. Springer.

Basadur, M. (2004). Leading others to think innovatively together: Creative leadership. *The Leadership Quarterly, 15*(1), 103-121.

Beer, S. (1984). The Viable System Model: Its provenance, development, methodology and pathology. *Journal of the Operational Research Society, 35*(1), 7-25.

Beer, S. (1994). *Beyond Dispute: The Invention of Team Syntegrity*. Chichester, UK: Wiley.

Birkinshaw, J., Hamel, G., & Mol, M.J. (2008). Management innovation. *Academy of Management Review, 33* (4).

Braun, W. (2002). The system archetypes. *The Systems Modeling Workbook (pp. 1-26)*.

Brkic, N., Chomyn, M., Fornes, A.F., Hanna R., & Morrell, A. (2021). *Why We Buy*. OCAD University, Toronto.

Bronfenbrenner, U. (1989). *Ecological Systems Theory* (Vol. 6). Greenwich, CT: JAI Press.

Christakis, A.N. & Bausch, K. C. (2006). *How People Harness their Collective Wisdom and Power to Construct the Future in Co-Laboratories of Democracy*. Greenwich, CT: Information Age Publishing.

Christakis, A.N. & Kakoulaki, M. (2021). Objectifying intersubjectivity through inclusion for a scientific [R] Evolution: Avoiding polarization by engaging stakeholders for saliency, priority and trust. In *From Polarisation to Multispecies Relationships* (pp. 699-728). Singapore: Springer.

Ciborra, C.U. (2009). The platform organization: Recombining strategies, structures, and surprises. In *Bricolage, Care and Information* (pp. 134-158). London: Palgrave Macmillan.

Collopy, F. (2009). Lessons learned–Why the failure of systems thinking should inform the future of design thinking. *Fast Company*.

Cooperrider, D. L. (1986). *Appreciative Inquiry: Toward a methodology for understanding and enhancing organizational innovation (theory, social, participation)*. Doctoral dissertation, Case-Western Reserve University.

Cooperrider, D., Whitney, D.D., & Stavros, J. (2008). *The Appreciative Inquiry Handbook: For Leaders of Change*. Berrett-Koehler Publishers.

den Ouden, E. (2012). *Innovation design: Creating Value for People, Organizations and Society* (p. 196). London: Springer.

Dervin, B. (1998). Sense-making theory and practice: An overview of user interests in knowledge seeking and use. *Journal of Knowledge Management,* 2(2), 36-46.

Dervin, B. (2003). Human studies and user studies: A call for methodological inter-disciplinarity. *Information Research, 9*(1), 9-1.

Design Council. (2005). *The 'Double Diamond' Design Process Model*. London: Design Council.

De Smedt, P. & Borch, K. (2021). Participatory policy design in system innovation. *Policy Design and Practice*, 1-15.

Dorst, K. (2006). Design problems and design paradoxes. *Design Issues* 2006; 22 (3): 4–17.

Dorst, K. (2015). *Frame Innovation: Create New Thinking by Design*. Cambridge, MA: MIT Press.

Engeström, Y. & Sannino, A. (2021). From mediated actions to heterogenous coalitions: four generations of activity-theoretical studies of work and learning. *Mind, Culture, and Activity, 28*(1), 4-23.

Fisher, S., Abdi, D. I., Matovic, V., Ludin, J., Walker, B. A., Mathews, D., ... & Williams, S. (2000). *Working with Conflict 2: Skills and Strategies for Action*. Zed Books.

Flach, J.M., Feufel, M.A., Reynolds, P. L., Parker, S. H., & Kellogg, K. M. (2017). Decisionmaking in practice: The dynamics of muddling through. *Applied Ergonomics, 63*, 133-141.

Flyvbjerg, B. (2004). Phronetic planning research: Theoretical and methodological reflections. *Planning Theory and Practice, 5*(3), 283-306.

Gall, J. (1975). *General Systemantics*. Quadrangle.

Geels, F.W. (2005). Processes and patterns in transitions and system innovations: Refining the co-evolutionary multi-level perspective. *Technological Forecasting and Social Change, 72*(6), 681-696.

Geels, F.W. (2011). The multi-level perspective on sustainability transitions: Responses to seven criticisms. *Environmental Innovation and Societal Transitions, 1*(1), 24-40.

Gharajedaghi, J. (2004). *Systems Methodology A Holistic Language of Interaction and Design Seeing Through Chaos and Understanding Complexities.*

Goodchild, M. (2021). Relational systems thinking: That's how change is going to come, from our Earth mother. *Journal of Awareness-Based Systems Change, 1*(1), 75-103.

Hanson, A. (2018). Have we reached Peak Toolkit? *OECD, Observatory of Public Sector Innovation*. http//oecd-opsi.org/have-we-reached-peak-toolkit

Heermann, B. (1997). *Building Team Spirit: Activities for Inspiring and Energizing Teams*. McGraw-Hill.

Holling, C.S. & Gunderson, L.H. (2002). *Panarchy: Understanding Transformations in Human And Natural Systems*. Washington, DC: Island Press.

Holtzblatt, K. & Beyer, H. (1997). *Contextual Design: Defining Customer-Centered Systems.* Elsevier.

Hugentobler, H. K., Jonas, W., & Rahe, D. (2004). Designing a methods platform for design and design research. *Design Research Society, Melbourne, November 2004.*

Illich, I. & Lang, A. (1973). *Tools for Conviviality*. New York: Harper & Row.

Inayatullah, S. (2009). Causal Layered Analysis: An integrative and transformative theory and method. *Futures Research Methodology, 3.*

Irwin, T., Kossoff, G., & Tonkinwise, C. (2015). Transition design provocation. *Design Philosophy Papers*, 13(1), 3-11.

Jackson, M.C. (2004). *Systems Thinking: Creative Holism for Managers*. John Wiley & Sons.

Jones, P. (2017). Social ecologies of flourishing: Designing conditions that sustain culture. In *Design for a Sustainable Culture* (pp. 38-54). Routledge.

Jones, P. & Bowes, J. (2017). Rendering systems visible for design: Synthesis maps as constructivist design narratives. *She Ji: The Journal of Design, Economics, and Innovation, 3*(3), 229-248.

Jones, P. (2018). Contexts of cocreation: Designing with system stakeholders. In *Systemic Design* (pp. 3-52). Springer, Tokyo.

Jones, P. (2018). Evolutionary stakeholder discovery: Requisite system sampling for cocreation. In *Proceedings of Relating Systems Thinking and Design (RSD7) 2018 Symposium*, Torino.

Jones, P. (2020). Systemic Design: Design for complex, social, and sociotechnical systems. G. Metcalf, K. Kijima, & H. Deguchi (Eds.), *Handbook of Systems Sciences*, 1-25. Tokyo: Springer Japan

Jones, P. H. (2009). Learning the lessons of systems thinking: Exploring the gap between thinking and leadership. *Integral Leadership Review, IX*, 4, 1-8.

Khan, Z. & Ing, D. (2019). Paying attention to where attention is placed in the rise of system(s) change(s). In *Proceedings of Relating Systems Thinking and Design (RSD8) 2019 Symposium.* Chicago, October 2019.

Klein, G., Phillips, J. K., Rall, E. L., & Peluso, D. A. (2007). A data–frame theory of sensemaking. In *Expertise Out of Context* (pp. 118-160). Psychology Press.

Klein, G., Ross, K. G., Moon, B. M., Klein, D. E., Hoffman, R. R., & Hollnagel, E. (2003). Macrocognition. *IEEE Intelligent Systems, 18*(3), 81-85.

Knowles, R. (2002*). The Leadership Dance: Pathways to Extraordinary Organizational Effectiveness*. The Center for Self-Organizing Leadership.

Kumar, V. & Whitney, P. (2007). Daily life, not markets. Customer-centered design. *Journal of Business Strategy.*

Ladner, S. (2019). *Mixed Methods: A Short Guide to Applied Mixed Methods Research*. Amazon Digital Services.

Latour, B. (2003). The promises of constructivism. *Chasing Technoscience: Matrix for Materiality*, 27-46.

Latour, B. (2007). *Reassembling the Social: An Introduction to Actor-Network Theory.* Oxford: Oxford University Press.

Leadbeater, C. (2013). The systems innovator. In G. Mulgan & C. Leadbeater (Eds). *Systems Innovation.* Discussion Paper. London: NESTA.

Manzini, E. (2015). *Design, When Everybody Designs: An Introduction to Design for Social Innovation*. Cambridge, MA: MIT Press.

Matthias, S. & McMullin, J. (2017). *Systemic Maturity Models and multi-organization collaborations.* In *Proceedings of Relating Systems Thinking and Design (RSD6) 2017 Symposium.* Oslo.

Meadows, D.H., Meadows, D.L., Randers, J., & Behrens, W. (1972). *The Limits to Growth: A Report for the Club of Rome's Project on the Predicament of Mankind*. New York: Universe Books.

Meadows, D.H. (1999). *Leverage Points: Places to Intervene in a System*. Hartland, VT: The Sustainability Institute.

Michura, P. & Ruecker, S. (2017). Design as production of presence – systemic approach to re-designing novelty. In *Proceedings of Relating Systems Thinking and Design (RSD6) 2017 Symposium.* Oslo.

Midgley, G. (2000). Boundary critique. In *Systemic Intervention* (pp. 135-158). Boston: Springer.

Mingers, J. (2014). *Systems Thinking, Critical Realism and Philosophy: A Confluence of Ideas*. Routledge.

Murphy, R. J. & Jones, P. (2021). Towards systemic theories of change: High-leverage strategies for managing wicked problems. *Design Management Journal, 16*(1), 49-65.

Nkwake, A. M. (2013). *Working with Assumptions in International Development Program Evaluation* (pp. 25-50). Springer.

Nogueira, A., Ashton, W. S., & Teixeira, C. (2019). Expanding perceptions of the circular economy through design: Eight capitals as innovation lenses. *Resources, Conservation and Recycling, 149*, 566-576.

Osterwalder, A., Pigneur, Y., Bernarda, G., & Smith, A. (2014). *Value Proposition Design: How to Create Products and Services Customers Want*. John Wiley & Sons.

Owen, C. (2001). Structured planning in design: Information-age tools for product development. *Design Issues, 17* (1), 27-43.

Owen, H. (2000). *The Power of Spirit: How Organizations Transform*. San Francisco: Berrett-Koehler Publishers.

Özbekhan, H., Jantsch, E., & Christakis, A. (1970). The Club of Rome—The Predicament of Mankind: A Quest for Structured Responses to Growing World-Wide Complexities and Uncertainties. *Philadelphia: University of Pennsylvania: Management and Behavioural Science Center.*

Patton, M. Q. (2017). *Principles-Focused Evaluation: The Guide.* Guilford Publications.

Polak, F. & Boulding, E. (1973). *The Image of the Future*. Elsevier.

Rittel, H.W. & Webber, M.M. (1973). Dilemmas in a general theory of planning. *Policy Sciences, 4(2)*, 155-169.

Roberts, C. J., Richards, M. G., Ross, A. M., Rhodes, D. H., & Hastings, D. E. (2009, March). Scenario planning in dynamic multi-attribute tradespace exploration. *3rd Annual IEEE Systems Conference* (pp. 366-371).

Russell, D. M., Stefik, M. J., Pirolli, P., & Card, S. K. (1993). The cost structure of sensemaking. *Proceedings of CHI'93 Conference on Human Factors in Computing Systems,* April 24-29, 1993 (pp. 269-276).

Sanders, E.B.N., & Stappers, P.J. (2012). *Convivial Toolbox: Generative Research for The Front End of Design*. Amsterdam: BIS Publishers.

Scharmer, O. (2018). *The Essentials of Theory U: Core Principles and Applications*. Berrett-Koehler.

Senge, P. M. (1990). *The Fifth Discipline: The Art and Practice of the Learning Organization.* Currency Doubleday.

Senge, P., Hamilton, H., & Kania, J. (2015). The dawn of system leadership. *Stanford Social Innovation Review, 13*(1), 27-33.

Sevaldson, B. (2022). *Designing Complexity: The methodology and practice of Systems Oriented Design*. Common Ground.

Sharpe, B., Hodgson, A., Leicester, G., Lyon, A. & Fazey, I. (2016). Three Horizons: A pathways practice for transformation. *Ecology and Society, 21*(2).

Skjerven, A. & Reitan, J. (Eds.). (2017). *Design for a Sustainable Culture: Perspectives, Practices and Education*. Routledge.

Snowden, D. (2005). Multi-ontology sense-making: A new simplicity in decision making. *Journal of Innovation in Health Informatics, 13*(1), 45-53.

Spinosa, C., Flores, F., & Dreyfus, H.L. (1997). *Disclosing New Worlds: Entrepreneurship, Democratic Action, and the Cultivation of Solidarity*. Cambridge, MA: MIT Press.

Swann, C. (2002). Action research and the practice of design. *Design Issues, 18*(1), 49-61.

Tsasis, P., Evans, J.M., Forrest, D., & Jones, R.K. (2013). Outcome mapping for health system integration. *Journal of Multidisciplinary Healthcare, 6*, 99.

Tufte, E. (1997). *Visual Explanations: Images and Quantities, Evidence and Narrative*. Cheshire, CT: Graphics Press.

Ulrich, W. (1987). Critical heuristics of social systems design. *European Journal of Operational Research, 31*(3), 276-283.

Upward, A. & Jones, P. (2016). An ontology for strongly sustainable business models: Defining an enterprise framework compatible with natural and social science. *Organization & Environment*, *29*(1), 97-123.

Vandenbroeck, P., Van Ael, K., Thoelen, A., & Bertels, P. (2016). Codifying systemic design: A toolkit. In *Proceedings of Relating Systems Thinking and Design (RSD5) 2016 Symposium.* Toronto.

Van Patter, G.K., & Jones, P. (2013). Understanding Design 1, 2, 3, 4: The rise of visual sensemaking. In in Tiiu Poldma (Ed.), *Meanings of Designed Spaces*, 331-342.

VanPatter, G.K., & Pastor, E. (2016). *Innovation Methods Mapping: De-mystifying 80+ Years of Innovation Process Design*. Humantific Publishing.

von Goethe, J. W. (1790). JW von Goethe Herzoglich Sachsen-Weimarischen Geheimraths Versuch die Metamorphose der Pflanzen zu erklären. Ettinger.

Waddell, S. (2016). Societal change systems: A framework to address wicked problems. *The Journal of Applied Behavioral Science, 52*(4), 422-449.

Waddock, S., Waddell, S., Jones, P.H., & Kendrick, I. (2022). Convening transformation systems to achieve system transformation. *Journal of Awareness-Based Systems Change, 2*(1), 77–100.

Warfield, J.N. (1974). *Structuring Complex Systems*. Columbus, OH: Battelle Memorial Institute.

Warfield, J.N. (1986). The Domain of Science Model: Evolution and design. *Proceedings of the 30th Annual Meeting, Society for General Systems Research,* H46-H59.

Weick, K.E., Sutcliffe, K.M., & Obstfeld, D. (2005). Organizing and the process of sensemaking. *Organization Science, 16*(4), 409-421.

Wenger, E. & Wenger-Traynor, B. (2021). *Systems Convening: A Crucial Form of Leadership for the 21st Century*. Social Learning Lab.

Weisbord, M., & Janoff, S. (2010). *Future Search: Getting the Whole System in the Room for Vision, Commitment, and Action*. San Francisco: Berrett-Koehler Publishers.

Wilber, K. (1997). An integral theory of consciousness. *Journal of Consciousness Studies, 4*(1), 71-92.

Relevant websites

- Contexts – The Systemic Design Journal: systemic-design.org/contexts

- Design Dialogues (Peter Jones): designdialogues.com

- Journeys tools download page: systemicdesigntoolkit.org/journeys

- Relating Systems Thinking and Design (RSD) Symposium proceedings: rsdsymposium.org

- Systemic Design Association (SDA): systemic-design.org

- Systems-Oriented Design: systemsorienteddesign.net

- Systemic Design Toolkit: systemicdesigntoolkit.org

Figure 5
A workshop participant looking at the visual scribing made during a workshop

Index